HEART AND SPIRIT

A FOOTBALLING HISTORY OF

THE REPUBLIC OF IRELAND

ALAN HANNIFY

First published in July 2020 by Kindle Direct Publishing.

Email the author at: alanhannify@gmail.com

A CIP catalogue record for this book is available from the British Library.

ISBN: 9798651963836

Cover art by Barry Masterson

website: www.barrymasterson.com

twitter: @BarryMasterson

All royalties from this book are being donated to **SOSAD Ireland**.

SOSAD Ireland is a mental health charity with five offices based in Carrickmacross, Cavan, Drogheda, Dundalk and Navan. The goals of the charity are as follows:

- To raise awareness of suicide in Ireland.
- To break the stigma surrounding suicide.
- To provide support and direction to those feeling depressed and/or suicidal.
- To provide support and direction to those who may know someone feeling suicidal.
- To provide support and direction to those who have been bereaved by suicide.

Through their offices, SOSAD Ireland offer a wide range of supports including:

- A safe and comfortable place to talk.
- Initial meeting to establish need.
- Professional counselling.
- Crisis or suicide interventions
- Bereavement support.
- Follow-up support.
- 24-hour helpline.
- Talks to schools and workplaces.
- Referrals to the best support services

All services are provided free of charge.

SOSAD Ireland are working towards a community that feels supported and to encourage and foster resilience, so that no one ever feels they have to cope alone. For more information, please visit: **www.sosadireland.ie**

CONTENTS

ACKNOWLEDGEMENTS

It is with deep gratitude that I acknowledge everyone who has assisted in the process of publishing this book.

I am particularly thankful to Brian Langan for editing the book and for the attention to detail, expertise and advice he provided.

I am very grateful to Barry Masterson who created the artwork and designed the book cover. Barry's outstanding illustrations have become synonymous with the Ireland matchday programmes.

I would like to express my sincere gratitude to Phil Dunphy who is a hugely committed and knowledgeable supporter of Irish football. Phil's thorough review, insightful analysis and encouragement were of crucial importance to the completion of the book.

I would like to thank Kevin Dunphy who runs the Eire Guide website and social media platforms for his advice and encouragement. Thanks also to Brendan Farrell and Darren Burke for their feedback and for the opportunity to tap into their football knowledge.

I would also like to take this opportunity to thank those people who have encouraged and facilitated my love of the Irish football team since I was a child. That includes family and friends who have taken me to matches, as well as those people I have travelled with and been fortunate to meet at matches over the years. In particular, I would like to thank my parents and my siblings, David and Christina.

Last but certainly not least, I would like to thank my wife and son, Leona and Cormac, for their patience and support.

ABBREVIATIONS

BBC:	British Broadcasting Corporation
DFB:	Deutscher Fußball-Bund
EU:	European Union
FA:	Football Association
FAI:	Football Association of Ireland
FAIFS:	Football Association of the Irish Free State
FIFA:	Fédération Internationale de Football Association
GAA:	Gaelic Athletic Association
IFA:	Irish Football Association
IRFU:	Irish Rugby Football Union
ITV:	Independent Television Network
NBA:	National Basketball Association
NFL:	National Football League
RTÉ:	Raidió Teilifís Éireann
RTL:	Radio Television Lëtzebuerg
TD:	Teachta Dála
UEFA:	Union of European Football Associations
UK:	United Kingdom
USA:	United States of America
USSR:	Union of Soviet Socialist Republics

For Leona and Cormac

Prologue

On a crisp November night at the Aviva Stadium, the early noise and sense of occasion have given way to a deafening silence from the home crowd, punctuated by the celebrations of the small section of travelling support. As the Irish fans contemplate the ramifications of the scrappy goal that their Danish visitors have just scored, the ball arrives at the feet of Stephen Ward in the opposition half of the field. It's the type of position where Ward might ordinarily clip the ball forward, but on this occasion, the left-back attempts to go past his Danish counterpart and concedes possession. A blistering counter-attack ensues, which culminates in Christian Eriksen firing home a second goal off the underside of Darren Randolph's crossbar.

By the end of the night, Eriksen has bagged three of his side's five goals against an Irish team left shell-shocked by the technical proficiency and tactical acumen of their visitors. It seemed a long time since Shane Duffy opened the scoring with a sixth-minute goal to stir the home crowd into a frenzy. It wasn't supposed to be like this. This was supposed to be the night when Martin O'Neill's team secured the country's place at a fourth World Cup finals tournament.

The Irish captain David Meyler had spoken in the days prior to the game of how he 'could only see one outcome' and that the Danish team 'don't have the character and the heart and the desire that we have'. The characteristics of heart and fighting spirit are positive attributes of the Irish sporting psyche that should be cherished and nurtured. However, the play-off defeat to Denmark was a stark reminder that such traits will only take a team so far. Unlike previous hard-luck stories accumulated during Ireland's storied history in play-offs for major tournaments, the comprehensive score-line in November 2017 meant that there could be no excuses or recriminations. The result was accompanied by the realisation that it would take some time to pick up the pieces from such a chastening defeat.

Of course, it could be argued that Irish football has found itself at a similarly low ebb in the past and that the loss to Denmark was a case of history repeating itself. The play-off defeat for Martin O'Neill's team occurred almost 32 years to the day since Eoin Hand's team suffered a 4-1 loss to the same opposition at Lansdowne Road. On that occasion, the circumstances were remarkably similar, as a sixth-minute goal from Frank Stapleton was followed by four unanswered goals from a Danish team that was marching towards the 1986 World Cup. The result signalled the end of Eoin Hand's managerial tenure and on that night in 1985, the prospects of the Republic of Ireland ever reaching the finals of an international tournament seemed increasingly forlorn. Little did the team's loyal supporters realise that a period of unprecedented success lay just over the horizon.

The arrival of Jack Charlton in 1986 and the success of his team in qualifying for major tournaments captured the public imagination. The journeys through Euro '88, Italia '90 and USA '94 became significant events in Irish popular culture and had a profound impact on cohorts of the population who had previously been indifferent to the sport. After decades of trying to establish some credibility on the international stage, Ireland under Jack Charlton emerged as one of the most difficult teams to beat in international football and were ranked among the top ten teams in the world.

The 'Boys in Green' became a source of great pride for the nation, but with success came higher expectations. The demanding nature of this new breed of Irish football fan was perhaps most acutely felt by Mick McCarthy, who succeeded 'Big Jack' in 1996. McCarthy had the unenviable task of having to rebuild an aging squad, while still under pressure to qualify for major tournaments. It was a task that the former captain set about in earnest by changing the style of play and introducing a new crop of talented young players. This process was helped in no small part by the success of Brian Kerr's teams at underage level.

The high-water mark of McCarthy's term in charge was a seismic 1-0 victory against the Netherlands in Dublin in September 2001. It was a star-studded Dutch team and a match that Ireland probably should have lost. It was not the most complete performance of McCarthy's reign but, as a standalone fixture, the result would prove to be a defining one. Irish fans leaving Lansdowne Road on that September evening were aware that they had witnessed a special result in the history of Irish football, but little did they realise it would take another fourteen years for the team to beat a higher-ranked nation in a competitive international.

In some respects, it is only with the passing of time that a single result or performance can be placed in its true context. A team and its manager are often defined by an individual fixture, its outcome and the subsequent narrative that emerges through the media and public discourse. Certain matches offer a snapshot of a team's identity and carry a significance that transcends time.

This book charts the evolution of the Republic of Ireland's football team through twelve landmark fixtures dating back to the nation's first involvement in a World Cup qualifier in 1934. Of the twelve fixtures detailed, there is limited footage available for the four earliest matches and as such, the analysis relies heavily on newspaper reports and archive material from the relevant period. The matches examined in the book are not necessarily the best performances by Irish teams, nor indeed are they all positive results. In this regard, the history of Irish football is characterised by fluctuations, from the high points of one-off wins against some to the leading powers in the world game to the disappointments of missing out on qualification for World Cups and European Championships. It is this ebb and flow between success and perceived failure, as encapsulated by era-defining fixtures, that frames the public perception of a qualifying campaign, a managerial tenure, or a particular generation of players.

Chapter 1
Irish Free State v Belgium
25 February 1934

'Moore shares the honours with Belgium.'

– Irish Press

The emergence of association football in Ireland can be traced back to the 1860s when the sport was largely focused around Belfast and the northeast of the island. The Irish Football Association (IFA) was established as the governing body in 1880 and a representative team from Ireland played its first international match against England two years later. However, it took longer for the sport to gain traction in the rest of the island.

The Leinster Football Association was founded in 1892 as the administrative organisation for football in the province and endured an uneasy relationship with the IFA during the early years of the twentieth century. There was a prevailing view amongst Dublin-based clubs that the IFA favoured clubs based in Ulster, particularly when it came to the selection of players for Ireland. This perception of bias was heightened by the IFA's preference for hosting international matches in Belfast. The backdrop of political tension added to the strain, with the southern affiliates becoming more outspoken following the Easter Rising in 1916 and during the subsequent War of Independence.

The relationship between the football authorities in Belfast and Dublin finally reached a breaking point in 1921. In his book, *The Irish Soccer Split*, Cormac Moore refers to the IFA's scheduling of an Irish Cup semi-final replay between Shelbourne and Glenavon as the catalyst. The first match had been played in Belfast and it was assumed that the replay would be in Dublin. However, an IFA committee ruled that it was unsafe for the fixture to be played in Dublin due to the on-going violence in the city. The replay was fixed for Belfast and following Shelbourne's refusal to comply, they were expelled from the competition.

In June 1921, a month after partition, the Football Association of Ireland (FAI) was founded in Molesworth Hall in Dublin. A Free State League was also formed, with eight teams involved. According to Paul Rouse in *Sport and Ireland: A History*, there were a series of factors contributing to the split, but 'it would also be wrong not to accept that political partition was at the heart of the partition of the governance of soccer'.

The new association soon started a campaign for recognition on the international stage and the British associations reluctantly recognised the FAI as an association with dominion status in 1923. The following year, the FAI gained full membership of FIFA on the condition that it would only govern football in the twenty-six counties of the Irish Free State. The FAI subsequently changed its name to the Football Association of the Irish Free State (FAIFS).

There were attempts at reconciliation between the IFA and FAIFS during the 1920s and early 1930s. A meeting brokered by the English FA in 1924 almost reached an agreement, but the IFA insisted on providing the chairman of the international team selection committee. A 1932 meeting agreed on sharing this role but failed to reach agreement when the FAIFS demanded one of the IFA's two places on the International Football Association Board.

The first opportunity for a team from the Irish Free State to play on the international stage was in 1924 at the Olympic Games in Paris. A squad of sixteen players travelled to the French capital under the auspices of the Olympic Council of Ireland. The squad was mainly comprised of players from Athlone Town, Bohemians and St James's

Gate. Under the captaincy of Athlone Town's Denis Hannon, the Irish team beat Bulgaria to advance to a quarter-final against the Netherlands. A Dutch goal in extra-time proved to be the difference, but the Free State team had performed credibly and demonstrated its potential. Given that the Olympic tournament pre-dated FIFA's introduction of the World Cup, it was the only global football tournament at that time and provided a valuable barometer for Irish football in an international context.

In the aftermath of the Olympic Games, the challenge facing the FAIFS was to find international opposition willing to play their team. This challenge was not helped by the association's fractious relationship with the British associations, which included the IFA in Belfast. The IFA's team took part in the annual British Home Championship alongside England, Scotland and Wales, which meant that the Irish Free State needed to look towards the Continent to arrange fixtures. This was difficult given the financial costs associated with travelling to Europe.

The first full international was held in March 1926 against Italy in Turin, which the home team won 3-0. A total of seven fixtures followed over the next six years, with Italy, Belgium, Spain and the Netherlands providing the opposition.

During this period, the IFA continued to select players from all thirty-two counties, which meant that certain players were often selected by both associations. This did not pose an immediate conflict, given that the respective associations were focused on fixtures against different opposition.

In addition to the inherent challenges posed by the relationship with the IFA, the growth of the game in the Free State was stymied by a nationalist fervour closely aligned to the ideals of the Gaelic Athletic Association (GAA). The GAA had enacted a ban in 1905 which forbade any member of the association from either participating in or watching 'foreign games'. In practice, the ban imposed on the GAA membership was to prevent their involvement in association football, rugby, cricket and hockey. In these circumstances, football struggled to establish a foothold outside of Dublin and some provincial towns.

The opportunity for meaningful competition finally presented itself in 1934 when the Irish Free State team was entered in the qualification process for the World Cup, which would be hosted by Italy. It was only the second World Cup and was the first to be held in Europe. The participation of an Irish team was noteworthy, as the four British associations were not members of FIFA and, as such, they were not taking part in the qualification process.

Thirty-two teams were entered in the qualifying groups for the World Cup and the Irish Free State was drawn in a three-team group along with Belgium and the Netherlands. The group format required each team to play each of the other teams once. FIFA informed the FAIFS that Belgium and the Netherlands feared that the receipts for a match in Dublin would not cover their travel costs and suggested that a triangular tournament be held in Amsterdam. This was deemed unacceptable by the FAIFS who wanted to play one game at home and the second away. Their proposal was eventually accepted by FIFA and it was determined that Belgium would travel to Dublin in February 1934, with the Irish team then travelling to Amsterdam to play the Dutch. The third and final game of the group would involve Belgium playing their home fixture against the Dutch in Antwerp.

During its relatively short history, the Irish Free State had already played Belgium three times. The first meeting of the teams took place in Liège in 1928, with the Irish winning 4-2. The sides met again in Dublin the following year and the home team registered a convincing 4-0 victory. The third encounter was in Brussels in 1930, with the Irish team once again confirming its superiority with a 3-1 win.

Despite those results, Belgian football had continued to progress, and their national team gained valuable experience through regular matches against other European teams. Indeed, Belgium were one of only four European nations to have taken part in the inaugural World Cup in 1930, although they returned home from Uruguay having lost both of their games without scoring a goal.

In contrast, it had been almost two years since the Irish Free State team had last played an international fixture. The Irish media recognised that this provided the visitors with a certain advantage and a match preview in the *Irish Press* advised its readers that 'since our last victory in 1930, football on the Continent has progressed by leaps and bounds'. The article went on: 'Belgium has naturally benefited by the development, and as they play against other countries much more frequently than do the Free State, their players have not only gained in experience, but should have developed an understanding.'

The Irish team was selected by the FAIFS and included nine players who were based in Ireland and two players who plied their trade in Scotland. The goalkeeper was Jim Foley of Cork FC, who was three weeks shy of his 20th birthday. The two full-backs were Miah Lynch of Cork Bohemians and Tom Burke of Cork FC.

Paddy Gaskins of Shamrock Rovers was picked at right-half and captained the side. Joe O'Reilly of Aberdeen was selected at centre-half. O'Reilly had scored against the Netherlands on his international debut two years earlier. Joe Kendrick was picked at left-half; at 28 years of age, he was one of the elder statesmen in the team. Indeed, Kendrick was part of the Irish team that had travelled to the 1924 Olympics and he had played for Everton prior to returning to Dublin where he had signed for Dolphin.

The two inside-forwards were David Byrne of Coleraine and Tim O'Keeffe of Cork FC. Byrne had won two previous international caps, one of which included a goal against Belgium in 1929. Billy Kennedy of St James's Gate was selected on the right wing, with Jimmy Kelly of Derry City on the left wing. Both Kennedy and Kelly were making their second international appearances, both having played against the Netherlands two years earlier.

Paddy Moore at centre-forward was undoubtedly the star player in the Irish team. Moore was 24 years old and hailed from Ballybough in Dublin. Following spells with Shamrock Rovers, Cardiff City and Tranmere Rovers, he had moved to Aberdeen in 1932. Moore had made two previous appearances for the Irish Free State, against Spain and the Netherlands, scoring in both of those games.

The Irish team's relative lack of international exposure meant that five of the players were making their first international appearances. William 'Sacky' Glen of Shamrock Rovers was originally selected to play at right-half, but an injury led to him being replaced in the team by Miah Lynch. This change also necessitated a positional switch with Paddy Gaskins moving from full-back to right-half.

The team could have been strengthened by eligible players from English clubs, such as Jimmy Dunne of Arsenal, Everton's Alec Stevenson and Harry Duggan of Leeds United. Securing the release of players from cross-channel clubs proved to be an on-going challenge for the Irish Free State, but there was an expectation that a team mainly comprised of home-based players would be capable of achieving qualification. Given that the World Cup finals would be played following the completion of the English League season, it was anticipated that the English clubs would release their Irish players for the tournament itself.

In theory, the Irish team lined up in a 2-3-5 formation. This is sometimes referred to as the pyramid formation and was regarded as the default system during this era. Teams were generally presented in newspapers and match programmes as comprising two full-backs who provided the last line of defence, with a line of three players in front of them – the right-half, centre-half and left-half. Historically, the centre-half role was akin to what might be considered as a central-midfield position in modern-day football and it was associated with creative players who were good passers of the ball.

However, the role of the centre-half had begun to change during the 1925-26 season, primarily in response to a change in the offside law. The old offside law required attacking players to have three opposition players between them and the opposition goal in order to remain onside. The three players tended to be the goalkeeper and two full-backs. Teams had become effective at applying an offside trap and this often resulted in matches becoming compressed into the middle third of the field.

The new offside law meant that the attacking players required only two opponents between them and the opposition goal and this made it more difficult, and risky, to perfect the offside trap. It also allowed teams to play the ball forward much more quickly and some managers adapted by dropping the centre-half into a deeper role.

Jonathan Wilson's book, *Inverting the Pyramid*, details how some English club sides began to utilise a deep-lying centre-half during the 1925-26 season. The new tactic involved the centre-half dropping back between the full-backs to offer more defensive cover, which effectively created a three-man backline. The two inside-forwards also dropped deeper, and this had the effect of creating what became known as the W-M formation, with the ten outfield players positioned at the notional points of the two letters. The W-M formation was a key factor in Herbert Chapman's managerial success at Arsenal in the late 1920s and early 1930s.

The tactical implications arising from the change in the offside law also became evident in Irish domestic football. An article appeared in the *Westmeath Independent* on 28 November 1925 observing that 'centre halves are playing farther back, and they are sticking to the opposing centre-forward'. Later that season, a writer in the *Wicklow News-Letter* discussed the changing style of play and noted that 'many full-backs are doubtful as to how far up the field they should go when their own team is advancing'.

The role of the centre-half as a 'third back' was almost certainly widespread in Irish football by the early 1930s. An article appeared in the *Irish Press* on 17 November 1931 which stated that 'centre-halves, owing to the change in the old offside rule, are nowadays nothing more or less than stoppers'. The same article referred to centre-halves as 'third backs, whose duty it is to hold up attacks coming through the centre'.

There is some footage available of the Irish Free State's match against Belgium in 1934 courtesy of *British Pathé* newsreel. Although it is only a couple of minutes in length, the footage shows a series of Belgian attacks, including two of their goals. During these passages of play, it is evident that the Irish team was defending with three men in the backline. The use of a deep-lying centre-half during this era serves to illustrate that Irish football was already mirroring tactical trends in the English game.

The Belgian players who travelled to Dublin were drawn exclusively from their domestic league. Four of the players were members of the Belgian league champions, the Union SG club in Brussels, including the goalkeeper and both full-backs. The forward duo of Jean Brichaut and Jean Capelle played their football with Standard Liège.

In advance of the game, the Irish newspapers referred to the speed and close passing movements of the Belgian team. A preview of the match in the *Irish Press* outlined an expectation of 'the Belgians outshining our players in ground work and close passing, but the long-swinging game, keen tackling and sharp, decisive attacks should turn the scale in favour of the Free State'. This could be viewed as an early reference to an Irish team placing an emphasis on a more direct style of play in contrast to the more refined approach of their Continental opponents.

Irish Free State

Foley

Lynch   O'Reilly   Burke

Gaskins   Kendrick
(captain)

Byrne   O'Keeffe

Moore

Kennedy   Kelly

S Vanden Eynde   Versyp

Capelle

Saeys   Brichaut

Bourgeois   Van Ingelgem

Welkenhuysen

Smellinckx   Pappaert
(captain)

Vandewyer

Belgium

The fixture was scheduled for a Sunday afternoon at Dalymount Park. A crowd of approximately 28,000 observed two minutes' silence before the game in memory of King Albert I of Belgium who had died in a mountaineering accident a week earlier. The Irish team kicked off, playing against the wind in the first half. Whether the wind was a pertinent factor in the game is difficult to determine. It was standard procedure for newspaper reports to reference the weather conditions during this era, irrespective of whether the conditions influenced the match.

With only a minute on the clock, Paddy Moore had the ball in the net, but he was adjudged to be offside. However, it was Belgium that settled into their stride with greater ease and they opened the scoring in the 13th minute. Louis Versyp dispossessed Tom Burke and swung in a cross from the right wing which was turned into the net by the unmarked centre-forward, Jean Capelle. The Irish team then launched an attack of their own and Billy Kennedy went close with a header from a pass by Tim O'Keeffe.

Much to the surprise of the home crowd, Belgium struck again after 24 minutes when another cross from Versyp forced Jim Foley to punch clear. The ball landed in front of Stanley Vanden Eynde who lobbed the ball into an empty net. The Irish team was facing an uphill battle, having conceded twice with just over a quarter of the game played. However, within a minute, they had a goal back when Paddy Moore raced onto a through-ball from Jimmy Kelly before unleashing a shot past the Belgian goalkeeper.

After 35 minutes of play, Stanley Vanden Eynde was involved in what was described as an innocuous challenge but unfortunately resulted in a broken leg for the Belgian left-winger. He was replaced by his brother, Francois Vanden Eynde.

O'Keeffe almost levelled the scores before half-time, but his shot hit the side netting. When the half-time whistle blew, the Irish team trailed 2-1 and although Moore looked menacing in attack, the home team was chasing the game.

The Irish defence had struggled in the first half. One potential explanation for their lack of cohesion and composure was the late positional changes arising from the injured William 'Sacky' Glen being replaced by Miah Lynch and the move of Paddy Gaskins to right-half. The Irish team sought to address this issue at the start of the second half with Gaskins and Joe O'Reilly switching positions. But this change failed to garner any immediate dividend, as Belgium scored their third goal three minutes into the second half. The substitute Francois Vanden Eynde side-footed to the net following a pass from André Saeys.

The home side replied almost immediately when Moore stretched out his leg to score from a cross by Kennedy. The Irish Free State then began to take control of the game and pressed for an equaliser, which duly arrived in the 56th minute. Moore latched onto a long pass from Kelly and the Aberdeen centre-forward completed his hattrick.

The ability of the two teams to create clear-cut goal scoring opportunities suggested that both sides had a carefree attacking approach in the second half. With the score-line at 3-3, the Irish team appeared to be in the ascendancy, but Belgium counter-attacked to good effect. The visitors scored their fourth goal on the hour mark when a quick attacking move led to Francois Vanden Eynde receiving the ball in the inside-left position. He cut inside Lynch to shoot past Foley.

The Irish keeper subsequently saved a shot from Capelle and at the other end, O'Keeffe went close to equalising, but his close-range shot was straight at Vandewyer. Then, with 15 minutes remaining, an Irish corner was cleared to Joe Kendrick who crossed for Moore and the diminutive centre-forward rose highest to head home his fourth goal of the game.

With the score tied at 4-4, the Irish team went in search of a winner. According to the match report in the *Cork Examiner*, the play was 'fast and furious' in the final fifteen minutes 'with the home team having rather the better of the exchanges'. Alas, the Irish team couldn't find a winner, with the Belgian defence holding firm to secure a draw.

The following day, the *Irish Independent* described the 4-4 draw as 'one of the most exciting matches seen at Dalymount Park for many a day'. The *Irish Press* reported that the Free State 'should have won' and that 'the tactics of the Belgians knocked them completely out of their stride'.

Unsurprisingly, much of the post-match reaction focused on the performance of Paddy Moore, the first player in the world to score four goals in a World Cup match. The *Irish Press* described each of his four goals as 'a masterstroke of precision and timing', whilst the *Cork Examiner* reported that 'never has a man given a cleverer or more courageous display'.

The Belgian media was less impressed with the quality of football on show. The Brussels-based *Het Laatste Nieuws* reported that 'the Belgians mainly owe this result to their courageous action because the play was generally mediocre'. The same publication also referred to the more physically robust approach of the Irish team:

> 'In Belgium, the game of certain Irish players would certainly have been punished with a few free kicks, but the English concept of the regulations does not fit in with the Belgian views and so it happened that they were at a disadvantage.'

The mention of 'English' was more than likely a reference to the English referee, Tom Crew, who officiated the game in Dublin. Nevertheless, the sentiment expressed was perhaps indicative of an emerging Continental perception of physicality in British and Irish football.

The Irish team had shown its determination in rescuing a draw, but the failure to beat Belgium was a blow to their hopes of qualifying for the World Cup. It meant that they would more than likely need to pick up a result in their second and final qualifying game away to the

Netherlands. The team that travelled to Amsterdam six weeks later included five changes from the side that had drawn against Belgium. The Netherlands won comfortably on a 5-2 score-line, with the Irish goals arriving courtesy of Paddy Moore and Shelbourne's Johnny Squires.

The Dutch team went on to beat Belgium 4-2 in the final group game in Antwerp to top the qualifying group. Belgium finished level on points with the Irish Free State, but had conceded one goal fewer, which was enough to secure second place and their progression to the World Cup.

Given the level of expectation before the qualifiers, the failure to reach the World Cup was a hugely disappointing outcome for the Irish team, not least as the side would have been bolstered by players from the English League clubs for the tournament itself. Despite the disappointment, the quest for World Cup qualification had provided the Irish public with a brief glimpse of the talents of Paddy Moore. The centre-forward had displayed his full repertoire of skills in achieving his four-goal haul against Belgium.

Sadly, the performance against Belgium was to be the high point of Moore's career. He fought an ongoing battle with alcoholism, which ultimately led to him leaving Aberdeen. He returned to Dublin in 1935 and signed for Shamrock Rovers, where he helped the club win the FAI Cup. At international level, Moore went on to play a pivotal role for the Free State when they beat Germany 5-2 in 1936, providing assists for four of the Irish goals. However, his off-field problems resulted in a premature end to his career, with just nine caps and seven goals for the Irish Free State.

Paddy Moore died in July 1951 at just 41 years of age. Following his passing, WP Murphy in the *Irish Independent* described him as 'a football genius' and 'one of a small circle of really great players which Ireland has produced'. He may never have achieved his full potential, but he was arguably the first truly great player to emerge from Dublin.

In 1936, the FAIFS reverted to the title of the Football Association of Ireland in anticipation of the change of the state's name in the pending Constitution of Ireland. The team would now be referred to as 'Ireland' or 'Éire'.

The qualifying campaign for the 1934 World Cup had highlighted the need for increased exposure to international football, which could only be achieved through regular fixtures with other national teams. In the three-and-a-half years between the qualifying campaigns for the 1934 and 1938 World Cups, the FAI organised a total of eleven full international fixtures.

The qualifying process for the 1938 World Cup pitted Ireland against an unfancied Norwegian team in a two-team group, with the first game held in Oslo and followed by the return fixture in Dublin. Prior to facing Norway, Ireland had won four of their last five internationals, including victories away to Germany, Switzerland and France. The expectation was that the Irish team would have too much experience and quality for their opponents, but they suffered a surprise 3-2 defeat in the first game.

In advance of the return fixture against Norway, a headline in the *Irish Press* stated that 'grit and fighting spirit should pull Ireland through'. This was an early reference to the characteristics which would eventually become synonymous with Irish football. Perhaps it says more about the Irish sporting mentality that fighting spirit was invoked as the reason why the team should advance, given that they were strong favourites to beat the unfancied Norwegians.

The second match against Norway was played at Dalymount Park. It was the first occasion that the Irish team wore numbers on their jerseys. Defensive frailties led to the concession of early goals and the home team was left chasing the game in a manner reminiscent of the Belgium fixture a few years earlier. The home team scored a late equaliser to salvage a 3-3 draw, but the result was enough for Norway to qualify for the World Cup. Ireland had narrowly missed out on qualification once again.

The failure to qualify for the 1938 World Cup was another lost opportunity, particularly as the Irish team appeared to be on an upward trajectory. Indeed, prior to the outbreak of the Second World War in 1939, the team drew with Hungary twice – impressive results given that the Hungarian team were runners-up at the 1938 World Cup.

It is worth speculating that, if an Irish team had qualified for either of the World Cups in 1934 or 1938, the history of football in the country might have evolved in a very different way. The platform and exposure offered by a World Cup played on European soil could have opened-up the game to a wider audience and increased football's credibility in a sporting landscape still dominated by the GAA.

Chapter 2
England v Republic of Ireland
21 September 1949

'Anybody who thinks the Irish have any chance should make an appointment with a Harley Street psychiatrist.'

– Henry Rose, *Daily Express*

The 1940s was a decade of significant change across Europe, with the Second World War and its aftermath having profound effects on the political landscape. International football slowly re-emerged from the embers of the War. After seven years without a fixture, the Irish team resumed action with a game against Portugal in 1946. In September of the same year, they finally played England. That match took place at Dalymount Park, with the legendary Tom Finney scoring an 83rd-minute goal to help England to victory. It was the first time that the FAI's team had faced one of the British associations, a legacy of the association's turbulent relationship with the IFA in Belfast.

In February 1949, Stanley Rous, Secretary of the English FA, wrote to the FAI advising that their International Committee had decided at a recent meeting to invite the FAI to send an international team to play England later in the year. Two possible dates in September were proposed, with Liverpool as the likely location. The FAI accepted the invitation and Goodison Park was confirmed as the venue.

The political terms of reference were also evolving around this time with the Republic of Ireland Act coming into force in April 1949, removing the country from the British Commonwealth and confirming its status as a republic. The FAI later complained to Stanley Rous that the FA had designated the fixture at Goodison Park as a game between England and Éire, noting that the team had been referred to as 'Ireland' in its previous fixtures. The FA apologised for any offence caused but advised that they needed to differentiate between this game and their annual fixture with Northern Ireland which, for many years, had been billed as England versus Ireland.

The fixture against England was the first opportunity for the FAI's team to showcase its talents on English soil, although their form was not at a level that would cause undue concern for their hosts. The Irish team had lost ten of their fourteen games since resuming competition after the War and had started their World Cup qualifying campaign with a loss to Sweden earlier in the year. They recovered to beat Finland at Dalymount Park, but few pundits were willing to give them any chance of causing an upset against England.

Frank Johnstone was an Irish reporter who travelled to Liverpool for the game. Writing in the *Irish Times* in 2006, he described his memories of the cross-channel voyage. The young reporter hopped on a bus in Sandymount, heading towards O'Connell Street. At Ringsend, the Shamrock Rovers' goalkeeper, Tommy Godwin, got onto the bus and sat down beside him. Following their bus journey, Johnstone and Godwin walked up the North Wall and boarded a boat to Liverpool, where they were joined by a second Shamrock Rovers player, Tommy O'Connor. According to Johnstone, there were fewer than 200 travelling supporters.

In contrast to modern-day standards, the preparations for the game were low-key. The Irish team were staying at the Palace Hotel in Birkdale and their training sessions took place at Southport's ground on Haig Avenue. The fixture was taking place in the days before substitutions and only the selected players travelled. As a result, only seven players took part in the training session on the day before the game. The four players missing from the training session, Con Martin, Davy Walsh, Tom Aherne and Tommy Moroney, had trained with their respective clubs before travelling to Southport in the afternoon.

The Irish training sessions were conducted by Billy Lord, who was associated with Shamrock Rovers for most of his career. During this era, the team was selected by a five-man committee, usually made up of FAI officials attached to League of Ireland clubs. There was no official manager, thereby meaning that the delegates on the selection committee could press the claims of their own club members. The team they picked had plenty of experience in its ranks and included seven players who were plying their trade in the English First Division, two in the English Second Division and two – Godwin and O'Connor – from the League of Ireland.

Godwin was selected as the goalkeeper, having made his international debut against Portugal four months earlier. At 22 years of age, he was the youngest member of the team but could rely on three experienced defenders in front of him. At full-back, the team was captained by the 30-year-old Jackie Carey, or Johnny as he was known in England. Carey was the Manchester United captain and had recently won the Football Writers' Association player of the year award. He was assisted in the backline by Con Martin, who was then at Aston Villa. Martin was an experienced centre-half who had played Gaelic football in his younger days, helping Dublin win a Leinster title in 1941. However, he had also been playing football for Drumcondra and when the GAA discovered this, Martin was expelled and his medal withheld. The third member of the backline was another 30-year old, Tom Aherne, who played with Luton Town in the Second Division.

Willie Walsh of Manchester City was selected at right-half. Born in Dublin, Walsh moved to Manchester with his family at the age of seven. He had turned professional at Manchester City as a teenager, but it had taken him a number of seasons to become established in the first team. At left-half was Tommy Moroney, who played in the Second Division with West Ham United. Moroney had scored in his international debut against Spain the previous year.

Peter Desmond of Middlesbrough was picked at inside-forward.

Desmond had spells at Waterford United and Shelbourne before moving to the English First Division in 1949. The Irish team was also able to call upon the Everton duo of Peter Farrell and Peter Corr who would provide their teammates with local knowledge, given their experience of playing at Goodison Park. Farrell was picked as an inside-forward with Corr at outside-right. A third Everton player, Tommy Eglington, was also available to play, but missed out on selection to Tommy O'Connor of Shamrock Rovers. O'Connor, who had made his international debut against Finland two weeks earlier, was picked at outside-left.

The team was completed by Davy Walsh at centre-forward. Walsh was in prolific form for West Bromwich Albion and had helped the West Midlands club gain promotion to the First Division earlier that year. Walsh had also scored a brace of goals in a 3-2 win against Spain two years earlier.

Of the eleven Irish players selected to face England, six were born in Dublin, two were from Cork, with one each from Limerick, Waterford and Dundalk. Another young Irish player, who travelled to Goodison Park to watch the game as a spectator, was 19-year-old Arthur Fitzsimons, who had made his international debut in the previous match against Finland. Fitzsimons had played for Shelbourne before moving to Middlesbrough at the start of the 1949-50 season as part of a two-player transfer that included Peter Desmond. Although Desmond was considered to be the makeweight in the deal, the FAI selectors opted for his greater experience to face England ahead of Fitzsimons. The FAI Archives include a letter, dated 15 September 1949, from the association's General Secretary Joe Wickham to Middlesbrough, explaining that Fitzsimons had not been included in the team as 'the Selection Committee think he is a bit young for this class of football'.

England were managed by Walter Winterbottom, who had been appointed as the country's first full-time manager in 1946. During his time in charge, Winterbottom succeeded in moulding England into a formidable team. Prior to meeting Ireland, England had won 15 of the 22 matches they played after the Second World War. Much of their success was based on the free-scoring exploits of a forward line of Stanley Matthews, Stan Mortensen, Tommy Lawton, Wilf Mannion and Tom Finney. However, that forward line was aging and by the time they faced Ireland at Goodison Park, only Mannion and Finney were available for selection. Finney needed no introduction to Irish followers, having scored the winning goal in the only previous meeting between the two nations.

The England team also included the experience of Neil Franklin and Billy Wright, with the latter captaining the side. Winterbottom named three debutants in his team – Bert Mozley, Peter Harris and Jesse Pye. The team included two members of Portsmouth's league-winning team and three players from the high-flying Wolverhampton Wanderers.

In the eyes of the English media, the Irish team had little or no chance of causing an upset. Henry Rose of the *Daily Express* was particularly dismissive, writing that 'anybody who thinks the Irish have any chance should make an appointment with a Harley Street psychiatrist', whilst a preview in *The Daily Telegraph* suggested that the match 'may end in a runaway home win'.

There was a slightly less complacent tone in *The Times*, which cautioned that 'it would be folly indeed to approach to-day's game in a light mood, and England we may be sure will not make that mistake'. Nevertheless, the same article concluded that 'on the face of it, there should only be one ending'.

England

1
Williams

2
Mozley

5
Franklin

3
Aston

4
Wright
(captain)

6
Dickinson

8
Morris

10
Mannion

7
Harris

9
Pye

11
Finney

11
O'Connor

9
D. Walsh

7
Corr

10
Desmond

8
Farrell

6
Moroney

4
W. Walsh

3
Aherne

5
Martin

2
Carey
(captain)

1
Godwin

Ireland

25

The Irish media provided a more rigorous analysis of the strengths of the respective teams. Three days before the game, the *Sunday Independent* expressed some concern that Ireland needed 'more weight on the wings' and that there was 'a big question-mark regarding goal-getting ability'. WP Murphy of the *Irish Independent* predicted that Jackie Carey and Willie Walsh would 'hold the English left, where Finney is only half the player he is on the other flank, as he is a natural right-footer who doubles back to cross the ball'.

The Irish players were in good spirits as they travelled by bus from Birkdale to Goodison Park. In an interview with the *Irish Independent* in 1999, Con Martin recalled the experience:

'There was a sing-song among the lads on the bus going to Goodison Park and one of the tunes they sang was When Irish Eyes are Smiling. And looking around, I remember saying to myself "we may as well sing about it now, because there won't be too many smiles after the match".'

The Irish team started the match with a strong wind behind them, but they were slow to settle. They almost went behind in the first minute when Jesse Pye headed a Finney cross wide from close range. It was almost a dream start to Pye's international career. Another move involving Johnny Morris and Billy Wright ended with a shot by Pye which was blocked. Finney then missed a one-on-one with the Irish goalkeeper, Tommy Godwin.

As the half progressed, England continued to dominate possession, but the threat posed by Finney was stemmed by Jackie Carey and a well-organised Irish defence. The match report in *The Times* suggested that there was too much lateral passing between Morris, Mannion and Pye and that none of the English players appeared willing to take the responsibility of having a shot.

The Irish team's only notable attempt on the English goal in the first half hour came from a counter-attacking move. First, Carey dispossessed Finney and initiated an attack from the full-back position, culminating in a clever back-heel by Davy Walsh and a shot from Peter Farrell that went just wide. According to *The Times*, Farrell and Walsh 'had begun to make the England defence look uncertain'.

The breakthrough arrived in the 32nd minute, against the run of play. Peter Desmond received a pass from Tommy O'Connor and was upended by Bert Mozley in the penalty area. The referee awarded a penalty and Con Martin was handed the responsibility of taking the spot-kick. According to the *Irish Press*, Martin struck the penalty 'with terrific force' and Bert Williams parried but was unable to prevent the ball crossing the line. The visitors had an unlikely lead.

The Irish team grew in confidence after the goal and Davy Walsh had two good attempts at increasing the lead, but his first effort went high and the second was saved by the advancing Williams. With half-time approaching, Williams failed to hold a lobbing shot from O'Connor, but he dived on the ball just as Corr was about to knock it into an empty net. The half-time whistle blew and although the score-line belied England's control of possession, the Irish team could quite conceivably have been two goals up.

At the start of the second half, England injected some pace into the game, laying siege to the Irish goal. It required a strong defensive effort to repel wave after wave of English attack. According to the match report in *The Daily Telegraph*, the Irish defence 'lived through a bombardment which, by all laws, should have produced three goals'.

Aherne cleared the ball off the toes of Pye inside the six-yard box before Godwin made a full-length save to prevent Peter Harris from scoring. Godwin then pulled off what the *Irish Press* described as 'a wonder save' to deny Finney the equaliser before the hour mark. Willie Walsh and Con Martin were both forced to clear shots off the line and then a corner-kick taken by Harris hit the underside of the bar and dropped neatly into Godwin's hands.

Billy Wright also went close to scoring when he struck a powerful shot from 30 yards, which Godwin somehow managed to parry away to safety. The Irish goal was leading a charmed life, but the team was defending heroically in the hope that they could hold onto their slender lead.

Then, with only five minutes remaining, the Irish team struck the decisive blow, ruthlessly capitalising on the disorganisation in the England defence. Tommy O'Connor's neat pass sent Peter Farrell clear and, with Bert Williams advancing from the English goal, Farrell lobbed the ball over his head and into the net. As an Everton player it was appropriate that Farrell should score on his home ground to seal the win. Meanwhile, O'Connor had justified his selection in the team by playing a key role in both goals.

When the final whistle blew, the Republic of Ireland celebrated as the first foreign team to beat England on English soil. England had previously lost to opposition in the British Home Championship, but this defeat marked a new departure. The English crowd was gracious in its applause as the Irish team left the field, with a noisy ovation reserved for Tommy Godwin who had performed heroics in the Irish goal.

There was little opportunity for the players to celebrate their historic victory as they needed to return to their clubs for training the following morning. Con Martin and Davy Walsh got a lift back to Birmingham on a bus with a group of West Bromwich Albion supporters who had travelled to Liverpool to cheer on England. They stopped at a pub for a few drinks and bought fish and chips before arriving in Birmingham.

The following day the English newspapers were generous in their praise of the Irish team but bemoaned the lack of a cutting edge from the home side's frontline. The various match reports provide the sense of an England team that was over-elaborate in its use of a short passing game, which was not enough to break down a packed Irish defence. By contrast, the Irish attacking play was more incisive, with their forwards making better use of their limited opportunities. The

Manchester Guardian described Ireland as 'a well-balanced team' which 'showed the value of direct methods'. *The Times* reported that 'all the evidence pointed to only one possible verdict, yet by the afternoon's end, that evidence was proved not worth the paper on which it was written'.

Aside from the goalkeeping performance of Godwin, both Jackie Carey and Con Martin were praised for their performances in suppressing the threats posed by Finney and Pye respectively. Davy Walsh also impressed, with *The Daily Telegraph* reporting that he led the Irish attack with 'dash and skill' and was 'the most dangerous forward on the field'. The local *Liverpool Echo* published a souvenir page to mark the occasion and according to the FAI Archives, General Secretary Joe Wickham ordered a copy so that the page could be framed and displayed at the FAI's headquarters in Merrion Square.

The Irish newspapers could barely withhold their excitement at the shock result, with the *Irish Independent* proclaiming that 'the British Lion was in a sorry state last night . . . his den had been invaded and tail twisted by the FAI soccer eleven who scored a sensational 2-0 win at Liverpool'. The *Irish Times* report was similarly jubilant:

> 'The vast majority of the 51,847 people streamed out of Goodison Park, Liverpool, yesterday with a dumbfounded look on their faces. The reason was that the cream of England's footballers had been beaten 2-0 at home by Ireland . . . It was one of the most amazing and thrilling internationals ever witnessed.'

The media coverage and publicity garnered by the victory was noteworthy at a time when Gaelic games constituted the primary sporting interest for most Irish people. The match in Liverpool took place four days before the centrepiece of the GAA calendar, the All-Ireland Football Final, involving Meath and Cavan. However, the win over England generated its fair share of sporting headlines. The result certainly helped to grab the attention of a cohort of Irish society that had previously been indifferent to the sport.

In the years that followed, it might have seemed as though the Irish victory at Goodison Park was wiped from the collective consciousness of the English media and supporters, with Hungary's 6-3 win over England at Wembley in 1953 often cited as the first victory for a foreign team on English soil. However, the newspaper reports in the immediate aftermath of the Irish win certainly indicated an awareness in England of the significance of the result. On the day after the game, *The Daily Telegraph* reported that the Irish team 'won fame as the first foreign team ever to make a successful invasion of England', whilst *The Manchester Guardian* adopted a similar tone, stating that 'it was England's first home defeat by a side other than from one of the home countries'.

As time passed, perhaps it became more palatable for the English media to focus on the 1953 defeat inspired by the genius of Ferenc Puskás and the team that became known as 'the Mighty Magyars'. Of course, it may simply be a case that an Irish team containing nine players from the English Football League conveyed a sense of familiarity and was certainly less exotic than the great Hungarian side.

Regardless of how the result was viewed in England, it was a momentous victory for football in the Republic of Ireland and certainly the most significant result the FAI's team had achieved up to that point. The win helped to establish some much-needed credibility for Irish football.

It is, however, worth noting that although it was only the Republic's second meeting with England, some of the players had featured regularly for the IFA's 'Ireland' team in the British Home Championship and had experience of playing against England. One such fixture was a match between England and the IFA's team at Goodison Park in November 1947. The match ended in a 2-2 draw, but the IFA's team contained no fewer than seven players born south of the border, five of whom would go on to represent the Republic at the same venue in 1949. Although the draw in 1947 tends to receive little attention, the experience of securing a result against England at Goodison Park would surely have stood to those players who would subsequently play for the Republic at the same venue two years later.

The FAI's ongoing relationship with the IFA also provided an important subtext to the 1949 fixture against England. Prior to the match at Goodison, FAI officials voiced their opposition to the Belfast-based organisation selecting Southern-born players in their teams. The IFA's team were due to play Scotland ten days later. When the IFA announced their squad, no Southern-born players were included and the *Evening Herald* reported that it was the first international team 'chosen in the North since the split in 1921 that has not included players born South of the border when any of the right standard were available'.

The Republic of Ireland's campaign to qualify for the 1950 World Cup in Brazil resumed two months later when they faced Sweden at Dalymount Park. The starting eleven contained ten of the players who had featured against England with the only change involving Tommy Moroney making way for Reg Ryan of West Bromwich Albion. Hopes were high that the team could secure one of the places on offer to European nations at the World Cup. However, with an expectant crowd of 41,000 watching, the Irish team slumped to a 3-1 defeat. Sweden sealed their passage to the following year's World Cup and would go on to claim third place at the tournament, making them the highest-placed European side.

In a remarkable series of events, the FAI subsequently received an invitation from FIFA to take part in the 1950 World Cup finals, following the decision of Scotland to withdraw. It was the first time that the British associations had participated in the World Cup and FIFA had offered two places in the tournament to the two highest-placed teams in the British Home Championship. George Graham, then secretary of the Scottish Football Association, inexplicably declared that Scotland would only accept the FIFA invite if they went as British champions. When they finished in the runners-up position, he was true to his word and Scotland withdrew.

With Scotland absent, the FAI weighed up the cost of taking part in the tournament and decided that it would bankrupt the association. An announcement was made by the FAI stating that the association was unable to accept the invitation due to short notice. As things transpired, only thirteen countries took part in the 1950 World Cup finals, but the participating nations actually reaped a financial dividend. With the benefit of hindsight, the FAI's failure to take up the invitation could be viewed as short-sighted. Participation in the tournament might have provided a significant step in shaping the future of Irish football.

During this period, the FAI appeared to be preoccupied with lobbying FIFA to prevent the IFA from picking Southern-born players. FIFA's response was to restrict the eligibility of players on the basis of the political border. A fixture between the IFA's team and Wales in March 1950 would prove to be the final occasion when players from the Republic would feature in the British Home Championship. In 1953, world football's governing body also ruled that neither team could be referred to as 'Ireland' in competitions which both teams were eligible to enter, decreeing that the official name for the FAI team would be the 'Republic of Ireland', with the IFA team to be referred to as 'Northern Ireland'.

It could be argued that the long-term development of Irish football would have been better served if the FAI had adopted a broader vision during this era, such as seizing the opportunities that might have arisen from an appearance at the World Cup finals. In hindsight, the aspiration to play and defeat England in a friendly international, coupled with the desire to restrict the IFA's remit, might seem like parochial objectives. Nevertheless, the victory at Goodison Park and the clarification of the eligibility criteria were important components in the creation of a discernible football identity for the Republic of Ireland.

The Irish team's quest to take part in the World Cup recommenced when they were drawn in a group alongside Luxembourg and France at the qualifying stage of the 1954 tournament. By that time, Arthur Fitzsimons of Middlesbrough had emerged as the team's creative force; he was joined by Con Martin, Peter Farrell and Davy Walsh – a trio of players who remained from the team that beat England in 1949. With Luxembourg effectively making up the numbers, qualification would be determined by the two fixtures against France.

But it was not to be. After losing 5-3 at Dalymount Park, the Irish team travelled for the return fixture in the Parc des Princes in Paris. A single goal was enough for France to defeat a gallant Irish effort and seal their passage to the World Cup. The disappointment of missing out on World Cup qualification in the city of Paris would eventually become an unfortunate theme in the history of Irish football.

Chapter 3
Republic of Ireland v West Germany
25 November 1956

'German giants were cut down.'

– Sean Piondar, *Irish Press*

On 13 April 1956, St Patrick's Athletic faced Shamrock Rovers at a packed Dalymount Park in a top-of-the-table clash between two sides competing for the League of Ireland title. Rovers prevailed on a 4-2 score-line, with the match report in the *Irish Independent* describing it as 'the best match of the season' during which the crowd was treated to '90 minutes of sparkling football'. St Pat's subsequently pipped Rovers to the title, but the fixture between the two clubs is noteworthy, as five of the players on the Dalymount pitch that day would go on to represent the Republic of Ireland against West Germany at the same venue seven months later.

The domestic game in Ireland in the 1950s was in a healthy state, with League of Ireland games regularly attracting large crowds. The league provided a viable pathway for players to make their way into the national team. It was also an era which produced a very successful Shamrock Rovers team, managed by Paddy Coad and which became known as 'Coad's Colts'.

Football had grown in popularity in the years following the victory over England at Goodison Park, but the continued expansion of the game faced the challenges of a conservative, nationalist society, which propagated the narrative that football, or soccer as it was often called, was a 'foreign game'. The struggle to gain the acceptance of the Irish establishment was perhaps best illustrated in the controversy surrounding two planned fixtures against Yugoslavia in the 1950s. Ireland were scheduled to play Yugoslavia in a friendly at Dalymount Park in 1952. However, the Catholic Church intervened, with Archbishop John Charles McQuaid stating that he did not want Ireland to play a 'Godless country'. The Catholic Church felt that it was being discriminated against by the Communist regime in Yugoslavia and McQuaid used this agenda to successfully lobby the FAI to withdraw the invitation.

Three years later, the FAI arranged another fixture with Yugoslavia in Dalymount, which was scheduled for October 1955. McQuaid was furious that his power had been undermined and that the FAI had not sought his permission. Lynda Slattery described in a 2007 article in *History Ireland* how the archbishop called on Irish people to boycott the match and warned schoolboys that attending the game would be a 'mortal sin'. The national broadcasting service, Radio Éireann, declined to cover the match, with their commentator Philip Greene making himself unavailable. No member of the Government attended the fixture, nor did the President, Sean T. O'Kelly. Despite the protestations, an impressive attendance of 21,400 turned up to watch a skilful Yugoslav team win 4-1. The fact that the match attracted such a strong attendance despite opposition from the conservative establishment merely served to illustrate the popularity of football amongst working-class people in Dublin.

Another opponent that Ireland faced regularly during this era was West Germany. In spite of the political upheavals in Continental Europe, the FAI had organised fixtures with the Germans, both prior to and after the Second World War. The Federal Republic of Germany – *Bundesrepublik Deutschland* – was created in May 1949, exactly five weeks after the Republic of Ireland Act came into force. The two nations subsequently met on the football field in 1951, 1952 and 1955, with one draw and two German wins during that period.

In the aftermath of the War, the West Germans had emerged as a formidable force in world football. They won their first World Cup in Switzerland in 1954 when they shocked Ferenc Puskás and his strongly fancied Hungarian team in the final. The victory became known as The Miracle of Bern, given the dominance of the Hungarian team prior to that final. The German success has always been mired in controversy, however, with a late goal by Puskás, which would have been the equaliser, ruled out as offside.

In November 1956, the world champions travelled to Dalymount Park once again to face Ireland in a friendly match. The West Germans were managed by Josef 'Sepp' Herberger, who had masterminded the World Cup success two years earlier. Despite their vaunted status, Herberger's team was not in a particularly rich vein of form. They had lost eleven of their sixteen matches following their World Cup triumph, including a loss to Switzerland in Frankfurt four days before playing against Ireland.

Notwithstanding their poor form, the strength of German football was highlighted in an interview with Dr Peco Bauwens, President of the German Football Association (the DFB), conducted in the days prior to their visit to Dalymount. Bauwens explained that the DFB had 54,000 teams and 1.7 million registered players, which did not include schoolboy teams. Their professional league comprised the first and second divisions, which permitted the payment of a maximum salary of 320 Deutschmarks per week, which was then equivalent to about £32 in Irish currency. The popularity and pre-eminence of football in West Germany was a far cry from the small domestic league and limited pool of players available in Ireland.

Unsurprisingly, West Germany travelled to Dublin as strong favourites, with the Irish media giving the hosts little chance of causing an upset. Two days prior to the fixture, the *Irish Times* posed the question, 'Who says that Ireland will shock Germany into defeat at Dalymount Park next Sunday? Not the student of the form book.'

The Irish team was now managed by Jackie Carey, who had

captained Ireland to their famous win over England seven years earlier. Carey's influence was limited, however, as the team continued to be selected by an FAI committee. The team they picked to face West Germany was backboned by a range of current and former League of Ireland players.

Alan Kelly was selected in goals to win his first international cap at 20 years of age. Kelly was from Bray and had joined Drumcondra earlier that year. The match programme included pen profiles for each of the Irish players, with Kelly's profile stating that he had 'a great chance of making this position his own for many years to come'.

Seamus Dunne of Luton Town was picked at right-back. Dunne, another Wicklow native, had played for Drogheda, Wicklow Town and Shelbourne before moving cross-channel. Gerry Mackey of Shamrock Rovers was selected at centre-half and handed the captaincy in what was only his second international appearance. The left-back was Noel Cantwell, a Corkman who had played for his local club Cork Athletic before moving to West Ham United in 1952. Cantwell was a talented sportsman and he also represented the Ireland cricket team during the 1950s.

Tommy Dunne of St Patrick's Athletic was picked at right-half, having won his first cap in a 4-1 win against the Netherlands in Rotterdam six months earlier. The son of Jimmy Dunne, who had played for Arsenal in the 1930s, Tommy was known as an attack-minded wing-half. Ronnie Nolan of Shamrock Rovers was selected at left-half to win his second cap, having made his international debut against Denmark the previous month.

Nolan's Rovers teammate, Jimmy McCann, was picked at outside right to make his international debut in what would prove to be his only full international appearance. The 20-year old Joe Haverty was selected at outside left. Haverty was a skilful player who had made a small number of appearances for St Patrick's Athletic before moving to Arsenal in 1954.

37

The inside-forwards were Noel Peyton and Arthur Fitzsimons. Peyton played his football with Shamrock Rovers and was making his international debut just nine days shy of his 21st birthday. Fitzsimons had started his career at Shelbourne before joining Middlesbrough in 1949. Known for his pace, dribbling and creativity, Fitzsimons formed a successful partnership at Middlesbrough with a certain Brian Clough. Indeed, Clough later described the Dubliner as the best goal-maker he ever played with.

Shelbourne's Dermot Curtis was picked at centre-forward to win his second cap. The day before the game, an interview with Curtis appeared in the *Irish Times*. 'We'll put up a good fight and, no matter how good the Germans are, I'll be surprised if they enjoy an easy afternoon,' said Curtis. 'For every one of the 90 minutes we'll be all out to give the Germans a shock.'

It is worth noting that the team selection initially included Liam Whelan, a wonderfully talented inside-forward who had established himself as an integral part of Matt Busby's Manchester United team. However, Whelan had played for his club against Tottenham Hotspur the day before Ireland faced West Germany. The FAI had taken a decision that players who turned out for their clubs the previous day would automatically be replaced in the national team. It was reported in the Irish newspapers five days before the West Germany game that if Whelan played for his club, he would be replaced by Noel Peyton. It appeared that this policy was not communicated by the FAI to Matt Busby, or to Liam Whelan who arrived into Dublin on the morning of the game. When Whelan discovered his place had been awarded to Peyton, he availed of the opportunity to visit his family home in Cabra, before returning to Dalymount in the afternoon, paying in to watch the match from the school end of the ground.

Whelan's exclusion meant that the Irish team included a total of seven League of Ireland players, including four members of the Shamrock Rovers team and one St Patrick's Athletic player who had all played in the pivotal league fixture between the two clubs seven months earlier. It was the first time in the post-War era that an Irish team included more players from the League of Ireland than from the English Football League.

By international standards, the Irish team was an inexperienced one; the eleven players had won a combined total of just 31 full international caps before meeting West Germany. The team included three debutants and only Seamus Dunne and Arthur Fitzsimons could be described as seasoned internationals. Of course, it should be noted that international fixtures were relatively sparse in the 1950s, so there were limited opportunities for players to earn caps. Nonetheless, the West German team was an experienced side, with a combined total of 92 full international caps accumulated before meeting Ireland. Sepp Herberger only selected one debutant, Elwin Schlebrosky, playing at right-half.

The legendary Fritz Walter was initially selected at inside-forward and was named in the match programme. Walter was a prolific goal scorer who had captained the team to their World Cup triumph. Although he was in the twilight of his career, he was still a key member of the West German team and had a wealth of international experience. However, he was forced to withdraw from the team at late notice, with the *Irish Times* reporting that his mother-in-law was seriously ill.

Walter's place in the team was taken by Hans Schäfer of FC Köln. Schäfer was one of four players in the team who had played in the World Cup Final two years earlier, the other three being Karl Mai, Max Morlock and Helmut Rahn. Indeed, Morlock and Rahn had combined to score the three goals that helped the Germans overcome Hungary in the final. In the absence of Fritz Walter, Morlock was named as captain.

Republic of Ireland

1
Kelly

2
S. Dunne

5
Mackey
(captain)

3
Cantwell

4
T. Dunne

6
Nolan

8
Peyton

10
Fitzsimons

7
McCann

9
Curtis

11
Haverty

11
Vollmar

9
Miltz

7
Rahn

10
Schäfer

8
Morlock
(captain)

6
Mai

4
Schlebrosky

3
Juskowiak

5
Wewers

2
Ehrhardt

1
Kwiatkowski

West Germany

The Irish team gathered in Milltown on the morning of the game before making their way to Dalymount Park for a 2:30pm kick-off. A crowd of approximately 35,000 turned up at Dalymount, with special 'excursion' trains laid on for fans travelling from outside Dublin. The FAI General Secretary, Joe Wickham, advised the press in advance of the game that they 'could have sold the Dalymount Park stand accommodation three times over'. Those fans without a stand ticket were able to pay in at the turnstiles on the day of the game to stand on the terraces.

Gerry Mackey won the coin toss and decided to defend the school end of the ground in the first half, availing of a strong breeze which was blowing in the direction of the German goal. The *Irish Independent* suggested that the breeze may have been a factor in West Germany's defensive approach in the first half. Despite this apparent disadvantage, it was the Germans who created the first meaningful attack. Heinz Vollmar combined well with his inside-forward Hans Schäfer, but Noel Cantwell came rushing across to clear the ball just as Schäfer was about to shoot.

Minutes later, Cantwell turned creator as he sent a long ball into the middle of the German box, which was headed by Curtis and saved by Kwiatkowski. That was quickly followed, at the other end of the pitch, by a shot from Morlock, which was saved by Alan Kelly.

With 17 minutes on the clock, West Germany suffered their first blow when Schäfer was forced off with an injury, incurred from the earlier tackle by Cantwell. Schäfer was replaced by Horst Eckel, who had also been part of the team that won the World Cup two years earlier. Indeed, Eckel holds the distinction of being the first substitute in the history of football when he was introduced in one of the qualifying games for the 1954 World Cup.

Following Schäfer's departure, the main threat was offered by Helmut Rahn, who had a couple of shots at the Irish goal. Curtis tried a long-range shot at the other end, but it was saved by Kwiatkowski.

The German attacks were more sporadic, but Rahn and Miltz combined well on the right flank, culminating in a shot from Miltz that forced Kelly into a save.

Ireland's inside-forwards linked up on the half-hour mark, with Noel Peyton putting Arthur Fitzsimons through, but the Middlesbrough man decided to pass inside rather than shooting and the move came to nothing. Six minutes later, Donal Curtis won possession and teed up Fitzsimons for an opening. Fitzsimons had two efforts at shooting, both of which were blocked, before Curtis followed up with an effort that was saved by Kwiatkowski. The match was scoreless when the half-time whistle blew and although Ireland had the better of the exchanges, the Germans were expected to come out strongly in the second half and avail of the stiff breeze.

To the surprise of the crowd, it was Ireland that emerged as the stronger team in the early stages of the second half. Curtis had a good effort which went just wide of the goal. That was followed by a jinking run from Nolan, during which Juskowiak appeared to handle the ball, but the referee was unconvinced. At this stage, the German defence appeared increasingly shaky and Joe Haverty delivered a dangerous corner, which was eventually cleared by Kwiatkowski.

With 62 minutes played, Donal Curtis was sandwiched between Wewers and Erhardt, just inside the angle of the box. The referee adjudged it to be a foul and awarded a penalty. Noel Cantwell stepped up to take the spot-kick and struck a low, powerful shot to the keeper's left to give Ireland the lead. It was a deserving reward for the second-half pressure that the Irish team had exerted.

Five minutes after Cantwell's goal, the Germans almost summoned up the perfect response when Miltz struck a powerful shot that hit the post. The world champions were forced to chase the game and, despite all the attacking talent at their disposal, they struggled to find a way through the Irish defence.

With just under 15 minutes remaining, they created an opening which owed much to the pace of the left-winger, Heinz Vollmar. The German defence cleared a corner kick upfield and Vollmar dispossessed Seamus Dunne as the Irish full-back was trying to control the ball. Vollmar raced clear and was bearing down on goal, but Alan Kelly advanced, diving at the feet of the German winger to take the ball off his toes.

With the Irish team holding on to their slender advantage, they seized upon the German's lack of defensive cover to score a second goal in the 87th minute, dispelling the visitors' hopes of a comeback. Fitzsimons took possession and played a pass inside to Joe Haverty, who eluded the attempted tackles of Wewers and Juskowiak before racing clear and beating the opposition keeper to double the Irish lead.

Two minutes later, as the crowd still celebrated Haverty's goal, Fitzsimons forced Kwiatkowski into a save at the expense of a corner on the right. Jimmy McCann took the corner short to Tommy Dunne, who quickly returned it to McCann. The Shamrock Rovers player unleashed a powerful left-footed drive, which was deflected past the goalkeeper by the head of Juskowiak. McCann was credited with the goal, the perfect way to mark his international debut. The final whistle blew shortly after McCann's goal and the Irish players and home crowd could celebrate an unlikely yet deserved 3-0 victory over the world champions.

After the game, Ireland's winning captain, Gerry Mackey, said: 'Naturally, I'm very proud of our team. It was a hard game, but we won well in the end.' German manager Sepp Herberger suggested that the Irish team were fitter and better prepared: 'It was a hard fight for our team, who were not as well equipped physically as the Irish. We were not as fit, but we should have done better. I was disappointed.'

Herberger's conclusion that the Irish team was fitter seems reasonable, given that the home side finished the game so strongly and scored their three goals in the final half hour. Nevertheless, it is important to draw a distinction between fitness and physicality in this instance. Indeed, it was the German team that had the greater physicality and apparent size advantage. This was a consistent theme in the following day's newspaper reports, with the match report in the *Irish Press* referring to the younger and smaller Irish team:

> 'The home-based players are very young – and allegedly inexperienced. Yet they blended well with the four from cross-Channel clubs, to master the bigger, older and stronger Germans.'

The same report went on to state that 'in the second half our lads' superior skill forced the Germans to adopt robust methods. These tactics put some of our lighter players on the ground, but they were no substitute for sound technique.'

The German media also recognised the quality of the Irish performance, with the match report in *Die Welt* stating that the game 'showed clearly what the Irishmen can do when playing in front of their own audience and how big their reserves of strength are'.

Frank Johnstone's match report in the *Irish Times* referred to some 'uncouth tackling' from the West Germans. The physically robust approach of the visitors, particularly in the second half, would appear to be borne out in the match statistics. The West Germans conceded a total of 22 free kicks, 16 of these in the second half. In contrast, Ireland only conceded four free kicks over the course of the 90 minutes.

The depiction of Ireland as a smaller and more technically proficient team in comparison to their German counterparts might appear to many as a role reversal of what we've become accustomed to in modern-day football. The match reports from this period are instructive of an Irish football culture which placed an emphasis on speed and skill.

It would, however, be wrong to suggest that the Irish team was unable to incorporate the more physical elements of the game when required. In a post-match interview, the injured Hans Schäfer said, 'at one time, I was injured when an Irish player went in with his boot up.

That should have been a penalty for us.'

Schäfer was referring to the incident in the opening minutes when Noel Cantwell cleared the ball just as the German was about to shoot. Although most of the match reports refer to Cantwell's speed and conviction in winning this challenge, WP Murphy of the *Irish Independent* stated, in two separate paragraphs of his report, that the referee might have awarded a penalty against Cantwell. The tackle resulted in West Germany losing one of their best players to injury, whereas the Corkman went on to be very influential in the game. Indeed, WP Murphy suggested that Cantwell was the man of the match, as 'his trenchant tackling, his formidable physique, allied to undoubted football skill, completely silenced the right-hand side of the German attack'.

The comprehensive result against West Germany capped off a successful year for the FAI, with the Republic of Ireland senior team winning all three of its fixtures. The 35,000 crowd in attendance at Dalymount Park also generated receipts of £6,000 for the association.

In the catalogue of great Irish football achievements, the success of this particular team in beating the world champions tends to be overlooked. This is partly due to the passing of time, but it likely didn't help that much of the attention of the media and sports fans was drawn towards the Olympic Games in Melbourne. The performances of Irish athletes in Australia were prominent in the sporting headlines of Irish newspapers in late November and early December 1956. Indeed, eight days after Ireland beat West Germany, Ronnie Delany won an Olympic gold medal in the 1,500 metres, which was at that time the Blue Riband event of the Games. Delany's gold medal is rightly considered as one of the great achievements in Irish sporting history and, as such, it almost certainly overshadowed the victory over West Germany.

The Irish team hoped that the result against the Germans would act as a springboard in their challenge to qualify for the 1958 World Cup in Sweden. In May 1957, they faced a strong England team in two fixtures during the qualifying stages. In the first game at Wembley Stadium, England proved too strong, winning on a score-line of 5-1. The return fixture at Dalymount Park was a different matter, however. In front of an estimated crowd of 47,000, Ireland took the lead in the fourth minute through a goal from Alf Ringstead of Sheffield United. With the team holding on for a famous victory, England scored a 90th-minute equaliser through John Atyeo, shocking the home crowd into an eerie silence. It was a disappointing outcome, as a win would have secured a play-off against England to determine which team qualified for the World Cup finals.

While he didn't feature in the team that had defeated West Germany, Liam Whelan played a key role in the home fixture against England. Tragically, the Munich Air Disaster would take the lives of Liam Whelan and four of the England players – Roger Byrne, Duncan Edwards, David Pegg and Tommy Taylor – less than nine months later. The devastation of losing the 'Busby Babes' was felt across the world and the loss of Liam Whelan had an enduring effect in Dublin. He had already made 98 first team appearances and scored 52 goals in four seasons at United. At the tender age of 22 and with only four caps for Ireland, his best days in a green shirt were still ahead of him.

Although the victory over West Germany was achieved in a friendly and against a team that wasn't at full strength, the result must rank as one of the finest achievements by an Irish football team in a standalone fixture, particularly as it comprised a team of homegrown players. It is remarkable that a side which included seven League of Ireland players and four former League of Ireland players could beat the world champions so comprehensively.

The result was a testament to the quality of domestic football at that time, although it should also be recognised that the League of Ireland's introduction to European club football a year later provided a rude awakening. Shamrock Rovers met Matt Busby's Manchester United in the European Cup in September 1957, with the English champions progressing to the next round on a 9-2 aggregate score-line. Nonetheless, the 1950s was undoubtedly a golden era for the domestic league when high attendances were commonplace, particularly for Dublin derbies between Drumcondra and Shamrock Rovers.

The crowds at League of Ireland fixtures slowly declined throughout the 1960s and with the reduced crowds came a perceived fall in the standard of players within the league. There are a series of reasons which might explain this. Firstly, socio-economic factors played a role, with a population shift in Dublin, as inner-city residents were moved to the outskirts as part of the government housing schemes of the 1960s. This impacted on the population catchment available to Dublin's inner-city clubs, making it difficult for fans to travel to watch their old clubs. Secondly, the growth of television provided an alternative form of entertainment. English football became accessible to Irish people when the BBC started screening highlights on *Match of the Day* in 1964. Thirdly, and perhaps most importantly, the lure of British clubs and the financial incentives on offer proved attractive to promising young players in Ireland. With the best young players being scouted at a young age, the influence of the League of Ireland on the national team was never the same after the 1950s.

Chapter 4
Spain v Republic of Ireland
10 November 1965

'Every man has his price: £25,000 was the FAI's.'

– Eamon Dunphy, *The Rocky Road*

The impressive results achieved by the Republic of Ireland in the late 1950s suggested that progress was being made, particularly on home soil, with Dalymount Park emerging as a fortress where visiting teams struggled. Nevertheless, the Republic still trailed behind their nearest neighbours, as evidenced by the fact that Northern Ireland, England, Scotland and Wales had all qualified for the 1958 World Cup.

The 1960s saw UEFA's creation of the European Nations' Cup, which is now of course known as the European Championship. Only seventeen teams entered the qualification process for the inaugural tournament in 1960, with just four teams qualifying for the finals. Ireland played Czechoslovakia in the preliminary round and despite winning the first game 2-0 at Dalymount, they lost 4-0 in the return fixture in Bratislava, thereby resulting in elimination. The Irish team once again encountered Czechoslovakia in the qualification campaign for the 1962 World Cup, but finished bottom of a three-team group which also included Scotland.

There was a marked improvement in the results achieved in the qualification campaign for the 1964 European Nations' Cup. The Irish team overcame Iceland in the first qualifying round. The next round, against Austria, was settled when Noel Cantwell scored a last-minute penalty to seal an impressive 3-2 win at Dalymount. That victory provided Ireland with passage through to the third qualifying round, which was effectively the quarter-final stage of the European Nations' Cup, with the winner progressing to the four-team tournament. However, a strong Spanish team stood in the way and qualification proved to be a step too far for Ireland. A 5-1 defeat in Seville was followed by a 2-0 loss in Dublin in April 1964. Spain hosted the tournament two months later and won their first major international trophy, beating the USSR in the final.

The Republic of Ireland's achievement in reaching the final eight teams in Europe as early as 1964 was perhaps too easily consigned to the history books. The comprehensive defeats to Spain left a sour taste and overshadowed the progress of the team. By beating a strong Austrian side in the previous round, the Irish team had once again demonstrated that, on their day, they could compete with some of Europe's leading nations. Despite being capable of such one-off victories, their prospects of qualifying for a major tournament were hindered by poor preparations, inconsistent selections, and the unavailability of some English-based players.

The qualification process for the 1966 World Cup in England once again pitted Ireland against the might of Spain. They were drawn in a three-team group which initially included Syria. However, the Syrian team subsequently withdrew from the qualifying process in solidarity with the African nations who decided to boycott the tournament. The African nations were aggrieved that the winners of their qualification process needed to enter a final round against the winners of the Asian and Oceanian zone in order to qualify for the World Cup. The withdrawal of Syria effectively meant that the two fixtures between Ireland and Spain would decide which nation qualified for the tournament.

Spain could call upon a formidable group of individual players, but they had a reputation as underachievers. Prior to becoming the European champions in 1964, they had struggled to make an impact on the international stage, failing to qualify for the 1958 World Cup and finishing bottom of their group at the 1962 World Cup. The travails of the Spanish national team were difficult to fathom, given the success of Real Madrid in the European Cup during the 1950s and the availability of naturalised players such as the Argentina-born Alfredo Di Stéfano and the Hungarian, Ferenc Puskás.

In the early 1960s, public discourse in Spain was framed in the context of the Franco regime, with the military dictator influencing the nation's sporting teams. David Goldblatt, in his global history of football, describes how the poor showing by Spain at the 1962 World Cup led to a tirade of nationalist anger from the sporting press, which was unhappy with the presence of foreigners and the use of what they perceived to be foreign tactics. In 1963, foreign players were banned from Spanish football and the success of the national team the following year was identified as vindication of that policy.

Spain were managed by José Villalonga Llorente, a former Real Madrid manager who steered the club to win the inaugural European Cup in 1956. As a 16-year old, Villalonga had enlisted as a nationalist soldier during the Spanish Civil War, which endeared him to Franco. He had taken the reins of the national team after the World Cup in 1962 and immediately translated his success at club level onto the international stage. With Villalonga at the helm, Spain were the undoubted favourites as they approached their two qualifying fixtures against Ireland.

The Irish team was still managed by the former Manchester United captain, Jackie Carey, but his role continued to be limited by the fact that the players were selected by the FAI's five-man selection committee, or the 'Big Five' as they had become known.

The first match was played at Dalymount Park on 5 May 1965 in front of an attendance of approximately 40,000. Spain were missing some key players, most notably Paco Gento of Real Madrid, Chus Pereda of Barcelona, and Luis Suárez of Inter Milan. The latter was missing due to his commitments with his Italian club in the European

Cup. In contrast, the Irish team was close to full strength and could rely on the experience and influence of Noel Cantwell, Charlie Hurley, Tony Dunne and Johnny Giles. In addition, the team had a prolific centre-forward in the shape of Blackburn Rovers' Andy McEvoy, who finished the 1964-65 season as the joint leading goal scorer in the English First Division.

The FAI had also taken advantage of a recent change in FIFA's eligibility rules to call up Shay Brennan, who was born in Manchester to Irish parents. Brennan, a part of Manchester United's league-winning team in 1965, is generally regarded as the first English-born player to play for Ireland. However, there have been suggestions that Mick O'Brien who played at centre-half for the Irish Free State team from 1927 to 1932 may have been the first. O'Brien was thought to have been born in Kilcock in County Kildare, but research by a historian at one of his former clubs, Brentford FC, indicated that he was actually born in Ushaw Moor, a village near Durham. Regardless of who holds the distinction of being the first non-Irish-born player, the arrival of Shay Brennan under the new FIFA eligibility rules was to signal the start of the FAI casting their net wide in search of suitably qualified players.

Brennan's international debut against Spain also coincided with a first senior cap for his Manchester United teammate Pat Dunne who played in goals, deputising for the injured Alan Kelly.

Match reports suggest that the game in Dalymount was a relatively evenly contested encounter. The key moment arrived just after the hour mark when Johnny Giles was fouled on the right wing. The resulting free kick was taken by Frank O'Neill of Shamrock Rovers, who sent the ball into the penalty area. Noel Cantwell jumped with a Spanish defender, but neither of them touched the ball. The Spanish goalkeeper, José Ángel Iribar, appeared to be distracted, letting the ball slip through his fingers for an own goal. The Irish defence, led by Charlie Hurley, held firm for the last half hour and kept Spain scoreless. It was a crucial win for Ireland and meant that a draw in Spain would secure qualification for the World Cup finals.

The return fixture took place in Seville in October 1965, almost six months after Ireland's win at Dalymount. The Irish defence was weakened by the absence of Shay Brennan and Charlie Hurley through injury, whilst Spain were strengthened by the return of Luis Suárez and Chus Pereda. Suárez was the reigning European Footballer of the Year and by that stage he had won two Serie A titles and two European Cups with Inter Milan.

The Spanish squad assembled two weeks prior to the fixture and trained together at the Sánchez Pizjuán Stadium in Seville. The Spanish authorities were clearly taking the game seriously and according to some Irish papers, the Spanish players were offered a generous win bonus in advance of the match. By comparison, the Irish preparations were somewhat amateur, with the players not assembling until a few days before the game.

The hosts dominated possession in the early stages and took the game to Ireland in front of a crowd of 50,000. After a difficult 20 minutes, Ireland won an indirect free kick in dangerous territory outside the Spanish penalty area. It was against the run of play, but Frank O'Neill touched the ball to Mick McGrath, whose shot flew past the Spanish keeper and into the net. However, the Portuguese referee inexplicably disallowed the goal and ruled that the free kick should be retaken. Although the disallowed goal was a blow to Ireland, it seemed to instil confidence in the team and six minutes later, Giles delivered a cross to McEvoy, who volleyed into the net to open the scoring.

With the home crowd growing increasingly impatient, Spain gradually took control again and two goals from Pereda before half-time put them into the lead. Spain resumed their dominance in the second half and, with pressure building, Pereda completed his hattrick before the hour mark. A fourth goal from Carlos Lapetra removed any doubt, giving Spain a comprehensive win.

Under modern-day protocol, the Spanish team's 4-2 aggregate victory over two legs would have put them through. This was, however, before the days of aggregate score-lines, which meant that a third match would be required at a neutral venue. It would be the Republic of Ireland's first experience of a play-off to reach a major tournament.

According to Paul Rowan's book, *The Team That Jack Built*, the FAI General Secretary Joe Wickham entered negotiations with the Spanish football authorities about the options for a neutral venue for the play-off match. The Spanish were pushing for a venue in Portugal, whereas the FAI wanted London or Manchester, which would have guaranteed a large contingent from the Irish community in Britain. After many hours of negotiation, the parties came up with the Parc des Princes in Paris as a compromise. Paris did not have the large Irish population that could be called upon in one of the English cities, nor was it particularly accessible for travelling supporters. It was, however, home to a significant Spanish community, many of whom had left Spain during the Civil War.

In the build-up to the match, Spanish and French newspapers reported that Ireland had agreed to Paris as the play-off venue in exchange for Spain's share of the gate receipts. The Madrid-based *ABC* newspaper reported that it would be 'a match that, from the economic point of view, will only benefit the Irish'. The total gate receipts for the play-off were estimated to be in the region of £25,000 – almost three times the annual FAI income at the time. The FAI had chosen a guaranteed financial sum, rather than optimising the team's prospects of qualifying for the World Cup.

According to Eamon Dunphy's autobiography, *The Rocky Road*, the Irish players became aware of the FAI's 'treacherous deal' when they were told by some travelling journalists while waiting at Heathrow Airport for their flight to Paris. 'We played our football in England, and London was home to tens of thousands of exiled Irish,' wrote Dunphy. 'Realising this, the Spanish had dangled a carrot: if the FAI agreed to play in Paris, they could keep the gate receipts. Every man has his price: £25,000 was the FAI's.'

The fixture in Paris was one of the first occasions that the British media took a genuine interest in the Republic of Ireland team. Prior to that, the Republic's results received little or no attention in the British newspapers, unless the game involved England. *The Times* depicted the Irish as the unfancied underdogs and reported that 'the plucky little Republic of Ireland side, limited in their resources, take on Spain, with their highly paid and publicized performers'. The *Irish Times* expressed a similar sentiment in stating that 'Irish fighting spirit has accomplished almost miraculous feats in the past but this one would appear to be beyond the capability of a team below full strength'.

Ireland were still missing Charlie Hurley for the play-off, as well as Mick McGrath and Jackie Hennessy, who had played in the win over Spain earlier that year. Pat Dunne retained his place in goals. The full-back positions were occupied by his Manchester United teammates, Shay Brennan and Tony Dunne. Brennan's inclusion was a boost following his unavailability for the previous match in Seville. The Irish team was captained by Noel Cantwell at centre-half.

The main talking point concerned the selection of Theo Foley at right-half, a position he was unfamiliar with. Foley was a hard-tackling full-back with his club, Northampton, but was selected to man-mark Spain's star man, Luis Suárez. Alongside Foley, the 31-year old Mick Meagan of Huddersfield Town was picked at left-half.

Johnny Giles was picked at inside-forward. Giles was emerging as one of the finest players in the English First Division, a key member of a strong Leeds United team that was making impressive progress under the management of Don Revie. Leeds were unlucky to miss out on a league and FA Cup double in 1965, losing out to Manchester United and Liverpool, respectively. Alongside Giles, the other inside-forward was 20-year old Eamon Dunphy, who was selected to make his international debut. Dunphy was five years younger than Giles, but the two men had grown up close to each other in Dublin's north inner city. Their early career trajectories were similar, both playing with Stella Marris before moving to Manchester United as teenagers. However, that was where the similarities ended. Giles had been part of Matt Busby's first team before signing for Leeds in 1963, whereas Dunphy left Old Trafford to sign for York City in the English Fourth Division.

Frank O'Neill and Joe Haverty, the only League of Ireland players in the team, were selected on the right and left wings respectively. O'Neill had returned to Ireland to sign for Shamrock Rovers after a spell at Arsenal. Haverty had a successful career in England and had recently returned to Dublin to play for Shelbourne. He was a survivor of the Irish team that beat West Germany in 1956 and provided a wealth of experience.

Andy McEvoy was picked at centre-forward and it was hoped that the Blackburn Rovers sharp-shooter could replicate his club form at international level. The Bray man had started his career as a half-back until the Blackburn manager, Jack Marshall, converted him into a forward. It proved to be an inspired move and McEvoy's poaching instinct meant that he was as prolific as Jimmy Greaves for a few seasons.

The Irish squad visited the Parc des Princes on the day before the game but were not allowed to train on the pitch. It was reported that no rain had fallen in Paris for about a month and the pitch had just been watered. The Parisian hosts were concerned that a training session would damage the pitch. Instead, the squad of thirteen players trained in the public park adjoining the Parc des Princes. According to a report in the *Irish Examiner*, Peter Fox from Dundalk conducted most of the training session, whilst Jackie Carey focused on his goalkeeper, Pat Dunne.

Much of the pre-match focus was on Theo Foley, who was selected to quell the threat posed by Luis Suárez. When questioned on the daunting prospect of marking the Spanish inside-forward, Foley said: 'I am not worried. In fact, I welcome this chance. I don't know yet what my instructions will be, but if I'm to follow Suárez, I'll chase him out of the park.'

In contrast to Ireland's build-up, the Spanish management and players were meticulous in their preparations. They spent a full week training together in Madrid, which included a match against a combined team selected from Real Madrid and Atlético Madrid. Afterwards, they watched a recording of their European Nations' Cup victory over the USSR the previous year. It was reported in the *Irish Examiner* that each of the Spanish players had been promised a £300 bonus if they won the game. The Spanish authorities were clearly providing the necessary support and incentives to ensure that José Villalonga and his team had the motivation and confidence to advance through the play-off.

Experience had taught the Spanish Football Federation not to leave any stone unturned in their pursuit of qualification. Spain had narrowly missed out on the 1954 World Cup after beating Turkey 4-1 at home and losing 1-0 away from home. The Spanish team entered a subsequent play-off against Turkey in Rome which ended in a 2-2 draw. Remarkably, lots were drawn to determine which nation qualified; a 14-year-old Italian boy was blindfolded and drew the Turkish team. In the long and storied history of the World Cup, Spain's failure to qualify for 1954 is perhaps one of the most unfortunate tales. Since their results against Ireland were identical to those against Turkey twelve years earlier, one could understand why the prospect of another play-off in a neutral venue might have left the Spanish feeling apprehensive.

Spain

1
Betancort

2   5   3
Revilla   Olivella   Reija
            (captain)

4   6
Glaria   Zoco

8   10
Pereda   Suárez

7   9   11
Ufarte   Marcelino   Lapetra

11   9   7
Haverty   McEvoy   O'Neill

10   8
Giles   Dunphy

6   4
Meagan   Foley

3   5   2
T. Dunne   Cantwell   Brennan
            (captain)

1
P. Dunne

Republic of Ireland

The difference on this occasion was that, if the play-off ended in a draw, the aggregate scores of the three matches would be used to determine which team qualified. With Spain ahead 4-2 over the previous two fixtures, the Irish team needed to win to progress to the World Cup.

Villalonga selected the same team that had beaten Ireland in Seville. Their pedigree was evident in the strength of the club sides that the players represented. Although Real Madrid was traditionally the main supplier of players to the national team, this Spanish team only included two players from the club. Their great rivals, Barcelona, also had two players in the team. In fact, it was Atlético Madrid and Real Zaragoza that were the main suppliers, with both clubs providing three players each. The 1960s was a golden age for Real Zaragoza with their forward line of Carlos Lapetra and Marcelino both becoming integral members of the national team.

The game was broadcast live on Radio Éireann, with Philip Greene providing the commentary. Although the Parc de Princes was supposed to be a neutral venue, there was a capacity crowd of 36,000 in attendance, which was overwhelmingly Spanish. It was estimated that fewer than 150 Irish fans travelled to Paris for the game. The crowd would provide a partisan backdrop for what was already an ominous task facing the Irish team.

Spain began the game on the front foot, dominating possession. The *Irish Press* reported that Ireland executed an astute tactical approach in the early stages as 'they played with a deep defence, bursting out every so often and driving an often-tottering Spanish defence to the wall'. According to the Spanish newspaper *ABC*, the Irish team showed its 'physical strength and well-planned scheme to mark, block and break the game of the Spanish attack'.

The first clear-cut chance arrived after 17 minutes when Suárez played a pass through the Irish defence for Pereda to run onto, but the Barcelona forward shot wide. Pereda once again provided a threat on the half-hour mark when he shot from inside the Irish penalty area but was blocked by Tony Dunne. The *Irish Times* reported that Theo Foley and Mick Meagan shadowed Spain's inside-forwards and that the Irish forwards 'had to give as much assistance as possible to their defence'.

Then, on 34 minutes, the Irish forwards created the best chance of the game, against the run of play. Giles received possession in the right-wing position, crossing the ball to find McEvoy in front of goal. McEvoy struck the ball first time from five yards out and beat the goalkeeper, but the Spanish left-half Zoco somehow managed to clear the ball for a corner. It was the same combination of Giles and McEvoy that had opened the scoring in the previous match in Seville and they were desperately unfortunate not to repeat the trick in Paris.

With half-time approaching, Pat Dunne was forced into saves to deny both Glaría and Zoco. By this stage, there was an increasing sense of Spanish impatience as they struggled to break down the well-organised Irish defence. The apprehension of the Spanish team was reflected in the crowd, which started a slow handclap before the half-time whistle blew. A 0-0 score-line was more than had been expected of Ireland in the first half and their ability to counter-attack had presented McEvoy with arguably the best chance of the half. The man-marking of Theo Foley had also helped to nullify the threat of Luis Suárez.

The pace of the game picked up in the early stages of the second half, with Spain looking the more likely to break the deadlock. Pereda and Ufarte both had opportunities but failed to score. Giles also had a long-range effort, which dipped and almost caught out Betancort in the Spanish goal. The *Irish Times* reported that the Spanish team 'became very ragged in their work for a long period after the interval when pass after pass went astray'.

Spain were finally presented with a clear-cut chance in the 74th minute when Giles was dispossessed by Pereda on the edge of the Irish box. Pereda sent Marcelino clear of the Irish backline and the centre-forward crossed a ball that Dunne could not hold, with Brennan forced to clear it off the line.

Moments later, Theo Foley raced into the Spanish box to meet a right-wing cross from Frank O'Neill. Foley jumped with the Spanish goalkeeper, Betancort and centre-half, Olivella. Betancort got his fist to the ball, but Foley crashed to the ground, caught on the cheek and above the eye by Olivella's elbow. He had to leave the field for treatment and with Ireland reduced to ten men, they needed to find a way to shore up their midfield. Up to that point, Foley had managed to keep Suárez quiet, but in his absence, Suárez finally began to find some space.

Just as Foley returned to the field, a Suárez pass released Pereda on the right wing, and he delivered a low cross towards the near post. Cantwell struggled to clear, and the ball broke quickly to an unmarked Roberto Ufarte, who struck a low shot which crept in at the far post. Spain had the lead and the Irish players had eleven minutes to save their dreams of qualifying for the World Cup.

The Irish team pushed forward in search of an equaliser and went close with a McEvoy chance. However, fatigue was setting in and gaps were opening at the back. Spain might have scored a second through Suárez who was denied by an excellent save from Pat Dunne.

The final whistle was blown, and tempers were briefly frayed between some of the opposing players. Spain's quality had proved too much for a strong and committed Irish team, with Suárez and Pereda once again proving their class.

Noel Cantwell spoke to Spanish journalists after the match, saying that 'Spain's win is fair, but if we managed to achieve extra-time, we would have imposed our greater fitness'. Cantwell concluded by congratulating Spanish football on reaching the World Cup. Luis Suárez spoke about how his team 'played a great match in defence and our tactics of waiting for the key opportunity gave the desired result'.

Suárez also observed: 'We should have won by a greater difference, but I also recognise that the Irish have played a great match.'

Ireland had earned the respect of their Spanish opponents and the opposition manager, Jose Villalonga, was somewhat surprised with the style of football they displayed. 'I expected the Irish team to play hard, decisively and to use every means possible to try and win,' said Villalonga. 'But what I really did not expect was for them to play such a good game of football.'

The following day, the *Irish Press* described the performance as 'an absolutely superb display' and according to the *Irish Examiner*, the match was 'the finest Irish performance of any era on the Continent'. The *Irish Times* reported that 'even though Ireland had failed they gained greatly in prestige by this tremendous fight against one of the best teams in the world'.

The media also heaped praise on Johnny Giles, with the match report in the *Irish Press* stating that 'Giles has blossomed forth into nothing short of a world class inside-forward'. The report continued to describe a complete performance from the Leeds United man: 'He was here, there and everywhere, moving smoothly from defence to creating openings in attack.'

The French press complimented the quality displayed by both teams, with *L'Équipe* reporting that 'Spain did not steal their victory, but it is fair to say that Ireland, by their courage and quality of play during certain periods, would equally have deserved to qualify for the finals'. *France-Soir* referred to the Irish team's reliance on 'their indomitable pluck, so characteristic of a nation of unweakening fighters'.

The slender loss, allied to the spirited display by the Irish team, left some players feeling that they had been let down by the FAI in agreeing to play the game in Paris. In his autobiography, Theo Foley wrote that 'we could have nicked it definitely, it was very close and, maybe, if we had played in London, it would have swung the game'.

That may well have been the case, but Spain had outscored Ireland on an aggregate score-line of 5-2 over the course of the three fixtures. In this regard, Spain displayed their superior quality, with their strength in depth and professional approach proving to be the difference. Ireland relied heavily on their marquee players and, even allowing for the absence of Charlie Hurley, the team was perhaps two or three players short of being a top-quality international side. In an interview with the *Second Captains* podcast in 2013, Eamon Dunphy reflected on the play-off defeat and noted that 'we always had wonderful players, but we never had enough of them'.

The difficulty of qualifying for a 16-team World Cup cannot be underestimated. Footballing heavyweights such as Czechoslovakia and Yugoslavia also missed out on qualification for the 1966 World Cup, despite finishing second and fourth respectively at the previous tournament four years earlier.

Spain marched on to the World Cup finals in England where they were faced with a difficult group, which also included West Germany, Argentina and Switzerland. They managed to beat the Swiss but lost to both the Argentines and Germans and were therefore eliminated at the group stage.

Considering the results that preceded the play-off defeat to Spain and the Irish team's fortunes in the years that followed, this match could be viewed as a notable fault-line in the history of Irish football. The performance in Paris should have provided an important building block in the evolution of the Irish team, but instead it signalled the start of a period of decline. The role of the FAI came into sharp focus after the play-off and, more specifically, the decision to agree to Paris as the venue. Poor preparation for games and inconsistency in decision-making from the 'Big Five' continued to provide obstacles to the team's development. Other nations had full-time managers with autonomy for selecting their teams. The late 1960s was a period of increasing tactical sophistication and Ireland's lack of off-field leadership left the team ill-equipped to keep pace.

The qualifying games for the 1968 European Nations' Cup were indicative of the problems in Irish football, as the team faced Spain for a third consecutive campaign. A scoreless draw at home was followed by a 2-0 defeat in Valencia, a match in which Johnny Giles was dropped from the team. The qualifying group also included Czechoslovakia and their visit to Dalymount attracted an attendance of just 6,257, the smallest crowd to ever attend an Irish home international.

Ireland were already out of contention by the time they travelled to Prague for their final match of the group against the same opposition. The squad was depleted and facing a team that only required a draw to qualify. Nonetheless, the game in Prague was noteworthy for a couple of reasons. First and foremost, Ireland scored two second-half goals to claim an unlikely away win against Czechoslovakia. Secondly, the Irish team adopted a 4-3-3 formation, which was a decision made by Charlie Hurley as captain. This was the first occasion that Ireland played with four players in their backline.

Notwithstanding this important tactical adaptation from Hurley, the team continued to be picked by the FAI's selection committee, meaning that the lack of consistency in team selection persisted. The malaise deepened during the qualifying campaign for the 1970 World Cup, with Ireland losing five out of their six games and finishing bottom of their group with a single point.

Whilst the previous twenty years had been underpinned by a strong team spirit and a sprinkling of skilful footballers, the culture within Irish football and the team's ability to upset the odds appeared to have dissipated by the end of the 1960s. The sense of entropy surrounding the national team would require a step change to a more professional approach.

Chapter 5
Republic of Ireland v USSR
30 October 1974

'Oh, it's a beautiful goal! Isn't it a beautiful goal?'

– Jimmy Magee, RTÉ

The FAI's reliance on a five-man committee to pick the team finally came to an end in 1969 when they made the decision to put in place a manager with responsibility for team selection. Mick Meagan was appointed on a part-time basis, shifting the responsibility for picking the team away from the 'Big Five'. However, Meagan could do little to address the continued decline in the team's fortunes and Ireland once again finished bottom of their group for the 1972 European Nations' Cup, with only a single draw from their six qualifying games.

Liam Tuohy took over as manager for the 1974 World Cup qualifiers, with Ireland drawn in a three-team group alongside the USSR and France. Tuohy sought to instil a more professional approach and one of the key changes he made involved the scheduling of home fixtures. The international matches in Dublin were generally played on Sundays, which was far from ideal timing given that they often followed the day after a round of English League fixtures. Tuohy insisted on moving the matches to Wednesdays to provide more preparation time and to ensure the availability of players. He also built up a rapport with club managers to ensure the release of key players.

With Tuohy at the helm, Ireland achieved an impressive 2-1 win at home to France in November 1972. Remarkably, it was the team's first home win in six years, a statistic that goes some way towards explaining the declining attendances during that period. However, the

Irish team lost both fixtures against the USSR, which paved the way for the Soviets to top the group. At the same time as managing Ireland, Touhy was also managing Shamrock Rovers and had a job outside of football as a sales manager. The challenge of juggling these roles with family commitments led to him making the decision to resign as Ireland manager at the end of the qualifying campaign for the 1974 World Cup.

Tuohy was replaced by Johnny Giles, who was appointed as player-manager. Although Giles had been a critic of the FAI, this was considered by many observers to be an astute appointment. He had made his international debut in 1959 and gone on to achieve a significant level of success at club level with Leeds. The first game for the new player-manager was a friendly at home to Poland in October 1973, which Ireland won 1-0.

It was an encouraging start for Giles and, the following May, he led the squad on a tour of South America, which included fixtures against Brazil, Uruguay and Chile. A credible 2-1 defeat to Brazil in the Maracanã Stadium was followed by a 2-0 loss against Uruguay and a 2-1 win against Chile in Santiago. The performances showed clear signs of progress, but the major tests for Giles and his team would arrive when they resumed competitive action the following autumn.

Ireland were drawn in Group 6 for the 1976 European Championship qualifying campaign alongside the USSR, Turkey and Switzerland. The opening fixture of the campaign was against the USSR in Dublin. The Soviets were amongst the heavyweights of European football. They won the first European Nations' Cup in 1960, were runners-up to Spain in 1964 and runners-up to West Germany in 1972. They had also claimed the bronze medal at the 1972 Olympics, but, for various reasons, they had failed to make a similar impact at World Cup tournaments. In fact, they missed out on the 1974 World Cup finals after refusing to fulfil the second leg of their play-off against Chile, in protest against Augusto Pinochet's regime and, specifically, his use of the Estadio Nacional in Santiago to imprison those who opposed his leadership.

The Soviets were also at the forefront of some of the most important tactical and stylistic innovations that football had undergone during the previous quarter of a century. In the 1940s and '50s, Boris Arkadyev introduced a style of play that involved quick passing, fluid movement and the interchanging of positions between different players. One of the leading coaches and visionaries of the 1960s was Viktor Maslov, who looked at the 4-2-4 formation being used by a number of club sides in the USSR and decided to drop both of his wingers back to create a midfield quartet and, by design, the 4-4-2 formation. Maslov's pioneering tactical approach became enshrined in Soviet football.

The USSR team that travelled to Dublin in 1974 was managed by Konstantin Beskov, who had been manager at Dynamo Moscow before being appointed to lead the national team. It was Beskov's second spell as manager of the national team, having previously managed the side that finished as runners-up at the European Nations' Cup in 1964.

Beskov could rely on a strong domestic league, with a significant geographical reach. The team he selected to play Ireland contained six players born in the modern territory of the Ukraine, four in Russia and one in Tajikstan. Their team was backboned by five players from Dynamo Kiev, with two players each from Dynamo Moscow, CSKA Moscow and Spartak Moscow. Somewhat surprisingly, Beskov's squad only contained one player from the reigning league champions, FC Ararat Yerevan – a club which just happened to be managed by Viktor Maslov. Incidentally, Ararat Yerevan had visited Ireland to play Cork Celtic in the second round of the European Cup one week prior to Ireland hosting the USSR. Cork Celtic lost the first leg 2-1 and would ultimately lose the tie 7-1 on aggregate.

Although Ararat Yerevan were the reigning champions, the new power base of Soviet football was Dynamo Kiev, a club that was emerging as a formidable force in European football. The Kiev duo of Oleg Blokhin and Volodymr Onyshchenko were identified as posing the main threat to the Irish defence. Blokhin was six days shy of his 22nd birthday but had already scored nine international goals and was in prolific form at club level. The more experienced Onyshchenko had scored the only goal when the USSR beat Ireland in Moscow the previous year. Onyshchenko offered a creative presence and was part of the Soviet teams that were runners-up in the European Nations' Cup and Olympic bronze medallists two years earlier.

The strength of the Soviet clubs clearly indicated the pedigree of their players, but Johnny Giles was measured in his praise of the opposition in the build-up to the game. Giles expressed the view that the USSR 'are a straightforward team, fit and well-disciplined in what you might call the Russian tradition, but though they may not have any particular brilliant individuals, they are good, and they are a hard team to beat'.

The Irish media seemed to share Giles's view of the opposition's defining characteristics, with Mel Moffat of the *Irish Press* writing that 'the Russians will play a dour, almost machine-like type of game, but they are super-fit'. Noel Dunne of the *Irish Independent* referred to 'Irish footballing skill and character', which he hoped would 'prove equal to the occasion and overcome the more stolid but so effective approach of the men from the USSR'.

In contrast to the Soviet team, which was comprised of players from just four club sides, Giles could not rely on the same level of cohesion or familiarity within his team. The eleven Irish players whom he selected were drawn from ten different clubs. Giles sought to compensate for this apparent disadvantage by arranging a collective training session in London in advance of the game – further evidence of the more professional approach being adopted by the new player-manager.

The squad trained at Blackrock College in the days leading up to the game. Giles was in the unusual position for an Irish manager of having almost a full deck to choose from. After naming his 18-man squad, Tony Dunne was the only player to withdraw due to injury. Steve Heighway was a late concern following a knock he picked up playing for Liverpool, but he was able to join the squad.

Giles named his team the day before the game and his chosen eleven had the look of a strong attacking side. The positive approach was clear from Giles's statement that 'we must win at home if we are to qualify from this group, we will be having a go'.

The team included Paddy Roche in goals. Roche's only previous international appearance had been three years earlier when he was part of an Irish team that conceded six goals against Austria in Linz. He later moved from Shelbourne to Manchester United and Giles felt he warranted another opportunity.

Joe Kinnear was picked at right-back. Kinnear was born in Dublin and moved to Watford with his family at the age of seven. He won an FA Cup medal with Tottenham Hotspur in 1967 and a UEFA Cup medal in 1972. Having made his international debut in 1967, he was one of Ireland's most experienced players. The centre of defence was led by Paddy Mulligan who was then at Crystal Palace, having previously played for Shamrock Rovers and Chelsea. Like Kinnear, Mulligan had also won a European medal, as part of the Chelsea team that claimed the UEFA Cup Winners' Cup in 1971.

Mulligan was joined in the centre of defence by Terry Mancini, who had recently signed for Arsenal. Mancini was born in London and was originally named Terry Seely. His father was Irish and died when Terry was seven. His mother later remarried, changing his surname to that of his stepfather. Mancini was unaware that he could play for Ireland until a chance conversation with Don Givens when they were teammates at QPR.

Coventry City's Jimmy Holmes was picked to play at left-back.

Hailing from The Liberties in Dublin, Holmes had become the Republic of Ireland's youngest-ever full international at 17 years and 200 days when he played against Austria in 1971.

In midfield, Johnny Giles captained the side and was accompanied by the experienced duo of Mick Martin and Steve Heighway. Mick Martin was at Manchester United, having started his career at Bohemians. His father, Con Martin, had been an integral part of the Irish team that beat England at Goodison Park in 1949. Heighway was a key member of Bill Shankly's Liverpool team and had already won his first league title, as well as winners' medals in the FA Cup and UEFA Cup. Like Joe Kinnear, Heighway was born in Dublin, but his family moved to England at a young age and he was educated in Sheffield.

The final member of the Irish midfield was a young Arsenal player by the name of Liam Brady, who was making his international debut. At 18 years of age, Brady had already established himself in the first team at Highbury and had a cultured left foot. The young midfielder came from a family steeped in football tradition. His great uncle, Frank Brady Senior, had played for the Irish Free State in the 1920s and his older brother Ray had won six caps for Ireland. Indeed, Liam's international debut was almost ten years to the day since Ray's final international appearance. Brady was a somewhat surprising selection to face the Soviets, as the more defensively minded Eoin Hand had performed well in that role during the summer tour to South America.

The front pairing comprised Don Givens and Ray Treacy. Givens was born in Limerick and had played for both Manchester United and Luton Town before signing for QPR in 1972. Ray Treacy was a product of Home Farm's underage system and had experienced a successful five years at Charlton Athletic before joining Swindon Town.

Republic of Ireland

1
Roche

2   4   5   3
Kinnear   Mulligan   Mancini   Holmes

7   10   6   9
Martin   Giles   Brady   Heighway
          (captain)

11   8
Givens   Treacy

11   7
Blokhin   Fedotov

8   10   9   6
Onyshchenko Veremeev Kolotov   Lovchev

4   3   5   2
Matviyenko Olshansky Kaplichny Nikulin
          (captain)

1
Pilgui

USSR

70

Although Giles selected the team in what appeared to be a conventional 4-4-2 formation, his comments the day before the game provided an insight into his philosophy on how football should be played. 'You have got to have a basic formation,' said Giles. 'But I don't believe in sticking to a rigid formation. It must be fluid, with the principle that when we have possession, we have ten players off the ball to move into position to receive it.'

The fact that Giles was espousing the benefits of a fluid playing style in the mid-1970s would suggest he was ahead of his time in terms of his understanding and tactical approach to football. Of course, Giles had played under both Matt Busby and Don Revie at club level, which almost certainly influenced his outlook on the game. Revie's Leeds United team were known for their combative approach and a perceived win-at-all-costs mentality, but Revie was also a manager who was respected for his tactical ingenuity.

The fixture against the USSR was scheduled for a Wednesday afternoon at Dalymount Park and a crowd of 35,000 packed into the Phibsborough ground. The Irish team showed an immediate sense of urgency, befitting of the occasion. From the first whistle, Liam Brady received the ball and drove forward across the halfway line. As an opening act, Brady showed the early intent and flair that would become emblematic of a great career.

The first opportunity of the game was presented when a Giles free kick found Terry Mancini in space, but Mancini headed narrowly wide. Moments later, a knockdown from Ray Treacy found its way to Don Givens, but he failed to capitalise. The QPR man's misfortune continued when the referee waved away his claims for a penalty when he went down in the box following a tackle from Sergei Olshansky. It looked like the correct decision from the referee.

With the Irish pressure building, the persistence of Givens was rewarded when he opened the scoring in the 23rd minute. The move started with Giles, who floated a beautiful pass from midfield to send

Joe Kinnear clear on the right wing. Kinnear delivered a perfect cross into the Soviet penalty area and Givens found himself in a position between the two centre-halves to head the opening goal. As Givens ran to receive the acclaim of the home crowd, Jimmy Magee of RTÉ provided one of his iconic pieces of commentary in an exultant tone: 'Oh, it's a beautiful goal! Isn't it a beautiful goal?'

With Giles and Brady dovetailing in midfield, the Irish team were dominating possession, carving the opposition open with some incisive passing. Kinnear's role was also noteworthy, as the Spurs full-back pushed forward on the right flank to add an extra man in attack. Kinnear's presence in a more advanced position allowed Ireland to dominate the midfield exchanges and when the Soviets did try to play the ball in behind him, Paddy Mulligan studiously covered the full-back position. This tactical approach illustrated the positivity with which the Irish team approached the game.

The USSR's first meaningful effort arrived when some nice one-touch football allowed Blokhin to get in behind the Irish defence, but his subsequent shot cleared the crossbar. It was a warning of the danger posed by the Soviets and particularly their ability to fashion a chance from very little.

On the half-hour mark, the Soviet goalkeeper decided to play the ball out from the back, but his defender failed to control the pass and it went out for a throw-in near the corner flag. With the throw-in on Ireland's right flank, Joe Kinnear went to take it, but left the ball as soon as he realised that Steve Heighway was running across to launch one of his long throws. Heighway delivered his throw into the penalty area, which the Soviet defence failed to deal with. Ray Treacy made a nuisance of himself and when the ball eventually landed on Treacy's head, he directed it towards Givens in the six-yard box, who hooked the ball across the keeper and into the net. Ireland were suddenly 2-0 up and there was an air of disbelief around Dalymount.

The celebrations were short-lived, however. Two minutes after the goal, Giles was preparing to take a free kick, as Terry Mancini and Vladimir Kaplichny jostled near the penalty spot. Mancini hit out in frustration and Kaplichny fell to the ground. The referee had no hesitation in showing a red card to the Irish defender and as soon as Kaplichny got to his feet, he also received his marching orders.

Only a few hours earlier, Muhammad Ali and George Foreman had boxed each other for the world heavyweight title in the historic 'Rumble in the Jungle' in Kinshasa. The exchange between Mancini and Kaplichny might have lacked the force and aggression of that heavyweight bout, but they left the referee with little choice but to send them off. Sadly, it would prove to be Mancini's last act in an Ireland shirt and a disappointing end to a short international career.

Mancini's dismissal led to some reorganisation, with Mick Martin moving into the centre of defence alongside Paddy Mulligan. This effectively created a 4-3-2 formation for the remainder of the game. The new central defensive pairing was soon under pressure as Onyshchenko went close to pulling a goal back for the Soviets. When the half-time whistle sounded, the Dalymount crowd responded by showing their appreciation for an outstanding first-half performance.

The second half predictably started with the USSR trying to find a way back into the game. The *Irish Independent* described how 'for the first twenty minutes of the second half, the Russian all-whites virtually took over complete control of the proceedings as they fought frantically to save the tie'. Blokhin wasted a good opportunity when he raced clear of the Irish defence but pulled his cross into Paddy Roche's hands with Onyshchenko in a scoring position. Their best opportunity arrived just after the hour mark when Vladimir Fedotov's shot forced Roche to parry. The rebound arrived at the feet of Viktor Kolotov, who was unable to convert the chance. Following their failure to capitalise on that opportunity, the hopes of the Soviet team appeared to fade.

Giles came under closer attention from the opposition in the second half and cleverly drifted onto the right wing, thereby opening up space in the midfield for Brady and Heighway to exploit. Ireland pushed on once again, sealing the win with twenty minutes remaining. Giles floated a perfectly flighted free kick into the box, which Givens met with a glancing header, directing the ball beyond the reach of the Soviet goalkeeper. The hattrick was complete for the QPR man, his ninth goal in an Irish jersey.

Three minutes later, Heighway could have made it four when he dispossessed Matvienko about 30 yards out, and with only the goalkeeper to beat, he sent a low shot just wide. The home team was now oozing confidence and playing with a real swagger. Heighway's influence on the game grew in the second half as he increasingly found space in the middle third.

Both Heighway and Brady had the ability to evade opposition players through a combination of close control and clever footwork. Their skills provided some variety to the Irish game plan, as Giles continued to pull the strings with his full range of passing on display in the middle of the park. Giles was central to the performance and he almost scored a fourth goal before the finish when his sweetly struck shot from 25 yards out forced an outstanding acrobatic save from Pilgui.

When the final whistle sounded, the crowd at Dalymount streamed onto the pitch in celebration. The players and fans were acutely aware that they had achieved a famous win for Irish football. Don Givens was presented with the man of the match award, whilst the fearless Liam Brady won many admirers for a stunning display in midfield. Giles and Brady might have been at opposite ends of their respective careers, but it's unlikely that Ireland had ever before fielded such a strong midfield pairing.

After the game, Giles expressed his satisfaction with the performance and result:

> 'We just went out there to play as well as we could. We did that and won 3-0. We have played at our best before and lost so this

was a great occasion for us. Certainly the happiest occasion I can remember for an Irish side.'

Don Givens described to the waiting press how he opened the scoring: 'From the moment I made contact with Joe Kinnear's cross, I knew the ball was on the way into the net for the first goal.'

The USSR manager, Konstantin Beskov stated that 'the sending off of Kaplichny affected our performance', but he went on to point out that 'there are a lot of matches yet to be played in this group and we have a good chance of qualifying'.

The following day, the *Irish Independent* described a 'scintillating display' and 'a glorious result which will astound the footballing world'. The match report in the *Cork Examiner* referred to 'the superiority of Ireland in the footballing sense' and their ability to 'mix it and dominate Russia by their skilled use of the ball and effortless teamwork,' concluding that it was 'unquestionably our best result after a footballing extravaganza of un-expected brilliance'. The *Irish Times* captured the public mood, illustrating an awareness that Irish football had been waiting for a result of this magnitude:

'Dalymount Park hasn't seen anything like this for a long time! . . . it is doubtful if there was one among the estimated 35,000 Dalymount Park attendance who was properly prepared for the 90 minutes of excitement, incident and splendour that marked this magnificent 3-0 victory.'

The Moscow-based *Sovetskii Sport* went with the simple headline of 'Reversal in Dublin' and, perhaps unsurprisingly, their match report focused on the shortcomings of the Soviet team, rather than the quality of Ireland's performance. The report in *Sovetskii Sport* reiterated that there was still sufficient time to recover in the group, noting that 'the USSR national team may be the first to qualify after the final match despite the heavy defeat'.

The Irish victory didn't go unnoticed in Britain either where the broadsheets lavished praise on Giles, for both his playing and coaching abilities. 'The Republic's captain and team manager, has achieved the framework of a spirited, organized side', reported Geoffrey Green in *The Times*. 'This largely was inspired by his own creative play as the midfield general. Possessing a football intelligence far above the average, Giles clearly has a future when he finally hangs up his boots.'

The hattrick by Don Givens was a significant milestone, the first Irish player in 38 years to achieve that feat in a senior international. Jimmy Dunne had scored three against Luxembourg in 1936 and of course Paddy Moore had scored four goals against Belgium in 1934.

The Irish football writer Peter Byrne later recounted in his book, *From the Press Box*, the bizarre circumstances encountered by Givens as he returned to London after scoring his hattrick. Givens had an early evening flight to catch, which left him with insufficient time to have a shower or get changed after the game. His taxi to Dublin Airport was caught up in traffic in Phibsborough, forcing him to abandon the taxi and flag down an unsuspecting motorist a mile further up the road. When Givens arrived in London that night and disembarked the plane in his muddied tracksuit, he was greeted at the airport by reporters and photographers from some of the British newspapers.

The majority of the Irish squad returned to the Central Hotel in Dublin to celebrate. In his autobiography, *A Football Man*, Johnny Giles described how the team was joined by various members of the Irish folk scene. Paddy Reilly, Patsy Watchorn, Tommy Byrne and Luke Kelly were all in attendance, having accepted an invite from Ray Treacy for 'a few drinks and a singsong'.

The win over the USSR was a huge statement for Giles as a player-manager and signalled the potential of his Irish squad. There was no doubting the individual and collective quality of the Soviet team that had travelled to Dublin. Dynamo Kiev went on to win the European Cup Winners' Cup later that season; their team included five players who had played against Ireland at Dalymount. Oleg Blokhin went on to win the Ballon d'Or award in 1975 and eventually became the all-time top goal scorer for the USSR with 42 goals, as well as becoming the only player to be capped over 100 times by the Soviets.

The Irish victory over the USSR was followed up by a disappointing 1-1 draw in Izmir against Turkey, with Givens once again the goal scorer. In the next match, at home to Switzerland, Ireland won 2-1 with the goals coming from Mick Martin and Ray Treacy. After three games, Ireland had five points out of a possible six.

Unfortunately, the campaign faltered in May 1975 when the squad travelled to play the USSR in Kiev, which was followed by their away fixture against Switzerland three days later. The Irish team lost 2-1 to the USSR in the same week as Dynamo Kiev won the European Cup Winners' Cup. On this occasion, the Soviet team comprised eleven players from Dynamo Kiev. The defeat to the USSR was followed by a 1-0 loss against Switzerland in Berne. The scheduling of the two most difficult away fixtures as part of a double-header at the end of a long, hard season raised further questions about the FAI's priorities.

Ireland's fate was now out of their hands and they were left hoping that Switzerland and Turkey would do them a favour. The team played its part in keeping the pressure on the USSR by beating Turkey 4-0 at Dalymount Park. Don Givens scored all four goals, almost a year to the day since his hattrick against the Soviets. Givens finished the qualifying campaign with eight goals.

In the last two matches, Turkey did manage to beat the USSR, but the Swiss lost 4-1, leaving the Soviets at the top of Group 6 by just one point. Considering the comprehensive win at the outset of the campaign, allied to the FAI's questionable decision to play the two key away games in the off-season, there was little doubt that Ireland missed out on a huge opportunity to top the group.

The USSR subsequently faced into a two-legged play-off with Czechoslovakia to qualify for the European Championship finals.

Czechoslovakia won on a 4-2 aggregate score-line and went on to win the European Championship the following summer. Despite the Republic's failure to qualify, the campaign proved to be an important turning point for Irish football, particularly in terms of preparation and professionalism. Giles had managed to buck the trend of the previous decade by providing consistency in team selection. He used just sixteen players over the twelve-month campaign, with six players playing in every qualifying game. This provided continuity and strengthened the team as a unit.

Giles had two further qualifying campaigns in charge of the Irish team. The qualifying group for the 1978 World Cup started with a defeat to France in Paris, but Ireland reversed the result at Lansdowne Road, with Liam Brady scoring the only goal of the game. The other team in the group was Bulgaria, with Giles's team once again losing away from home, but drawing in Dublin. The results left Ireland at the bottom of a tight group.

The qualifying campaign for the 1980 European Championship once again included Bulgaria, as well as Denmark and near neighbours England and Northern Ireland. The Republic started the group strongly, securing impressive home wins against Denmark and Bulgaria. However, the campaign finished on a disappointing note with defeats to Northern Ireland in Belfast and England at Wembley. Those results left the Republic in third position in the group and Giles subsequently stepped down.

During his time as manager of the national team, Johnny Giles had also returned to Ireland to take up a role as player-manager of Shamrock Rovers. He was joined by Eamon Dunphy and they had ambitious plans for the Glenmalure club. Their vision involved professionalism and a revamped youth system. Giles hoped that his plans for Rovers would help to rejuvenate the League of Ireland and provide a viable pathway for young players to carve out a career at home. The project, however, was met with resentment from some opposition clubs and after spending over five years at Rovers, Giles eventually resigned from the club in February 1983.

Chapter 6
Belgium v Republic of Ireland
25 March 1981

'I can think of no reason for that goal being disallowed and in my estimation there's only one word to sum up the referee . . . disgraceful.'

– Eoin Hand

Eoin Hand took over as manager of the Republic of Ireland in 1980, tasked with leading the nation into the qualifying campaign for the World Cup finals, due to be held in Spain two years later. As a player, Hand had won twenty international caps before starting his managerial career with Limerick United, a club which he guided to the League of Ireland title in 1980. At 34 years of age, he was the youngest international manager in Europe.

Hand and his squad faced a daunting task in a qualification group which in modern-day parlance might be referred to as a 'Group of Death'. The group included the Netherlands, World Cup runners-up in 1974 and 1978, and Belgium, runners-up at the European Championship in 1980. Then there was France, led by Michel Platini, who were very much on an upward curve and building towards major tournament success. Finally, Cyprus fulfilled the role of group minnows.

Notwithstanding the calibre of the opposition, Eoin Hand was able to call upon a hugely talented group of Irish players, many of whom were at the peak of their careers. In the centre of defence, Liverpool's Mark Lawrenson and David O'Leary of Arsenal formed a formidable partnership for much of the campaign. To this day, it is doubtful that

Ireland has ever fielded a more competent pair of ball-playing centre-backs. In midfield, the team was led by Liam Brady, who had signed for Juventus in 1980 and was regarded as one of the finest midfield players in Europe. Up front, Frank Stapleton of Arsenal provided the physicality and link-up play which enabled him to act as the focal point of the team's attack.

Ireland started the group strongly with victories over Cyprus and the Netherlands. These wins were followed by a home draw against Belgium and a disappointing 2-0 loss to France in Paris. The loss to France was controversial, as Michael Robinson scored a goal that was subsequently disallowed for an apparent handball. The disallowed goal came at a crucial time, with France leading 1-0, and the match very much in the balance. Hand's team recovered their momentum in the group with a comprehensive 6-0 win at home to Cyprus the following month. The win left Ireland with seven points out of a possible ten.

In March 1981, the squad travelled to Brussels for what would prove to be a pivotal encounter with Belgium. After starting the qualifying group with a draw in Dublin, Belgium had gone on to beat the Netherlands in Brussels and followed that with two unconvincing wins over Cyprus. Like Ireland, the Belgians had amassed seven points in the group, but they were struggling to keep pace with Ireland and France in the goal-scoring stakes.

The consensus in the Irish media was that Belgium would need to beat Ireland, as Liam Brady pointed out in his column for the *Sunday Independent* the weekend before the game. 'They will have to change their policy against us because of their result against Cyprus and because of the away games they face in France and Holland,' wrote Brady. 'That may give us the opportunity to counter-attack to good effect.'

Contrary to Brady's assertions, there was a view in the Belgian media that the pressure was on Ireland to secure a result, with the match preview in the Brussels-based *Le Soir* newspaper stating that the Irish team would be 'morally animated by the fact that it is playing for its last chance in Brussels'.

Ireland's prospects were not helped by the absence of Mark Lawrenson through injury and his loss was compounded by David O'Leary failing a fitness test before kick-off. The team would be missing their first-choice central defensive pairing. In any previous era, the loss of players of that calibre would have left an Irish team severely weakened, but this squad had greater strength in depth.

Eoin Hand's teams often lined up in a 4-3-3 formation, which was a system that facilitated the likes of Robinson and Heighway in linking-up with Stapleton. This formation also allowed the team to adopt a more defensive shape when required, with Heighway capable of dropping into a deeper role to create what was effectively a 4-4-2 system.

Seamus McDonagh was picked in goals to win only his second cap, having made his debut against Wales in a friendly at Tolka Park the previous month. McDonagh was born in Rotherham and had moved to Everton at the start of the 1980-81 season. Dave Langan of Birmingham City was selected at right-back, with Tottenham Hotspur's Chris Hughton at left-back. Hughton qualified to play for his country through his Irish-born mother and he was the first mixed-race player to represent Ireland.

With Lawrenson and O'Leary missing from the centre of defence, Hand paired Kevin Moran of Manchester United with Mick Martin of Newcastle United – two men with connections to Dublin GAA. Moran won two All-Ireland football medals with Dublin in 1976 and 1977 before moving to Manchester the following year. Moran's success in both codes was reminiscent of the path pursued by Mick Martin's father, Con, who had won a Leinster title with Dublin in 1941 before going on to play for the Republic of Ireland and be part of that famous win against England at Goodison Park.

In midfield, Hand was able to select the creative talents of Liam Brady alongside Tony Grealish and Gerry Daly. Brady was the captain and a hugely respected figure within the team. In the 1980-81 season, he would go on to be top scorer for Giovanni Trapattoni's Juventus as they won the Serie A title. Grealish was also a player that was comfortable in possession and with an ability to get forward and support the frontline. Grealish played for Luton Town and although he was born in London, he was fiercely proud of his Irish roots. He even represented London in a Gaelic football challenge match against New York at Wembley. Gerry Daly had started his senior career with Bohemians before moving to Manchester United in 1973. He had a subsequent spell at Derby County and, somewhat unusually for a younger player, a two-year loan spell in the North American Soccer League before signing for Coventry City.

Michael Robinson was picked on the right side of the front three and at 21 years of age, he was the youngest member of the team. Born in Leicester and playing for Brighton and Hove Albion, Robinson was already displaying all the tenacity and intelligence that would later define his career on and off the pitch. Steve Heighway was picked on the left of the front three and he offered a wealth of experience. At that stage in his career, Heighway had won four league titles with Liverpool, as well as an FA Cup, two European Cups and two UEFA Cups. The centre-forward role was filled by Frank Stapleton who came through the Arsenal youth system at the same time as David O'Leary and Liam Brady. Stapleton had made over 200 first team appearances for the Gunners and won an FA Cup winners' medal in 1979.

There was an acknowledgement in the Belgian press that the Irish team posed a significant threat, with a match preview in *Le Soir* stating that 'Ireland is a team that cannot be taken lightly'. The preview also noted that the Irish team was 'composed of players with practice of the rigours of the English championship'.

The Belgian team was managed by Guy Thys, who had been

appointed to the position in 1976. His squad was comprised primarily of players based in the Belgian league which, despite only turning professional in 1972, offered a decent production line for the national team.

The side which Thys selected to face Ireland included seven players who had played in the final of the European Championship nine months earlier, including each of the back four. Their experienced goalkeeper, Jean-Marie Pfaff, was missing through injury and was replaced by the 22-year-old Michel Preud'homme. Three members of their defence – Eric Gerets, Walter Meeuws and Michel Renquin – played together at Standard Liège and were renowned for their effective use of the offside trap. Gerets, arguably one of the best full-backs in Europe, captained the team. The Belgian defenders had a familiarity with each other and understood their respective roles implicitly, which ensured that they were a difficult team to break down.

The Belgian midfield quartet was athletic and workmanlike, with Albert Cluytens providing pace on the right wing and René Vandereycken posing a danger from set-pieces. Erwin Vandenbergh and Jan Ceulemans, both tall and physically strong strikers, were expected to be a handful for the Irish defence.

The venue for the fixture was the Heysel Stadium in Brussels and it attracted a large travelling support, with an estimated 5,000 Irish fans in attendance. Eight special Aer Lingus flights arrived in Brussels on the Monday, two days prior to the match, whilst a large Irish contingent also travelled by overnight Sealink ferry from Folkestone to Ostend the night before the game. Some Irish papers reported that there was trouble on the overnight ferry and that the Irish fans were met by riot police with dogs on their arrival in Ostend.

Belgium

| 1 | |
| Preud'homme | |

2	4	3	5
Gerets	Meeuws	Millecamps	Renquin
(captain)			

| 8 | 10 | 7 | 6 |
| Cluytens | Coeck | Vandereycken | Mommens |

| 9 | 11 |
| Vandenbergh | Ceulemans |

| 8 |
| Stapleton |

| 9 | | | 11 |
| Heighway | | | Robinson |

6	10	7
Brady	Grealish	Daly
(captain)		

| 3 | 4 | 5 | 2 |
| Hughton | Martin | Moran | Langan |

| 1 |
| McDonagh |

Republic of Ireland

The match in Brussels is regarded by some Irish fans of that vintage as one of the earliest occasions on which large numbers travelled for an away fixture. The travelling support made their voices heard with a loud rendition of 'Amhrán na bhFiann' before kick-off and their singing was audible throughout.

The match kicked off in wet and windy conditions. The pressure was on Belgium to take the game to their visitors and they set about their task in the early minutes, with Gerets and Cluytens combining well on the right flank. Belgium won their first corner after three minutes and Vandereycken delivered a dangerous ball to the near post which Mick Martin managed to clear. The ball eventually made its way out to Cluytens, whose shot took a deflection. The television footage suggested that the deflection might have been off a Belgian player, but the referee had no hesitation in awarding another corner. It was a marginal call, but the type of decision that home teams often receive.

Despite the early pressure, Ireland looked composed, with both Brady and Grealish eager to get on the ball in midfield. Stapleton was also leading by example; in the 10th minute, he collected the ball in his own half before starting on a powerful run which eventually yielded a throw-in deep in the opposition half.

Belgium posed their first real threat when Vandenbergh took possession on the left and crossed a dangerous ball to the edge of the six-yard box, but Hughton managed to clear. Hughton would again prove to be Ireland's saviour in the 26th minute when a Belgian corner was met by a powerful header from Ceulemans, which was cleared off the line by the Irish left-back. This was the closest Belgium had come to scoring, with both sides struggling to create clear-cut opportunities.

Belgium looked at their most dangerous from set-pieces and long throw-ins from Gerets, which allowed Vandenbergh and Ceulemans to threaten in the air. Nonetheless, the Irish central defensive pairing of Kevin Moran and Mick Martin looked well prepared for this tactic and Moran's no-nonsense approach ensured that he was winning the aerial battle.

With three minutes remaining in the first half, Belgium almost opened the scoring when a cross from Mommens on the left wing went over Hughton's head and evaded Heighway at the back post before landing into the path of Gerets. The Belgian full-back controlled the ball well and struck a right-footed shot which flew inches wide of the far post.

The Irish midfield had managed to retain possession impressively without putting together any incisive moves, but that changed with only a minute remaining in the first half. Stapleton collected the ball on the right wing and threaded a forward pass into the feet of Michael Robinson, who turned first time and ran at the opposition defence. The Belgian centre-back, Luc Millecamps, rushed across and took Robinson down, giving Ireland a free kick on the angle of the penalty box. What happened next was to become a seminal moment, not only in the match, but in the careers of Eoin Hand and his players.

Brady stood over the free kick, with Daly and Grealish on either side of him. Ireland had three players on the edge of the box – Stapleton, Robinson and Moran – and in position to attack the imminent cross. Just as the referee blew the whistle, Stapleton made a quick run towards the six-yard box and in doing so, he stole a march on the Belgian centre-back, Walter Meeuws. Brady immediately spotted the run and chipped a perfectly placed delivery into the path of Stapleton, who got to the ball before the Belgian keeper and finished it to the back of the net.

The Irish celebrations were cut short, however, as the Portuguese referee, Raul Nazaré, blew his whistle to disallow the goal. It was unclear what infringement had taken place to warrant the referee's intervention. The linesman subsequently raised his flag, but no explanation was given as the Irish players protested.

On closer viewing of the incident, it is evident that the referee's positioning was poor. He ran from the area where the free kick was awarded towards the middle of the penalty area, turning his back on the ball as Brady took the free. As he ran, the referee inadvertently impeded the run of Walter Meeuws, who had been marking Stapleton. The referee and Meeuws collided and as the goal was scored, Meeuws lay on the ground, with some of the Belgian players protesting.

There was no apparent reason to disallow the goal. Some commentators suggested that the referee panicked, as he realised he had clumsily checked the run of Meeuws and wanted to avoid a hostile response from the home crowd. Although the referee impeded Meeuws, it is extremely unlikely that the Belgian defender would have got back into a position to prevent Stapleton from scoring. Regardless of this, the referee is merely part of the field of play and any effect his positioning might have on the play would not be a legitimate reason to disallow the goal.

The referee's positioning in this instance also meant that he did not have a clear enough view of either Brady or Stapleton to determine that the goal was offside. In any case, the television footage indicates that there were at least four, possibly five, Belgian defenders who played Stapleton onside.

The half-time whistle was blown a minute later and although the Irish team had survived a couple of decent Belgian chances, they knew they should have been walking into the dressing-room with a valuable lead. Tempers were frayed as the players left the field with Stapleton having to calm Brady, who was embroiled in a heated dialogue with some of his Belgian counterparts.

Brady had been central to everything Ireland did well during the opening stages. The match report in the *Irish Examiner* described the Juventus midfielder as 'the most compelling figure in the first half' and that 'his captain's sense of responsibility lifted Ireland to heights that could not have been foreseen'.

By the time the second half kicked off, the weather conditions had deteriorated, with a thunderstorm leaving the pitch sodden. Ireland started with more conviction and the half was only five minutes old when Brady dribbled inside from a left-wing position and skipped past the Belgian challenges before striking a shot from the edge of the box, which was saved by Preud'homme.

Ireland were looking increasingly comfortable, with the back four holding a high line in defence. With 57 minutes on the clock, Dave Langan took a free kick from the right flank. The ball travelled over the top of the Belgian defence and landed into the path of the on-rushing Robinson, whose first-time shot was firmly struck but saved by Preud'homme. Aside from the disallowed goal, it was the most clear-cut chance Ireland had created.

With the Irish team seemingly gaining the upper hand, Belgium almost struck back. Cluytens took possession on the right wing and delivered a superb ball towards the back post where Ceulemans had stolen in behind Langan. The Belgian striker headed downwards and McDonagh somehow managed to pull off a point-blank save.

Frank Stapleton was substituted for Mickey Walsh with just under 20 minutes remaining. Stapleton had led from the front and run himself to a standstill on a heavy pitch. Within a minute of Stapleton being replaced, his teammates created another opportunity for Robinson. Daly hit a long ball upfield for Robinson to run onto. With one touch, his pace took him away from Millecamps and into the Belgian penalty area. However, he was forced to strike from a tight angle and his shot was blocked by Preud'homme. Robinson had become increasingly influential in the second half and the Belgian defence was struggling to deal with his pace and direct approach.

Ireland continued to look the most likely side to score and were presented with another opportunity in the 78th minute. A corner from Heighway was punched clear by Preud'homme and landed at the feet of Grealish, but his shot was blocked before the ball arrived to Gerry Daly twelve yards out. Daly rushed his shot and it flew well wide of the Belgian goal.

89

With the clock ticking down, the Belgians became increasingly frantic in their attempts to break the deadlock. A corner landed at the feet of Ceulemans, whose shot was blocked by Langan inside the six-yard box. A minute later, Ceulemens dribbled into the Irish penalty area and teed up his strike partner, Vandenbergh, but his shot was straight at McDonagh.

Then, with three minutes remaining, another controversial refereeing decision helped to determine the outcome of the match. A through-ball was played for Eric Gerets to chase, but it was over-hit and Gerets threw himself to the ground in what appeared to be an exaggerated dive. The footage of the incident shows that the nearest Irish players were Heighway and Walsh and that neither player made any attempt to tackle him. Inexplicably, the referee blew his whistle, awarding Belgium a free kick on the edge of the Irish box. The player with the best view of the incident, Chris Hughton, was clearly incensed with both Gerets and the referee.

After the referee had waved away the Irish protests, Vandereycken took the free kick, which was floated towards the goal. The ball rebounded off the top of the crossbar and back into a crowded goalmouth where Ceulemans jumped highest and headed into the Irish net. It was a cruel goal to concede and exacerbated the sense of injustice at the referee's earlier decision to disallow Stapleton's goal.

The decision to award the free kick was further evidence of poor officiating from the referee. There is the possibility that the match officials were subconsciously influenced by the fact that Gerets had become increasingly vocal as the match wore on. There were a couple of occasions in the second half when the Belgian captain had spoken to the referee and was seen gesturing to the Portuguese official to brandish yellow cards to Irish players. His increasing prominence may have contributed to the referee's decision to award the free kick.

In the aftermath of the Belgian goal, the television cameras panned to the Irish bench where Eoin Hand and his colleagues were holding their heads in their hands. The final whistle blew minutes later, consigning Ireland to a second defeat in the group. It was a bitterly disappointing outcome for an Irish team that had battled hard and were deserving of a result.

At the final whistle, some of the Irish players surrounded the referee to remonstrate, with both Mickey Walsh and Liam Brady particularly upset. Eoin Hand also made his way onto the field to confront the referee. 'You're a disgrace,' said Hand. 'You've been paid off. You've robbed us.' When speaking to the media after the game, Hand was scathing of the Portuguese official's decision-making. 'I can think of no reason for that goal being disallowed and in my estimation there's only one word to sum up the referee . . . disgraceful.'

A certain Jack Charlton, then manager of Sheffield Wednesday, was in the Heysel Stadium watching on as an interested spectator. Charlton was quoted in the following day's *Irish Independent* and described the disallowed goal as 'a disgrace', adding that 'it was as good a goal as I have ever seen'.

Unsurprisingly, the performance of Raul Nazaré and his match officials dominated the headlines in the Irish newspapers. The *Irish Press* went with the headline, 'Robbed Again', and the accompanying match report by Mel Moffat described Nazaré as 'the villain of the piece' after he 'disallowed a Frank Stapleton goal just before half-time and then a free kick he awarded on the edge of the Irish area, after Belgium captain Gerets seemed to take a dive, led to the killer goal only three minutes from time'. The abysmal officiating, allied to the horrendous weather conditions in Brussels, created an emotive sense of an opportunity lost for a golden generation of players. Bill George in the *Irish Examiner* eloquently described how 'the electrical storm that flashed and thundered over the stadium mirrored the maelstrom of emotions that tore at the very heart of our heroic team'.

The performance of Raul Nazaré didn't go unnoticed in the Belgian press. Writing in *Le Soir*, Jacques Thibaut stated that 'the Irish even scored a goal at the end of the first half, which was cancelled for an offside that was not obvious'. There was also a tacit acknowledgement of the poor officiating in *La Libre Belgique* with the match report stating that 'we would not dare to insist that sporting fairness is entirely respected in this case'.

Although the Belgian press showed a degree of empathy for the Irish team's misfortune, one might have expected greater introspection, given that Belgian football had been subject to a similar refereeing injustice eight years earlier. In their final qualifying game for the 1974 World Cup, Belgium's Jan Verheyen had an 89th minute goal against the Netherlands erroneously disallowed for offside. That decision cost Belgium a place at the World Cup, thereby paving the way for Johann Cruyff and his Dutch team to take centre stage the following summer with their display of 'Total Football'.

Following the defeat in Brussels, the FAI wrote to Artemio Franchi, the Chairman of the FIFA Referees' Committee and requested that FIFA publish the report by the refereeing official who was assessing Nazaré's performance. FIFA responded, declining the request. However, the governing body noted that the refereeing assessor Anton Bucheli rated Nazaré's display as 'good to excellent' and that the decision to disallow the Irish goal was correct.

In 2002, Paul Howard tracked down Raul Nazaré and travelled to Lisbon to interview him for the *Sunday Tribune*. The journalist was armed with a video recording of the game, which he had sourced from Eoin Hand. He sat through the key incidents with Nazaré, starting with the disallowed Stapleton goal. At first, Nazaré claimed the goal was offside, but on seeing it again, he accepted that was impossible. However, he then changed his story, saying that he had awarded an indirect free kick and that Liam Brady had shot directly at goal. When Paul Howard pointed out that the ball had changed direction as Frank Stapleton had side-footed it into the net, Nazaré changed his mind once again. The former referee asserted that the goal had been ruled out because Stapleton hadn't touched the ball, but that the ball had actually deflected in off his own back. 'The ball hits off me,' said Nazaré. 'It hits off my back and into the goal. I remember now that that is why I disallowed it. Yes, you were right, it does change direction. But this is only because it hits me and not Stapleton.' Nazaré's explanation was scarcely credible, as he was almost two metres away from the ball when Stapleton put it in the Belgian net.

Nazaré also recalled how Mickey Walsh approached him after the game and said: 'Raul, I am very sad. The hearts of all the Irish nation are crying.' In fact, Walsh was not quite so philosophical and actually called Nazaré a cheat. Meanwhile Liam Brady asked Walsh for the Portuguese word for thief, then confronted Nazaré with his new word, jabbing a finger in the direction of the referee to emphasise the point.

The disappointment of the result in Brussels was left to fester for Eoin Hand and his team, as there was a six-month gap until their next qualifier against the Netherlands. The team travelled to Rotterdam to take on the Dutch in the autumn of 1981. Hand's team showed their resilience by twice coming from behind to salvage a 2-2 draw, with Robinson and Stapleton scoring the goals. The result meant that Belgium were now assured of qualification, but with two to qualify from the group Ireland were still in with a chance. They needed to beat France in their final match and hope that the Netherlands or Cyprus could claim a draw against the French in their last two fixtures.

Ireland's final qualifier against France was played in front of a capacity attendance at Lansdowne Road and the home side started the game with pace and attacking intent. The early pressure forced an own goal from French defender Philippe Mahut, but Bruno Bellone equalised three minutes later. In the second half, Ireland produced some wonderful football, with Stapleton and Robinson scoring to give the team a 3-1 lead. Michel Platini cut the deficit to ensure a tense finish to a great game. The 3-2 win over France capped off a qualifying campaign in which the Irish team demonstrated that they could hold their own with the leading European nations, but qualification was now out of their hands.

France subsequently went on to beat Cyprus and then the Netherlands in their two remaining games. They finished level with Ireland on ten points, but a 7-0 thrashing of Cyprus earlier in the group ensured that the French, with a better goal difference, qualified instead of Ireland. The misfortune endured by Eoin Hand's team was further illustrated by the fact that both England and Northern Ireland qualified from their respective groups with just nine points.

It was the closest the Republic of Ireland had come to qualifying for a major tournament and the poor refereeing decisions in Brussels added to the sense of disappointment. A draw away to Belgium would have been sufficient for the team qualify. In his 2017 autobiography, Eoin Hand was forthright in his view that if Raul Nazaré's 'truly shocking refereeing display had not intervened' and Ireland had held onto a point in Brussels, they would have travelled to the World Cup in Spain. Hand's autobiography also stated, with more than a hint of regret, that 'a wonderful group of Irish players were denied the opportunity to compete in football's greatest showcase'.

The qualifying campaign for the 1982 World Cup should have provided a strong foundation for the Irish team to grow and evolve, perhaps even channelling their disappointment and using the setback as motivation to qualify for the subsequent European Championship. However, the manner in which the team missed out on the World Cup merely added to the sense of fatalism that pervaded Irish football at this time. In a manner reminiscent of the years that followed the play-off defeat to Spain in 1965, Eoin Hand's squad struggled to reach the same heights thereafter. Once again, poor decision-making by the FAI played its part, with an ill-conceived tour of South America in May 1982 proving particularly damaging.

The South American tour included fixtures against Chile and Brazil, as well as a hastily arranged game against Trinidad and

Tobago. The schedule originally included a fixture against Argentina in Buenos Aires. However, Argentina had just invaded the Falkland Islands, leading to a war with Britain.

In this political climate, most of the English clubs refused to release their players, which meant that Hand was forced to travel with a severely depleted squad which included a number of League of Ireland representatives. The Argentina fixture was subsequently cancelled, but the FAI's travel arrangements still involved the farcical situation of the squad flying to Santiago via Buenos Aires, where the flight was grounded for several hours. Three defeats followed, including a record 7-0 loss to a Brazilian side which included the likes of Zico, Falcão and Sócrates.

The following month, the same Brazilian team would captivate football fans across the world with some scintillating displays at the World Cup. They were joined at the tournament by France and Belgium, the two teams that had pipped Ireland to qualification. France went on to reach the semi-finals of the tournament before being controversially eliminated by West Germany following a penalty shoot-out. Belgium beat the reigning champions Argentina and topped their group before being knocked out in the second round. The performances of both nations left Irish fans wondering what might have been and a lingering regret for a generation of Irish players who could have held their own on the world stage.

Hand remained in charge for the subsequent qualifying campaign for the European Championship, but the Irish team finished behind Spain and a resurgent Netherlands. The campaign for the 1986 World Cup began with an impressive home win over the USSR, but the Irish challenge floundered after a comprehensive defeat to Denmark in Copenhagen. By the time Ireland faced the same opposition in their final group game, the wheels had well and truly come off. A crowd of approximately 12,000 turned up at Lansdowne Road to witness a 4-1 defeat to a team spearheaded by Michael Laudrup and Preben Elkjær

Larsen. The defeat marked the end of Eoin Hand's term as Irish manager.

While his team had achieved some outstanding results, missing out on qualification for the 1982 World Cup would prove to be the enduring narrative of Eoin Hand's tenure. The poignant footage of him holding his head in his hands following the Ceulemens goal would become an abiding image of his time as Irish manager. It also served to highlight the fine margin between success and perceived failure. Hand was denied the opportunity to take the nation to its first major tournament, and one wonders how the history of Irish football and the style of play might have evolved if his team had qualified.

Many Irish players and supporters strongly suspected that there were more sinister forces at play on that ill-fated night in Brussels, although it is important to emphasise that nothing was ever proven. Belgian football would later become embroiled in a series of match-fixing scandals. Eric Gerets, whose theatrics won the free kick that led to Belgium's winning goal, was later implicated in a bribery scandal involving his club, Standard Liège. The scandal occurred at the end of the 1981-82 season and Gerets was forced to serve a one-year suspension for his involvement.

One of the more infamous stories of match-fixing involved Brian Clough's Nottingham Forest, who lost to Anderlecht in the UEFA Cup semi-final in April 1984. In that case, the truth finally emerged in 1997 when the Belgian club admitted that their former president, Constant Vanden Stock, had used a local gangster to pay the Spanish referee £18,000.

In October 2017, *Sports Illustrated* published an article which listed the eleven best teams in history to miss out on qualification for the World Cup finals. Eoin Hand's Irish team from the 1982 qualification campaign was included on the list. Many seasoned followers contend that the team in question remains the most talented Irish team of all time. With several of the players at the peaks of their careers, it was a case of what might have been.

Chapter 7
England v Republic of Ireland
12 June 1988

'Somebody once told me fortune favours the brave and God,
our lads were brave this afternoon.'

– Jack Charlton

Jack Charlton was appointed as the new Republic of Ireland manager in February 1986, the first non-Irish manager of the national team. Although Charlton had won a World Cup winners' medal with England in 1966, he had experienced relatively modest success in club management. He was a somewhat surprising choice, pipping the highly decorated Bob Paisley to the position, and the public reaction was mixed. Charlton was known to be outspoken and had applied for the England manager's job when Don Revie quit in 1977 but had lost out to Ron Greenwood.

At his first press conference in Dublin, Charlton's gruff persona was in early evidence and the occasion was marked by an altercation with Eamon Dunphy after Charlton took issue with his line of questioning. Dunphy and Johnny Giles had moved on from their playing days to become the main television pundits for Irish matches. The disagreement between Charlton and Dunphy was to set in motion a relationship which would become increasingly acidic over the following decade.

The early turbulence continued when Charlton attended a youth game against England at Elland Road and entered the dressing-room at half-time to address the Irish team. The youth team manager Liam Tuohy felt he was being undermined and he subsequently resigned, along with his assistants, Noel O'Reilly and Brian Kerr. The departure of Tuohy and his colleagues was a significant loss to Irish football, as they were nurturing a crop of talented young players and had already managed to qualify for three European Championships and one World Championship at underage level.

Big Jack's first match in charge of the senior team ended in a disappointing home defeat to Wales, but he soon set about redefining Ireland's playing style. His preference was for a more direct approach, or 'route one' as it was sometimes referred to. This strategy necessitated a high work-rate from his midfielders and strikers, who were required to pressurise the opposition and give them little time on the ball. When Ireland gained possession, the ball was generally directed over the opposition defence, forcing their defenders into the more uncomfortable role of having to turn and face their own goal.

The phrase 'put them under pressure' would become part of Charlton's lexicon over the subsequent years. The change in approach yielded some initial success as Ireland won a triangular tournament in Iceland which was also contested by the host nation and Czechoslovakia. It was a low-key tournament, but it was noteworthy as the Irish team had never won an international trophy before.

The qualification process for the European Championship started in September 1986. The Irish team was drawn in Group 7 alongside their old foes, Belgium, as well as Scotland, Bulgaria and Luxembourg. The campaign started with a well-earned 2-2 draw away to Belgium, with the goals scored by Frank Stapleton and Liam Brady. A subsequent scoreless draw against Scotland at Lansdowne Road was followed by the return fixture at Hampden Park in Glasgow. That night, Charlton picked a starting eleven which is arguably one of the strongest teams to ever represent the country. An early goal from Mark Lawrenson was enough to secure a valuable away win.

After putting themselves into a strong position, Ireland's campaign hit a significant speed bump when they lost away to Bulgaria and endured another scoreless home draw against Belgium. Two consecutive wins over Luxembourg were followed by their final fixture of the group against Bulgaria at Lansdowne Road. With the prospects of qualification appearing unlikely, Charlton's team beat Bulgaria 2-0 through second-half goals from Paul McGrath and Kevin Moran. Liam Brady was in excellent form but was sent off with six minutes remaining for retaliating to the incessant fouling of the Bulgarian midfielder, Ayan Sadakov.

The remaining fixtures involved the other four teams in the group, with the pivotal match taking place in Sofia as Bulgaria hosted Scotland. A draw would have been sufficient for Bulgaria to qualify and Irish expectations of an upset were understandably low. Indeed, it later transpired that Jack Charlton didn't even watch the game, preferring instead to spend his time fishing. With four minutes remaining in Sofia, Gary Mackay, a Scottish substitute winning his first cap, broke the deadlock to score a goal that would win the game for his country and earn him a cherished place in Irish football folklore.

Less than two years after taking up the job, Charlton had led the Republic of Ireland to its first ever major championship finals. After coming close on previous occasions, particularly under Johnny Giles and Eoin Hand, the Irish team would finally have an opportunity to dine at the top table as one of eight teams at the European Championship in Germany.

The achievement of securing qualification came at a price, however. Charlton's relationship with some of the older players had become strained. The most publicised example of this occurred when David O'Leary chose to go on a family holiday despite being given a late call-up by Charlton to the triangular tournament in Iceland. Charlton clearly took offence and the Arsenal man was not selected again for a squad until November 1988. Liam Brady also struggled under Charlton as the manager's direct playing style often bypassed the midfielder, failing to make best use of his natural talents. Brady's sending-off in the final qualifier against Bulgaria meant that he was suspended for the first two group games at Euro '88. This scenario would have placed Charlton in a difficult position were it not for the fact that a subsequent knee injury ruled Brady out of the tournament entirely. For some Irish fans, the delight at qualifying for a first major tournament was tempered somewhat by the regret that two of the country's most celebrated players would not have the opportunity to grace that stage.

The European Championship finals comprised two groups with four teams in each. Ireland were drawn in Group 2, alongside England, the USSR and the Netherlands. It was a daunting prospect, with Ireland scheduled to face England in Stuttgart in their opening match. It seemed appropriate that the country's first game at a major tournament would be against the 'Old Enemy' – and, of course, Jack Charlton's homeland.

The tournament promised to be a momentous occasion for Irish football, but expectation levels were relatively measured in advance of the squad's departure. A pre-tournament friendly against Poland attracted a crowd of only 18,500 to Lansdowne Road. The relatively low-key build-up was somewhat surprising given the excellent form of the Irish team in the run up to the tournament, which comprised of eight consecutive victories before a draw in Oslo against Norway in their final fixture.

The Irish squad was backboned by seasoned professionals, a number of whom were steely characters. The starting eleven had an average age of 29 years, which was almost two years older than the average age of the England team.

Packie Bonner of Celtic was the first-choice keeper, with two of his clubmates, Chris Morris and Mick McCarthy, forming part of the back four. Born in Cornwall, Morris was an assured right-back who had only emerged as a viable candidate following the end of the qualification campaign. At 24 years of age, Morris was the youngest member of the starting eleven. Mick McCarthy, a no-nonsense central defender, was very much in the mould of his manager. However, he was not necessarily a favourite of the purists, many of whom would have preferred to see the stylish David O'Leary in the centre of defence.

McCarthy was partnered by the equally robust Kevin Moran, who had carved out an impressive career at Manchester United. The final member of the back four was Chris Hughton of Tottenham Hotspur. Moran and Hughton were survivors from the infamous fixture against Belgium in 1981.

The central midfield was anchored by Paul McGrath, a teammate of Kevin Moran at Old Trafford. Although McGrath had built his reputation as a central defender, Big Jack felt that his footballing ability and athleticism would allow him to play a key role in the Irish midfield. This was an approach that Charlton had used to good effect during the qualifying campaign when Mark Lawrenson fulfilled the defensive midfield role in certain fixtures. McGrath would act as the foil for his central midfield partner, Ronnie Whelan, to provide the creativity. Whelan was comfortably the most decorated member of the Irish team, having already won five league titles and a European Cup as part of a hugely successful Liverpool side.

Whelan's Liverpool teammate Ray Houghton was selected on the right side of midfield. Houghton was born in Glasgow but qualified to play for Ireland through his Donegal-born father. He made his international debut in Jack Charlton's first game in charge at a time when he was playing his club football at Oxford United. On the left wing, Tony Galvin of Sheffield Wednesday would provide the direct running that was integral to the Irish game plan. Prior to becoming a professional footballer, Galvin had secured a degree in Russian Studies, after which he had spent nine years at Tottenham Hotspur.

Charlton partnered Frank Stapleton and John Aldridge up front.

Stapleton was the Irish captain and, having spent most of his career at Arsenal and Manchester United, he had signed for Ajax in 1987 before returning to England to play for Derby County. After missing out on qualification for the World Cup in 1982, it was fitting that Stapleton finally had an opportunity to perform at a major tournament. Aldridge was the third Liverpool player in the starting eleven and, like Ray Houghton, he had also made his international debut in Charlton's first game, at a time when he was still at Oxford United. Although he was prolific at club level, Aldridge had yet to find the net in an Irish shirt.

England were strongly fancied to win the European Championship. Bobby Robson's squad had qualified for the tournament in a very impressive manner, winning five out of their six qualifiers, scoring 19 goals and only conceding one. The experienced Peter Shilton of Derby County was in goals, with Gary Stevens and Kenny Sansom in the full-back positions. The centre of defence was a cause of concern for England fans, as Terry Butcher had broken his leg in advance of the tournament. In his absence, the central-defensive partnership included two relatively inexperienced players in the shape of 24-year-old Mark Wright and 21-year-old Tony Adams.

In midfield, England could call upon the Manchester United captain, Bryan Robson, and he was partnered by Neil Webb who was selected ahead of Glenn Hoddle. The manager opted for two wingers in the form of Chris Waddle on the right and John Barnes on the left. Up front, Gary Lineker of Barcelona was partnered by Liverpool's Peter Beardsley.

England might have steamrolled their way through their qualification group, but they were also reliant on the goal-scoring exploits of Gary Lineker and Bryan Robson. Going into the tournament, Lineker and Robson had a combined total of 47 goals for England, more than the rest of the squad put together. If Ireland could cut off the supply line to either or both of those players, it would certainly enhance their prospects of securing a result.

103

England

1
Shilton

2
Stevens

19
Wright

6
Adams

5
Sansom

12
Waddle

4
Webb

7
Robson
(captain)

11
Barnes

9
Beardsley

10
Lineker

10
Stapleton
(captain)

9
Aldridge

11
Galvin

6
Whelan

7
McGrath

8
Houghton

3
Hughton

4
Moran

5
McCarthy

2
Morris

1
Bonner

Republic of Ireland

In the days leading up to the game, the English media expressed some concerns about potential defensive frailties and a series of niggling injuries that were hampering preparations for Bobby Robson's squad. Concerns about the availability of key players led to Robson cancelling the squad's scheduled training session 48 hours before the game in favour of the players going for a swim.

Nevertheless, the attitude in the English media remained confident, with some of the cross-channel press quite dismissive of Ireland's style of play. An article in *The Guardian* stated that 'it is certainly simple, but just how effective the long-ball game is going to be against sides who do not surrender possession that easily must be open to doubt'. A preview in *The Times* likened the Irish style of play to 'the direct approach that Wimbledon have honed to a fine art at club level'.

The fact that Wimbledon had beaten Liverpool in the FA Cup Final four weeks earlier might have created a heightened sense of unease amongst the English broadsheets. However, the comparisons to Wimbledon did a disservice to an Irish team which did, after all, include three Liverpool players. Indeed, a cursory glance at the Irish team indicated that it was not short of quality, with every member of the starting eleven having experience of winning major honours at club level. Whelan, Houghton and Aldridge had just won the English First Division with Liverpool. Bonner, Morris and McCarthy had just won the Scottish League title with Celtic. Hughton and Galvin had won FA Cup and UEFA Cup winners' medals during their time at Tottenham Hotspur, whilst Moran, McGrath and Stapleton had each won FA Cup winners' medals during their careers.

The English media acknowledged that the Irish team had a strong central spine, particularly with McGrath in a holding midfield role, but the prevailing view was that Waddle and Barnes could target Morris and Hughton on the flanks. David Lacey of *The Guardian* wrote that 'if Bobby Robson's faith in wingers is born out England ought to begin the tournament with an encouraging victory by at least two goals'.

Prior to the game, the television coverage from ITV featured Brian Clough, who was working as a pundit. Clough was particularly dismissive of Mick McCarthy, whom he identified as the weak link in the Irish team, due to a perceived lack of pace.

Undeterred by the commentary in the English media, Jack Charlton exuded a sense of confidence, cutting a relaxed figure on the day before the game. 'I feel very guilty as I have no anxiety whatsoever about my team playing England,' said Charlton. The manager's self-assured approach seemed to transmit itself to the players, whereas the Irish media conveyed the sense of giddy excitement taking hold back home. The *Irish Press* reported that 'a nation will come to a stand-still for 90 minutes tomorrow afternoon when a 52-year-old English man leads out eleven green-shirted players for the most important game in the 67-year history of the Football Association of Ireland'.

And so it was that on 12 June 1988, the Republic of Ireland entered the Neckarstadion in Stuttgart to make their first appearance at the finals of a major tournament. A crowd of 51,373 was in attendance to witness a landmark moment in the history of Irish football. It was estimated that 13,000 Irish fans had travelled to Stuttgart. Most of those fans were located on one side of the main grandstand, which the Irish team would be playing into in the first half.

The match started at a frenetic pace, as one might expect for what was effectively a derby fixture. Ireland were the quicker team to settle and the English defence looked somewhat uneasy. In the sixth minute, Kevin Moran stood over a free kick deep in the Irish half of the field and launched a long ball down the left. In their eagerness to beat Frank Stapleton to the header, Mark Wright and Gary Stevens collided awkwardly and only served to cushion the ball into the path of Tony Galvin, who in turn hooked the ball back towards the penalty area. Kenny Sansom miscued his clearance, with the ball spinning into the air for John Aldridge to head. The ball then dropped invitingly for Ray

Houghton to head it back across goal and beyond the reach of a helpless Peter Shilton. As the net rippled, the Irish fans in the stadium erupted in delirious celebration. Jack Charlton stood on the side-line rubbing his head, having hit it off the roof of the dugout during the celebrations. The English team looked shell-shocked, their fears about defensive frailties realised.

Buoyed by the goal, the Irish players continued to press the opposition defence and midfield. When in possession, they sought to put the ball in behind the English back four and force their defenders to turn. Chris Morris tested Shilton with a long-range shot; this was followed by a fine passing move involving Stapleton, Galvin, Whelan and Aldridge. It was the best passing move of the first half and the type of interplay which demonstrated that Charlton's team could play neat, passing football when required.

The Irish players displayed an insatiable appetite for hard work, with Aldridge harrying the English defenders and Stapleton dropping into midfield to help McGrath and Whelan. Aldridge's role in pressing opposition players was a characteristic associated with the Liverpool teams of the 1980s, especially his teammate Ian Rush, who was particularly adept at performing the role.

McGrath's athleticism was evident throughout the first half and he continued to pressurise his Manchester United teammate Bryan Robson. With Robson and Webb forced deep to receive the ball, Waddle and Barnes were starved of possession on the wings. On those rare occasions when the English wingers received the ball, they were met with tenacious tackling from Morris and Hughton in the full-back positions.

It took 35 minutes for England to get a proper shot on goal, which was a weak effort from Lineker. England's first half could be summed up by one simple misplaced pass from Webb, which was intended for Waddle but went out over the side-line, preventing them from building a dangerous attack.

As the teams left the field for the half-time break, there was genuine astonishment in the stadium that Ireland were in control of proceedings. Liam Brady was working as a pundit for ITV and used the half-time interval to compliment the performance of Mick McCarthy, which appeared to be a subtle dig at Brian Clough for his earlier dismissive remarks about the Irish centre-back.

The teams returned for the second half with England under pressure to salvage something from the game. They set about their task with some urgency and had a series of opportunities in the first ten minutes. A long ball from Sansom found Lineker, but his shot was parried by Bonner and when the rebound came to Beardsley, the Liverpool man blazed his shot high over the bar. Robson and Beardsley then combined well, with Beardsley creating space on the edge of the box, only for the striker to put his left-foot effort wide.

On the hour mark, Robson sent Lineker clear once again, but Bonner narrowed the angle and Lineker's shot flew high over the goal. Lineker's latest miss was followed by the substitution of the ineffective Neil Webb, who was replaced by Glenn Hoddle. One of the more notable aspects of Ireland's performance up to this point was the team's high defensive line, which effectively squeezed England when they were in possession. In order to counteract this tactic, England had started to play long balls over the top of the Irish defence. Hoddle's vision and ability to execute a long pass meant that the Irish back four needed to drop deeper.

Ireland almost made it 2-0 against the run of play. Another long ball forward was headed across the English box by Stapleton, which Robson could only half clear. Ronnie Whelan arrived on the edge of the penalty area and struck a sweet shot with his right foot which cannoned off the top of the crossbar. It was a wonderful piece of technique from the Dubliner.

After 62 minutes, 21-year-old Arsenal player Niall Quinn was introduced in place of Frank Stapleton. Stapleton had played a key role in the defensive effort by dropping deep and providing the Irish central midfield with a numerical advantage over Robson and Webb. It is unclear whether it was Charlton's original intention to deploy Stapleton in this role, or simply a tactical response from the player himself, but the surprise of scoring the early goal was likely to have been the determining factor. The towering figure of Quinn would provide the Irish team with a target and give the English defence something different to think about.

Stapleton's departure did, however, open-up some space in midfield. This, combined with the fresh legs of Glenn Hoddle, immediately altered the dynamic of the game, with Hoddle and Robson getting on the ball and moving it with greater pace and purpose. A Hoddle pass over the top of the Irish defence provided another chance for Lineker, but his half-volley went just wide of the goal. Moments later, Lineker turned provider for Robson, who saw his effort saved by Bonner. At the other end, Ireland went close when Quinn got in front of his Arsenal teammate, Tony Adams, but the centre-forward's glancing header went just wide.

Another opportunity presented itself to Lineker, as the ball fell to the Barcelona striker about eight yards out from the Irish goal, but Bonner somehow managed to block the goal-bound attempt with his left knee. The Irish defence had dropped progressively deeper during the second half and fatigue appeared to be setting in after their first-half exertions. Kevin Sheedy replaced Tony Galvin on the left side of midfield, as Ireland tried to retain some possession.

Hoddle again went close with a volley and Waddle headed a decent chance over the crossbar. The frustration on the faces of the England players suggested that they may have realised this was not going to be their day.

With the game in injury time, Ireland looked to be on the brink of a famous result. However, England were presented with one final roll of the dice when they were awarded a free kick on the left wing, deep inside the Irish half. The free kick was taken by Hoddle and it appeared that the Irish defence momentarily switched off, allowing Lineker space to head the ball towards goal. Once again, Bonner somehow found a way to repel the shot, getting his hand to the ball and directing it onto the post and out for a corner. The subsequent corner was dealt with by the Irish defence and the referee blew the full-time whistle, signalling the start of the celebrations.

The Irish players looked physically exhausted, which was to be expected following their efforts in the heat of the German summer. The physical fatigue was combined with a sense of relief, as Packie Bonner's goal had lived a charmed life in the second half. Bonner had put in the performance of his life; reflecting on his heroics after the game, he modestly declared that 'God was definitely on my side'.

Jack Charlton also acknowledged that Ireland 'got away with a lot of things' but noted that the hot weather had 'made it doubly hard' for his team to retain their intensity. 'When we took a 1-0 lead it was difficult for the rest of the game because the day and climate did not suit the type of performance we give,' said Charlton.

The man of the moment, Ray Houghton, adopted a similar theme in his post-match interview. 'It was a marvellous win for us, but we always felt confident going into the match,' said Houghton. 'The heat and humidity was a bit of a problem for some of the lads but we coped with that, too, as the game progressed.'

For Bobby Robson and England, there was a huge sense of regret that the team had not managed to salvage something from the match. Robson stated that his team 'had 18 chances in the second half to score goals, but we did not take any of them'. The England manager was gracious in defeat, paying tribute to Big Jack's players: 'It's a marvellous win for the Irish. Their fighting spirit saw them through all afternoon. After the goal they were very inspired.'

The following day, the Irish newspapers reported the feeling of unbridled joy and pride in the Irish team, whilst also commending the exemplary behaviour of the supporters in celebrating their team's victory. The *Irish Examiner* reported that it was 'a magnificent performance' and 'ranks as one of the greatest in the history of Irish football'. Charlie Stuart in the *Irish Press* wrote that 'even hard-bitten journalists had tears of joy in their eyes when East German referee Siegfried Kirschen signalled the final whistle'.

The sense of jubilation in the Irish newspapers was in stark contrast to the downbeat mood in the English media, as the broadsheets gave the plaudits to the Irish team. *The Times* went with the headline, 'Bonner blocks inept England', whereas *The Guardian* went with 'England put to green sword'.

It was 39 years since the Republic of Ireland had registered their only previous victory over England at Goodison Park. Indeed, it is possible to draw some parallels between the two fixtures. Tommy Godwin's heroic goalkeeping performance in 1949 was matched by Packie Bonner in Stuttgart. Jesse Pye's failure to convert goal-scoring opportunities at Goodison was outdone by Lineker's profligacy in front of goal at the Neckarstadion. Moreover, there was a correlation between the aspirations of the respective England teams to play what they considered to be a more cultured, short passing game against what they believed to be a more unsophisticated Irish style of play. The comparison between the two fixtures suggest that the simplicity of Ireland's more direct approach during two different eras proved successful for both generations.

Jack Charlton's philosophy might not have been one for the purists, but his players had clearly bought into it, and none more so than John Aldridge. The Liverpool striker was in free-scoring form at club level and, although he had yet to register a goal at international level, he showed an unquestioning desire to follow Charlton's tactics. 'People keep at me about not scoring,' said Aldridge after the game. 'Of course I wish I got one, but Big Jack wants me to close down and push in on the full-backs.'

In the Neckarstadion, Aldridge had chased the English defenders into corners and across the width of the pitch. In doing so, he was the one who led the pressing of the opposition players and was arguably the key component in ensuring the effectiveness of Charlton's game plan.

Although the team's victory over England required a large slice of good fortune, their subsequent match against the USSR is often regarded as one of the finest performances in the history of Irish football. The USSR were a powerful force in the late 1980s and managed by one of football's most innovative coaches, Valeriy Lobanovskyi. Under Lobanovskyi, the Soviet team played a structured style of football, built on key principles that included the pressing of opposition players and an emphasis on the collective strengths of the team.

In their opening game, the USSR had beaten the Netherlands 1-0, but there was a notable shift in their tactical approach when facing Ireland. Rather than pressing high up the pitch, the Soviets sat in a deeper defensive block to counteract the anticipated long-ball tactic. Conversely, the Irish team adopted a much more nuanced approach and played some constructive passing football in the Soviet half of the field. A spectacular volley from Ronnie Whelan gave Ireland a deserved lead after 38 minutes. The ball appeared to strike Whelan's shin, but that didn't take away from the audacity of the strike. In truth, Ireland could easily have been two or three goals to the good by half-time. They continued to exert control in the second half. However, with Charlton's team standing on the brink of another famous win, the USSR salvaged a draw when Oleh Protasov equalised 16 minutes from the end.

The Irish team went into their final game of the group against the Netherlands in Gelsenkirchen. The Dutch had recovered from their opening loss against the USSR by comprehensively beating England 3-1 courtesy of a Marco van Basten hattrick. A draw would be sufficient to see Ireland through to the semi-finals and the Boys in Green were on course to achieving their objective until Wim Kieft scored for the Dutch with eight minutes remaining. It was a cruel blow for an Irish team that had performed beyond all expectations.

The USSR and the Netherlands progressed to the semi-finals where they beat Italy and West Germany respectively. A masterclass from van Basten in the final helped the Dutch to avenge their earlier defeat to the Soviets, securing their first major international trophy. For Ireland, there was solace in the fact that they had travelled to their first major tournament and more than held their own against the two eventual finalists. It might seem somewhat fantastical to imagine an Irish team in the semi-finals of the European Championship but, for spells against the USSR and the Dutch, such an outcome appeared to be within touching distance.

Although the Irish team exited at the group stage, their tournament was in marked contrast to that of their English counterparts. Bobby Robson's squad was eliminated from the tournament with three defeats, despite being one of the pre-tournament favourites.

Jack Charlton's much-maligned style of play had posed significant questions for three of the most respected managers in world football – Robson, Lobanovskyi and Rinus Michels. Indeed, Lobanovskyi and Michels were two of the foremost tacticians in the game, yet both struggled to counteract the Irish approach.

Charlton's direct style of football differed from the short passing styles preferred by his predecessors, but he made no apologies. It was difficult to question the conviction with which Charlton implemented his strategy. The game against England in Stuttgart was perhaps the least complete performance from Ireland at Euro '88, as there was a demonstrable quality in the way they dominated the Soviets and went toe-to-toe with the Dutch in the subsequent group games.

Kevin Moran succinctly explained the context and significance of the result in Stuttgart in an interview with Paul Kimmage in the

Sunday Independent in June 2015. Moran described it as 'the biggest game' before observing that 'it was our first time to qualify, the first major time to play against England in a big game; it was a neutral venue, we were underdogs and we beat them'.

The victory over England would become part of Irish sporting folklore and for many Irish people, it remains the single greatest moment in the country's sporting history. It was a transcendent occasion for the Irish fans in attendance, the experience of which was wonderfully encapsulated by Christy Moore in his song, 'Joxer Goes to Stuttgart'.

Jack Charlton and his squad returned to a heroes' welcome in Dublin. The country's introduction to tournament football had provided a glimpse of what was possible and created a yearning amongst the squad and supporters to return to football's top table.

Chapter 8
Republic of Ireland v Romania
25 June 1990

'The nation holds its breath.'

– George Hamilton, RTÉ

The success of Euro '88 created a feel-good factor around Irish football and Big Jack's squad sought to continue the momentum by securing the Republic of Ireland's first ever qualification for the World Cup. In a qualification group containing Spain, Northern Ireland, Hungary and Malta, the team faced three away fixtures at the start of the campaign. A scoreless draw in Belfast was followed by a 2-0 defeat in Seville and a further stalemate in Budapest. A total of two points with no goals scored in the opening three games did not suggest the sort of form that would lead to Charlton's team qualifying for the tournament.

However, the team then had the benefit of four consecutive home fixtures, where a packed Lansdowne Road would provide a raucous and colourful backdrop for the visiting teams. The home games started with a hard-earned 1-0 win against Spain in April 1989, which acted as the catalyst for the remainder of the campaign. That seismic result was followed by two successive 2-0 wins against Malta in May and Hungary in June.

By the autumn, the Republic were well placed in the group and momentum was building. When Billy Bingham's Northern Ireland visited a heaving Lansdowne Road, they were treated to what had become a regular home crowd rendition of 'Que sera sera, whatever will be will be, we're going to Italy'. Swept away by the increasing tide of excitement, Jack Charlton's men defeated Northern Ireland with a resounding 3-0 score-line. Qualification was secured the following month, as a brace of goals from John Aldridge was sufficient to beat Malta on a memorable afternoon in Valletta.

The growing maturity of Charlton's team was evident in the fact that they kept seven clean sheets in those eight qualifying games. After the disappointments of losing the play-off to Spain in 1965 and missing out on the 1982 tournament on goal difference, the significance of qualifying for a first World Cup felt like vindication for long-suffering Irish fans. The success also grabbed the attention of the wider population in a country where, for some, football had been a peripheral sport for so long.

When the draw for the World Cup finals was made, Ireland were placed in Group F and faced with a schedule which looked remarkably similar to the European Championship two years earlier. The group would start with a fixture against England in Cagliari, followed by Egypt in Palermo and a final group game against the Netherlands, also in Palermo.

The anticipation and excitement in Ireland grew in the months leading up to the World Cup. The players were now household names across the country and the team was an attractive commercial brand. For thousands of fans, the opportunity to travel to Italia '90 was a once-in-a-lifetime experience that could not be missed. In a struggling economy where emigration levels remained high and the unemployment rate was around fourteen per cent, the credit unions were busy processing loans for the travelling hordes.

With the World Cup returning to Italy for the first time since 1934, there was an expectation that the tournament would offer the perfect opportunity for the leading nations to showcase their talents. Italy was already home to the strongest domestic league in world football and many of the world's best footballers were based there. Amongst those players residing in Italy was Diego Maradona, who had lifted the

World Cup for Argentina four years earlier with an unstoppable *tour de force*. However, the opening game of Italia '90 proved that there are no guarantees in football as Maradona and Argentina were surprisingly beaten 1-0 by a vibrant Cameroon side in Milan.

Ireland opened their tournament three days later against England on a wet and stormy night in Cagliari as Jack Charlton sought once again to outwit his old friend Bobby Robson. Gary Lineker had posed the main threat in Stuttgart two years earlier but failed to find a way past Packie Bonner. Yet after only eight minutes in Cagliari, a defence splitting pass from Chris Waddle allowed Lineker to take a touch past the onrushing Bonner before bundling the ball into the net.

In a reversal of roles, Ireland would now be tasked with trying to claw back an equaliser against an English defence that was more experienced and cohesive than two years previously. The breakthrough arrived with 73 minutes on the clock, as a long punt from Bonner created indecision in the English defence. Kevin Sheedy latched onto the ball and his sweetly struck left-foot shot nestled neatly in the bottom corner of Peter Shilton's net. A scrappy game yielded a 1-1 draw that left England frustrated once again but provided Ireland with a solid platform to build on.

The second fixture against Egypt was identified by the fans and media as a great opportunity for Ireland to put themselves in pole position to win the group. Despite managing a draw against the Netherlands in their opening game, Egypt were perceived to be the minnows of the group and Jack Charlton identified it as a fixture Ireland needed to win. The match proved to be one of the poorest performances of the Charlton era, with Ireland's lack of invention allied to the opposition's absence of ambition, resulting in a drab scoreless draw. The performance led to some sharp criticism of Charlton's tactics, with Eamon Dunphy particularly vocal in expressing his aversion to the style of play.

Once again, Ireland's fate would be determined by a pivotal group decider against the Netherlands. As the reigning European champions, the Dutch were strongly fancied to win the tournament and were backboned by the AC Milan trio of Frank Rijkaard, Ruud Gullit and Marco van Basten. This threat materialised in the 11th minute when Gullit scored the opening goal following a slick one-two. Ireland battled hard to find a way back into the game and with less than twenty minutes remaining Niall Quinn pounced on a fumble by Hans van Breukelen to score the equaliser. The source of the goal was once again a long kick downfield from Bonner. The latter part of the game was effectively played at walking pace with what a number of the Irish players later referred to as a gentleman's agreement between the two sides to settle for a draw.

With England beating Egypt in the other fixture to top the group, the Dutch and Irish both finished the group with identical records. However, with the four best third-placed teams qualifying for the last 16, three points was enough for both teams. Lots were drawn to decide which team would face West Germany and which would face Romania. The draw was kinder to the Boys in Green, as they were handed a second-round tie with Romania in the Stadio Luigi Ferraris in Genoa. The Irish squad duly moved north to their new base at the Grand Bristol Hotel overlooking Rapallo Bay.

Jack Charlton seemed more relaxed following the team's passage to the last 16 and was quick to express his satisfaction with the relocation to the Italian mainland. 'This is the real thing here in Genoa,' said Charlton. 'We felt a little removed from the competition down in Sicily and Sardinia. There was so much pressure on us when we were down on the islands and trying to get out of one of the toughest groups in the competition.'

By qualifying for the last 16, there was almost certainly a realisation for the management and squad that they had fulfilled the expectations of the Irish public and were now in bonus territory. The Irish team were also acquiring the respect of other nations. After drawing with the Dutch, Ruud Gullit expressed his admiration for Jack Charlton's team. 'I think they surprised everybody, for not only were they strong but on this occasion they mixed their game,' said the Dutch captain. 'I like them so much that I think they could go all the way. I admire the way they play and nobody will relish playing against them. I thought there were times when they looked the complete team.'

The side that Charlton picked to face Romania remained unchanged from the starting eleven that drew with the Dutch. Niall Quinn's goal was enough for him to retain his place ahead of Tony Cascarino. The experience in the Irish team was implicit in the fact that nine of the starting eleven had featured in the win over England in Stuttgart two years earlier.

Bonner was in goals, whilst the back four included Morris, McCarthy and Moran. At left-back, 21-year-old Steve Staunton was the youngest member of the team but had established his credentials as part of a Liverpool squad that had just won the league title in England.

The midfield included Paul McGrath in the holding role with Ray Houghton on the right flank. Andy Townsend was picked in central midfield, having made his international debut less than eighteen months earlier. Townsend played his football at Norwich and quickly established himself in Big Jack's team. The midfield quartet was completed by Kevin Sheedy on the left. Sheedy, who had scored the vital equaliser against England in the group stage, had made his international debut in 1984 and was an established member of a strong Everton squad for much of the 1980s. Up front, the in-form Quinn was partnered by John Aldridge.

In contrast to Ireland, Romania were playing at their fifth World Cup finals. They had successfully negotiated a difficult group which contained Maradona's Argentina. The Romanians started their tournament with a 2-0 win over the USSR in Bari, followed by a 2-1 defeat against Cameroon at the same venue, before earning a 1-1 draw against Argentina in their final group game in Naples. Those results were enough to secure second place in the group.

The four goals they had scored in the tournament included two each from Marius Lăcătuş and Gavril Balint, both members of a hugely talented Steaua Bucharest team that won the European Cup in 1986. Unfortunately, from Romania's perspective, Lăcătuş had picked up two yellow cards in the group stage and as a result, he would miss the game against Ireland. His replacement in the team was Florin Răducioiu, who at 20 years of age was the second youngest player at the World Cup.

The undoubted star of the Romanian team was a 25-year-old by the name of Gheorghe Hagi. Standing at 5 foot 7 inches in height, Hagi was a pacey dribbler and packed a powerful shot off his left foot. His low centre of gravity, combined with his close control and change of pace had earned him the nickname, 'The Maradona of the Carpathians'. Hagi also played his football with Steaua Bucharest and his record included 76 goals in 97 games during his three seasons with the club. Hagi's time at Steaua coincided with the club's astonishing 104-match undefeated streak in the Romanian league from 1986 to 1989.

Prior to the World Cup, all but one member of Romania's 22-man squad was playing in the domestic league. Romanian football had established a strong pedigree, as illustrated by Steaua's European exploits, which included their success in 1986 and finishing runners-up against an outstanding AC Milan side in the European Cup Final in 1989.

Steaua's supremacy ended during the 1989-90 season when their great rivals Dinamo Bucharest won the league and cup double, as well as reaching the semi-finals of the European Cup Winners' Cup. Dinamo's recent rise to ascendancy was reflected in the national squad for the World Cup, which included ten of their players. Seven members of the squad played for Steaua. Despite the bitter rivalry that existed between Dinamo and Steaua, the predominance of playing resources from the two Bucharest clubs benefitted the national team's style of play in terms of cohesion and fluency. The valuable experience gained by the Romanian clubs in European competitions was an advantage their players had over most of their Irish counterparts, given that English clubs were banned by UEFA from competing in Europe following the Heysel Stadium tragedy in 1985.

Romania's participation in the World Cup was, however, set against a backdrop of political change that was sweeping through Eastern Europe. After months of violent protests and unrest throughout 1989, the Communist regime in Romania had been overthrown, with President Nicolae Ceauşescu and his wife executed on Christmas Day and a new government formed.

Ceauşescu's regime had played an important role in the development of Romanian football. Simon Hart's book, *World in Motion*, details how the state identified the best young footballers and took them to the Luceafărul school in Bucharest where they were educated and trained on a daily basis. This system created a strong pipeline of playing talent, which helped to explain the strength of Romanian football in the 1980s and early '90s.

One of the effects of the revolution was that the Romanian players were now free to go abroad, and this attracted the attention of Western scouts. There were reports during the World Cup that Romanian players were being plagued by representatives of foreign clubs. Ovidiu Ioaniţoaia, a spokesman for the Romanian team, spoke about this issue during the tournament. 'There's incredible pressure on the players,' said Ioaniţoaia. 'We're trying to stop it. All the time there are phone calls, letters and people trying to get players to sign.' Hagi was being linked with Real Madrid, Răducioiu with Fiorentina, and Ioan Sabău with Feyenoord.

A further distraction for the Romanian squad during the course of the tournament was the political climate in their homeland. The

Mineriad protests in Bucharest took place in mid-June, arising from the frustration and anger of people at the lack of meaningful change following the revolution. Indeed, the Romanian manager, Emerich Jenei, was forced to return home briefly during the tournament to visit his daughter who had been injured in the protests.

In terms of playing style, Jenei's team would present a very different challenge to what Ireland had faced up to that point. The Romanian team focused on building play from the back. The defence included a sweeper who performed an important role in dictating the tempo of their play with an ability to select a range of passes. The sweeper role was deeply embedded in Romanian football and could be traced back to the 1950s when a player called Alexandru Apolzan played for Steaua Bucharest. Apolzan is often credited as being the first sweeper in world football.

The player who might have been expected to assume the sweeper role at Italia '90 was Miodrag Belodedici, another member of Steaua's successful European Cup winning team. However, Belodedici had fled his homeland in 1988 and sought refuge in Yugoslavia, where he joined Red Star Belgrade. Under the Ceaușescu regime, he was found guilty of treason and although the charges were dropped after the revolution, he was not called up to the World Cup squad. This meant that the all-important sweeper role at the tournament was fulfilled by the 22-year-old Gheorghe Popescu.

With Popescu orchestrating play from his position in defence, the Romanian team utilised two deep-lying midfielders, and their full-backs had licence to get forward. The full-backs would seek to link up with two attacking midfielders in the shape of Hagi and Sabău. Hagi had a free role in the team, although his preference was to drift inside from the right wing where he could use his left foot to good effect.

Republic of Ireland

| 1 | Bonner |

2 Morris
4 McCarthy (captain)
5 Moran
3 Staunton

8 Houghton
7 McGrath
13 Townsend
11 Sheedy

9 Aldridge
17 Quinn

14 Răducioiu
18 Balint

8 Sabău
10 Hagi

5 Rotariu
21 Lupescu

3 Klein
6 Popescu
4 Andone
2 Rednic

1 Lung (captain)

Romania

123

The Romanian team were capable of transitioning from a slow and patient build-up before exploding into life in the opposition half of the field. Hagi and his teammates had demonstrated during the group stage that they could put together quick combinations of play, with a fluent tempo and rhythm in their passing.

In the build-up to kick-off, Charlton discussed his uncompromising style of play with the same type of conviction that he had demonstrated during his previous four years in the job. 'Our game is designed to upset teams from that part of the world and I don't think Romania will like the way we play today but, then again, we might not like the way they play either,' said Charlton.

Following Ireland's passage through the group stages of the tournament, thousands of supporters descended on Genoa for what was, at that point, the biggest game in Irish football history. It was estimated that somewhere in the region of 20,000 Irish fans had found their way to Genoa.

It was a late Monday afternoon kick-off, but the weather was warm and humid. As the teams walked onto the pitch, they were greeted by a wall of sound from the predominantly Irish crowd which made it look like a home game for Jack Charlton's team.

Steve Staunton had the first shot at goal after only three minutes, but his 35-yard effort was speculative and easily gathered by Silviu Lung in the Romanian goal. The first warning sign of Hagi's ability came just a minute later, as he combined well with Sabău on the left before leaving three Irish defenders in his wake. Hagi then picked out Sabău in the box, but his shot went narrowly wide of Bonner's left post. Romania had started the game with intent and Ireland were struggling to contain their movement and quick interplay. Sabău then gained possession in his own half, before driving forward and laying the ball off to Balint, whose subsequent shot was straight at Bonner.

Ireland's first chance arrived on 19 minutes when a long ball from McCarthy was headed down by Niall Quinn to Andy Townsend, but the Norwich man's effort was comfortably saved by Lung. Within minutes, Hagi was once again threatening the Irish goal when he played a one-two with Balint before unleashing a shot that Bonner palmed away.

The Irish midfield struggled to close down Hagi, and his pace and left foot looked increasingly menacing. In his *World Cup Diary*, Jack Charlton later described his concern about the threat that Hagi posed: 'We weren't coping with Hagi nearly as well as I had hoped. As a matter of policy, we had decided against man-marking him – the player closest to him at any particular time would pick him up – but in the event, we were doing neither.'

By the midway point of the first half, the Irish players were looking a little lethargic and struggling with the warm conditions. Their prospects of gaining a foothold in the game were not helped by John Aldridge's struggle to shake off an injury. In Ross Whitaker's documentary, *The Boys in Green*, Aldridge advised that, upon realising he was unfit to continue, he decided to take out Hagi with a tackle. Viewed through a contemporary lens, the subsequent challenge by Aldridge on Hagi was aggressive and he was fortunate to escape with just a yellow card. Hagi was also fortunate that he was able to continue playing.

Aldridge was replaced by Tony Cascarino, who had started the two earlier matches against England and Egypt. Cascarino had signed for Aston Villa three months earlier, having worked his way up the English Football League with spells at both Gillingham and Millwall. The decision to opt for Cascarino as a second target man alongside Quinn suggested that Jack Charlton had already seen enough of the game to determine the approach that he felt would work best. Aldridge was an integral part of Charlton's normal game plan, as there was an onus on him to run the channels and pressurise opposition defenders. Neither Quinn nor Cascarino offered that type of mobility, but Cascarino was the only striker on the bench. The alternative would have involved introducing an extra midfielder in the shape of Ronnie Whelan or John Sheridan.

With Quinn and Cascarino up front, Ireland looked to be at their most threatening from set-pieces. One free kick from Townsend was taken short to Sheedy, who took a touch to lift the ball and then volley it, forcing Lung into a save. As half-time approached, the Irish team carved out their best opportunity of the game when Cascarino headed the ball down for Sheedy who stretched out a toe and directed the ball towards the goal. However, Lung got across quickly to save. The chance proved that Ireland could create openings and it provided a positive end to the first half.

In the opening minutes of the second half, the Irish team created another good chance when Houghton played the ball into Quinn's feet inside the penalty area. Quinn then managed to work some space before crossing for Cascarino at the back post, but Cascarino couldn't keep his header down. That opportunity signalled the start of Ireland's most encouraging spell in the game, with the full-backs pushing forward in support.

On the hour mark, Ray Houghton picked out the run of Chris Morris down the right wing. Morris pulled the ball back towards Sheedy in the penalty area, but a Romanian defender got there ahead of him and the ball went behind for a corner. Moments later, another chance to attack from out wide came to nothing, as Morris was unable to provide a decent delivery.

Although Romania were lacking the early pace and fluidity that they showed in the first half, they still posed a threat. A clever corner-kick routine in the 71st minute culminated in the ball being played into an unmarked Răducioiu, who got his shot away first time and forced Bonner into a save. Moments later, Hagi received possession in midfield and ran at the Irish defence before unleashing a rasping shot from 25 yards, which Bonner saved at full stretch.

As the match approached the 90-minute mark, the Irish team

attempted to find a breakthrough, with Cascarino heading off target and a subsequent header from Quinn earning a corner-kick. Those efforts were followed by the Brazilian referee blowing his whistle to signal the end of normal time.

The temperature in the stadium had dropped, but the earlier exertions had clearly taken their toll on both teams, as the pace of the game was slower during the first period of extra-time. The one player still showing a different gear was Hagi. Four minutes into extra-time, he played a one-two with a teammate before striking another powerful shot which required a smart save from Bonner.

Jack Charlton decided to make his second substitution, introducing David O'Leary in place of Steve Staunton. It had become increasingly apparent that Staunton was struggling to keep pace with Hagi and get close enough to make a challenge. O'Leary had over fifty caps for his country and at the very least he would offer fresh legs. The introduction of O'Leary coincided with a decent period of possession for Ireland, as they began to force Romania back. Some fine play from Sheedy on the left wing led to a header from Houghton, but he couldn't direct it on target.

Romania made another substitution with Sabău exiting for Daniel Timofte, a 22-year-old attacking midfielder from Dinamo Bucharest. As the end of the first period of extra-time approached, Townsend and McCarthy charged down two goal-bound shots following a Romanian corner.

The teams swapped ends and the second period of extra-time began at an almost pedestrian pace. Townsend had an opportunity with a volley from the edge of the area which was comfortably dealt with by the Romanian keeper, and Quinn had a shot which was off target. The game slowly petered out, as both sides struggled with fatigue and appeared satisfied to take their chances in a penalty shoot-out.

After 120 minutes of football, it was fair to conclude that this match had pitted two teams against each other with diametrically opposed styles of play. The technical ability of Romania's players was apparent throughout but particularly in the opening half hour. Ireland, on the other hand, relied on a more direct and physically robust approach to the game, which became even more pronounced following the substitution of Aldridge for Cascarino. The two distinguishing features of the match were the predominance of Gheorghe Hagi as the fulcrum for the Romanian attack and the remarkable ability of Mick McCarthy to avoid a yellow card.

Hagi took ten shots over the course of the match and although only three of them hit the target, the majority were struck with enough venom to cause concern for Bonner and his defenders. McCarthy committed seven fouls in total, four of them on Răducioiu and three on Hagi. Indeed, the match was only four seconds old when McCarthy conceded the first free kick. As things transpired, the Irish captain conceded more free kicks than any other player at the tournament and yet avoided a booking. That statistic was an indicator of the tight marking and imposing approach which Jack Charlton encouraged from his central defenders and it was probably more prevalent against Romania than in any other fixture during Charlton's managerial tenure.

A penalty shoot-out represented an unknown quantity for Charlton and his team, but the manager and players looked relaxed. Packie Bonner had been involved in a shoot-out for Celtic the previous month when they faced Aberdeen in the Scottish Cup Final, which went to 'sudden death' with Aberdeen eventually converting nine out of their ten penalties to claim the trophy. Bonner had been asked about the possibility of a penalty shoot-out in the days prior to facing Romania. The Donegal man said that it would be 'a chance to make amends for the Scottish Cup Final', adding that 'there's no pressure on the goalkeeper, it's all on the guy taking the penalty'.

Romania's contingent of Steaua Bucharest players had experience of penalties from their involvement in European club football. The 1986 European Cup Final was decided by a shoot-out when penalties from Marius Lăcătuş and Gavril Balint helped the club to defeat Barcelona. However, Lăcătuş was not on the pitch against Ireland and curiously, Balint was not selected to take a penalty.

While the absence of both players from Romania's list of penalty-takers was welcome news from an Irish perspective, Big Jack's men were also arguably missing their two strongest candidates, with neither John Aldridge nor Ronnie Whelan on the pitch at the end of extra-time. Steve Staunton and John Sheridan, two other accomplished players with a placed ball, would also have to look on from the side-line. And yet, the Irish team could still rely on other decent strikers of the ball, with both Kevin Sheedy and Ray Houghton putting themselves forward.

Romania won the coin toss and would have the advantage of taking the first penalty, but they would be taking them at the northern end of the stadium, which was occupied by Irish supporters. Gheorghe Hagi had been the best player on the pitch over the course of 120 minutes and he stepped forward to commence proceedings. Hagi dispatched his spot-kick with aplomb. He was followed by Kevin Sheedy, who smashed the ball with conviction past Silviu Lung. The success rate continued as Danut Lupu, Ray Houghton, Iosif Rotariu, Andy Townsend and Ioan Lupescu all converted in turn.

Romania had a 4-3 lead as Tony Cascarino stepped forward to try and keep Ireland on level terms. In his autobiography, *Full Time*, Cascarino described the self-doubt he experienced as he made the long walk towards the penalty-spot and how his legs 'felt like rubber sticks'. This lack of confidence manifested itself in his subsequent spot-kick, as his striking foot made contact with the ground at the same time as he struck the ball. Fortunately, the ball flew under the body of Lung and the Irish supporters breathed a huge sigh of relief as the net rippled. The television replays showed that Cascarino had managed to take a large divot from the ground as he struck his penalty.

Daniel Timofte then stepped forward to take Romania's fifth penalty. Bonner had been guessing the right way for the previous spot-kicks and it felt as though he was getting closer to saving one. Timofte placed the ball and took a short run-up from an acute angle before striking the ball with the inside of his right foot. Bonner dived to his right and the ball was at a perfect height for the Donegal man to reach and palm away. The save handed the initiative to Ireland and suddenly the team was standing on the brink of the quarter-finals of the World Cup.

David O'Leary made the lonely walk forward for what Irish fans hoped would be the deciding penalty. O'Leary had endured a difficult relationship with Jack Charlton and had not featured in the previous group games. Like Timofte, O'Leary had been introduced as a substitute in extra-time and, like the Romanian midfielder, his involvement in the shoot-out would have a defining effect on the outcome. Although the Arsenal man was recognised as a cultured central defender, he was not readily associated with penalty-taking.

O'Leary took his time in placing the ball, which added to the unbearable tension in the stadium. The suspense and significance of the moment was perfectly encapsulated by the RTÉ commentator, George Hamilton, who uttered the immortal words, 'The nation holds its breath,' as O'Leary started his run-up. O'Leary struck the ball with his instep to Lung's left, with the goalkeeper diving to the right. As the ball hit the back of the net, it provided the cue for frenzied celebrations amongst the Irish players and staff.

Ireland had achieved the unthinkable and reached the quarter-finals in their first appearance at a World Cup. The performance may not have been the most impressive of Charlton's tenure, but it epitomised many of the traits associated with his team. The players had managed to dig in and defend belligerently in warm and humid conditions against a technical and pacey Romanian frontline. The nature of the performance served to illustrate that the Irish team included seasoned professionals who were hard to break down and fiercely competitive, irrespective of the opposition.

In the post-match interviews, Charlton compared his team's achievement to England lifting the World Cup twenty-four years earlier and stated that '1966 was a wonderful day, but this is an even more wonderful day'. The manager spoke of his admiration for the heroes of the shoot-out but reserved heartfelt praise for O'Leary. 'I'm delighted for Dave O'Leary,' said Charlton. 'He volunteered to take the last penalty. Only a player with real courage and confidence would make that decision.'

O'Leary himself described to reporters what was going through his mind as he walked up to take the decisive penalty: 'I thought about what scoring would mean to everybody, my Mum and Dad, my kids, my family and my friends. It is one of the greatest feelings in my whole life.' The penalty kick appeared to be a cathartic moment for O'Leary after the disappointment of missing out on the squad for Euro '88, and a deserving reward, given his dignified behaviour throughout.

The following day, Peter Byrne wrote in the *Irish Times* that 'moments of imperishable drama under a hot Italian sun yielded the result to illuminate Irish sporting history'. Tony Leen in the *Irish Examiner* proclaimed that 'Ireland's death-defying heroes climbed to astonishing new heights last night – and sent a nation into unprecedented rapture'. The headline in *Gazzetta dello Sport* read 'Little Invincible Ireland' and was accompanied by an action photograph of Bonner making the crucial penalty save.

After the drama in Genoa, the Irish squad moved on to a new hotel and the FAI arranged to show them video footage of the euphoric scenes back in Ireland. Given that the tournament was being played out long before the advent of social media, it is hardly surprising that the recorded footage took some of the players by surprise. That was the moment when the enormity of their achievements began to sink in. In Alan McLoughlin's autobiography, *A Different Shade of Green*, he describes how the squad watched footage of people 'with their hands raised high, hugging one another, crying, applauding, slapping each other's backs and falling off chairs'. McLoughlin noted that it was 'not just young men but women, children, old people – all delighted, all grinning and laughing and cheering'.

Some of the television footage captured in the immediate aftermath of the penalty shoot-out included a man in tears as he watched the action at the EU Summit which was taking place at Dublin Castle. The footage would later be used as part of RTÉ's *Reeling in the Years* episode for 1990. The man in question was John Healy, a journalist from Charlestown in Mayo who in 1968 had published a book entitled *No One Shouted Stop*. His book chronicled the economic and social decline in the west of Ireland during a time of poverty and mass emigration. Although John Healy was not known as a football fan, his deeper understanding of Irish emigration suggested that there may have been a symmetry between his emotional outpouring and the achievement of a squad of players that was largely comprised of the sons and grandsons of Irish emigrants. Of the thirteen players who featured against Romania, seven had grown up in Britain. The significant contribution of the Irish diaspora added to the poignancy of the occasion.

Ireland's reward for overcoming Romania was a quarter-final tie against the hosts in the Stadio Olimpico five days later. Following their arrival in Rome, the Irish management and players were granted an audience with Pope John Paul II in the Vatican. The excitement had reached fever pitch in Ireland and even the government was getting in on the act. The Taoiseach, Charlie Haughey, availed of the government jet to fly himself and a select group of TDs to Rome for the game. Haughey had turned up in Paris three years earlier when Stephen Roche won the Tour de France, so it was hardly surprising that he identified Ireland's World Cup progression as an opportunity to be seen on board the latest sporting bandwagon. In some respects, the build-up to the quarter-final demonstrated how Irish football's relationship with the Church and the political establishment had changed beyond recognition from the controversial fixture against Yugoslavia in 1955.

From a footballing perspective, Italy would pose the sternest test that Jack Charlton's team had faced in the tournament. The Italians were strongly fancied to win the World Cup and had yet to concede a goal. Their striker, Totò Schillaci, was emerging as one of the surprise stars of the World Cup, having already scored three goals in the tournament. The sight of the Irish team walking out to face the hosts at the quarter-final stage of a World Cup was beyond the reasonable imagination of seasoned football fans and an achievement that might never be repeated.

The fairy tale ended with the Italians advancing to the semi-finals, as another Schillaci goal proved to be the difference. In truth, Italy were good value for their win, and it is open to debate as to whether the Irish team truly believed that they could upset the host nation. By that stage, Charlton's team had exceeded all expectations and would return to Dublin to a heroes' welcome.

The squad arrived home on the same day as Nelson Mandela was being presented with the Freedom of the City of Dublin. The South African anti-apartheid leader had been released from prison in February 1990 after serving 27 years.

Following their arrival into Dublin Airport, the management and players boarded an open-top bus which crawled between the tens of thousands of people who lined the route between the airport and city centre. The profile of Irish football had ascended to another level and impacted the nation in a truly profound way.

Although Italia '90 was a significant moment in Irish popular culture, the tournament itself is generally regarded as one of the most negative and least entertaining World Cups. The tournament produced an average of 2.21 goals per match, still the lowest in World Cup history. Both semi-finals were decided by penalty shoot-outs and the final was decided by a spot-kick for West Germany which defeated Maradona's Argentina. Ireland's style of play didn't go unnoticed in the tournament, including the pivotal role played by Packie Bonner. In Jonathan Wilson's book, *The Outsider*, he wrote that the 1990 World Cup prompted a general rethink about the laws of the game and particularly 'one passage of play in the group match between the Republic of Ireland and Egypt in which the Irish keeper Packie Bonner held the ball for almost six minutes without releasing it'. FIFA finally took action with the introduction of the back-pass rule in 1992 to discourage time-wasting and defensive play.

Bonner's penalty save catapulted him to legendary status in Ireland. It would become the Donegal man's defining moment in an Irish jersey, but his joy was in stark contrast to the pain experienced by Daniel Timofte. The Romanian midfielder returned to his homeland as the man who cost his nation a place in the quarter-finals of the World Cup. Indeed, three months after the penalty miss, Timofte travelled to Dublin as part of a Dinamo Bucharest team that played St Patrick's Athletic in the first round of the European Cup. Timofte went on to have a decent career but missed out on the Romanian squad that travelled to the 1994 World Cup.

In 2015, Graham Clifford of the *Irish Independent* travelled to Romania to interview Timofte and discuss the penalty. During the interview, Clifford arranged a telephone call between Timofte and Bonner, where the two protagonists spoke to each other a quarter of a century on from that defining moment. Timofte told Bonner: 'I wanted to hit it right down the middle like I always did with penalties, but a teammate told me that you were having trouble diving, that you stay in the centre of the goals and he changed my mind.' Timofte also referred to the effect of the previous penalty by Cascarino in which 'he took part of the pitch', thereby creating a hole on the penalty spot.

The Romanian squad of the early '90s became known as the *Generația de Aur* ('golden generation') in their homeland and were at their peak by the time the 1994 World Cup came around. They finally went one step further by reaching a quarter-final after knocking out Argentina. The disappointment of being eliminated on penalties four years earlier almost certainly proved to be a motivating factor in their success. A month prior to USA '94, Gheorghe Hagi spoke to the *New York Times* and expressed the hurt he felt following the penalty shoot-out loss to Ireland. 'It wasn't fair,' said Hagi. 'We played better than the Irish did. We had all the scoring opportunities. Even the Irish players said that we deserved to win. I still have a bitter taste in my mouth from that match.'

The Irish team might have gone through Italia '90 without winning a match in normal time, but the events of that summer had captured the public imagination like no previous sporting event in the country's history. The squad's musical offering, 'Put 'Em Under Pressure', remained at No. 1 in the Irish singles charts for thirteen consecutive weeks and would become the soundtrack of the Charlton era. The story of the World Cup would also form the backdrop to Roddy Doyle's novel, *The Van*, which was published the following year and made into a film in 1996.

The World Cup experience resonated with people in a country that was about to go through a period of significant socio-economic change. The scenes of unbridled joy were also symptomatic of an innocence that would be almost impossible to repeat in a contemporary context.

Chapter 9
Italy v Republic of Ireland
18 June 1994

'That was the moment somebody turned down the sound and everything slowed. The moment I felt unbreakable.'

– Paul McGrath, *Back from the Brink*

Following Italia '90, the Republic of Ireland sought to qualify for a third major tournament on the trot by making it to the European Championship in 1992. The Boys in Green were drawn in a four-team group which included familiar foes, England, as well as Poland and Turkey. It was a campaign that ended in disappointment with England topping the group and narrowly sealing qualification through a late Gary Lineker goal in their final qualifier away to Poland.

Both of Ireland's matches against the 'Old Enemy' ended in 1-1 draws, but Jack Charlton's team failed to capitalise on a dominant display when they visited Wembley. In what was one of the finest performances of Charlton's tenure, the Irish team spent long periods camped in the English half but were unable to score a winner. It was the matches against Poland though, that would ultimately cost Ireland qualification. A scoreless draw at Lansdowne Road was followed by a 3-3 draw in Poznan in which the Irish team were 3-1 up and seemingly coasting before conceding two late goals.

The failure to qualify for Euro '92 was a missed opportunity for Charlton's squad, which was arguably stronger than the one that went to Italia '90. The squad was evolving, with younger players such as Denis Irwin and Terry Phelan emerging and the likes of Steve Staunton and Niall Quinn becoming increasingly influential. The

European Championship was subsequently won by Denmark, a team that hadn't actually qualified for the tournament and were effectively called from their summer holidays to replace the war-torn Yugoslavia.

As fate would have it, Denmark were drawn in the same qualifying group as Ireland for the subsequent World Cup qualifying campaign. In what was described as the 'Group of Death', Charlton's squad was faced with the prospect of playing the Danes, Spain and Northern Ireland, with difficult away trips to navigate against Albania, Latvia and Lithuania.

The first half of the campaign included two valuable scoreless draws away from home against Denmark and Spain. The latter fixture in Seville was one that Ireland were unfortunate not to win, with a second half goal from John Aldridge incorrectly ruled out for being offside. The same night, a 21-year-old Roy Keane put in a performance that marked his coming-of-age as an international footballer. The Nottingham Forest player had left Cobh Ramblers two years earlier and provided a new source of energy and drive in the Irish midfield.

By the time Spain visited Dublin in the penultimate round of fixtures, Ireland were looking to seal qualification for the World Cup finals. Spain had other ideas, however, and three goals inside the first half hour left the home side shell-shocked. The Republic's qualification hopes were left hanging by a thread, but John Sheridan scored a second-half consolation which would ultimately prove crucial. The following month, Northern Ireland hosted the Republic in Belfast, but there wasn't much in the way of hospitality on display. On a tense night in Windsor Park, Alan McLoughlin struck a priceless equaliser to keep the World Cup dream alive. The game finished 1-1 and with Spain beating Denmark in Seville, the Republic qualified in second place. Both the Republic and Denmark finished with the same number of points and the same goal difference, but Jack Charlton's team had scored more goals over the course of the campaign.

Ireland were one of 24 teams in the draw for the World Cup finals, which took place in Las Vegas in December 1993. On a night when Roberto Baggio was crowned FIFA World Player of the Year, Ireland were drawn in Group E alongside Baggio's Italy. The other teams in the group were Norway, who had qualified at the expense of England, and World Cup regulars, Mexico. The Irish team would start the tournament by facing Italy in the Giants Stadium in New Jersey, followed by Mexico in the heat of Orlando, before returning to the Giants Stadium to conclude the group against Norway.

In the two months prior to the tournament, Ireland beat both the Netherlands and Germany in friendly matches away from home. Those results pointed to an increasing level of confidence within the squad. Indeed, the Irish team had only lost a single competitive fixture since Italy beat them in the quarter-final of the World Cup four years earlier. The sense of expectation continued to grow as Charlton supplemented his squad with an injection of young talent in the shape of Phil Babb, Gary Kelly and Jason McAteer. The 'Three Amigos' as they became known had all made their debuts in a friendly against Russia in March 1994 and continued to impress in the warm-up games prior to the World Cup.

One of the main talking points in the build-up to the tournament was how the Irish players would deal with the heat and humidity in the United States, particularly as the fixtures against Mexico and Norway were scheduled to kick-off shortly after midday. Jack Charlton was vocal in expressing his concern that players might suffer from dehydration and should be provided with easy access to water during games. The FAI decided to base the squad in Orlando with a two-week training camp to allow the players time to acclimatise. The squad flew from Orlando to New Jersey two days before they were due to face Italy, staying at the Sheraton Tara Hotel in Parssipanny, some 35 miles from downtown Manhattan.

The World Cup kicked off on 17 June, with Germany facing Bolivia in Chicago. As Irish fans descended on the 'Big Apple', the attention of the city's inhabitants was consumed by other matters. The New York Rangers ice hockey team were celebrating the end of their 54-year wait for the Stanley Cup with a ticker-tape parade on Broadway. Later that evening, basketball took centre stage as the New York Knicks hosted the Houston Rockets in the NBA Finals at Madison Square Garden. Television coverage of the basketball was interrupted by a surreal story which was unfolding at the same time in Los Angeles, as the police chased after a white Ford Bronco containing OJ Simpson. The police pursuit of the former NFL player provided the focus for the US media on the eve of Ireland's opening fixture, and the subsequent trial of Simpson for two counts of murder captivated a worldwide television audience.

The match against Italy represented a huge challenge for Ireland, particularly given their pedigree in a tournament they had won on three previous occasions. Nevertheless, the point was consistently made by pundits in the months prior to the World Cup that Italian teams traditionally made sluggish starts to tournaments. This was true and was perhaps most evident in 1982 when they drew their three group games before going on to lift the trophy.

Italy were managed by Arrigo Sacchi, the architect of AC Milan's success in the late 1980s and early '90s. Sacchi was not only one of the most tactically astute managers in world football, but also one of the most innovative. In an era when Italian club football was very much focused on strong defensive play, Sacchi preferred a fluid, yet organised attacking 4-4-2 formation. His tactical approach involved a move away from *Catenaccio* and the traditional *libero,* or sweeper system, which had been at the heart of Italian football since the 1950s.

Sacchi's team to face Ireland was backboned by AC Milan players, with the entire back four and two of the midfielders from the *Rossoneri.* A month earlier, AC Milan had won the UEFA Champions League with a resounding 4-0 win over Barcelona. Serie A was undoubtedly the strongest league in the world at that time and the

Italian national team was able to call on some of the league's biggest stars.

The defensive unit of Mauro Tassotti, Franco Baresi, Alessandro Costacurta and Paolo Maldini commanded respect as four of the best defenders in world football. Dino Baggio and Demetrio Albertini provided a combination of athleticism and creativity in the centre of the park. Sacchi also had an embarrassment of riches in the forward positions. The Italian manager opted for Roberto Baggio and Lazio's Giuseppe Signori up front. The Italians had the luxury of leaving some of Europe's leading strikers on the bench, including AC Milan's Daniele Massaro, Pierluigi Casiraghi of Lazio, and Parma's Gianfranco Zola. Gianluca Vialli of Juventus and Sampdoria's Roberto Mancini didn't even make the squad.

By contrast, Ireland were seriously lacking in options to play up front. Niall Quinn missed the tournament as he was recovering from a cruciate ligament injury, whilst Tony Cascarino and John Aldridge were also struggling for fitness. The lack of fit strikers led Charlton to change the formation from his preferred 4-4-2 to what appeared to be a more defensive 4-5-1.

Packie Bonner was still Ireland's first-choice goalkeeper, although he had spent most of the season out of favour at Celtic. Manchester United's Denis Irwin was picked at right-back. Although Irwin played his club football at left-back, Charlton preferred to play the Cork man on his more natural right side. Terry Phelan of Manchester City, a firm favourite of the Irish manager, was selected at left-back.

The centre of defence included Aston Villa's Paul McGrath and the 23-year-old Phil Babb, who played for Coventry City. At 34 years of age, McGrath was entering the twilight of his career and recurring knee injuries meant that he was not quite as mobile as when he anchored the Irish midfield at Euro '88 and Italia '90. McGrath had also struggled with a virus in his shoulder in the months leading up to the tournament, but his performance alongside Babb in the friendly win over Germany provided a timely reassurance for his manager. Babb's display in the same match was also enough to convince Charlton that he should start ahead of Alan Kernaghan.

The central figure in the Irish midfield was Roy Keane of Manchester United. The young Cork man's career was on a rapid upward trajectory, having moved from Brian Clough's Nottingham Forest to Old Trafford in 1993 for a British record transfer fee of £3.75 million. Big Jack was faced with a selection dilemma on the right side of midfield, as Jason McAteer's form was putting pressure on Ray Houghton. The manager decided to opt for experience, and Houghton was named in the starting eleven. He was joined in midfield by his Aston Villa teammates, Andy Townsend and Steve Staunton. Townsend had become a very influential player within the squad and assumed the captaincy two years earlier. The final member of the midfield, John Sheridan of Sheffield Wednesday, was a creative midfielder with a fine range of passing.

Tommy Coyne of Motherwell was entrusted with the role of lone striker. Coyne was an unlikely starting player but had emerged as a viable candidate following an excellent performance in the friendly win over the Netherlands, scoring the only goal of the game. His selection was ultimately sealed due to the absence of Quinn and the on-going fitness issues experienced by Aldridge and Cascarino.

Whilst Italy had their AC Milan contingent, the fact that Ireland had four players from Aston Villa and two from Manchester United meant that there was also a strong sense of familiarity within the team, which was further borne out by consistency of selection. The Irish starting eleven had an average age of 29 years and two months, with five of the players over the age of 30. Six of the starting team had played against Italy in Rome four years earlier – Bonner, McGrath, Houghton, Townsend, Staunton and Sheridan. The Italian side had four survivors from that fixture – Baresi, Maldini, Roberto Donadoni and Roberto Baggio.

Italy had won all seven of the previous fixtures between the two nations and the general consensus amongst the Irish media and fans was that a draw would represent a fine result and would set the team up for a win against Mexico in their subsequent outing. Andy Townsend cautioned that 'the one thing you don't want to do in the first game is lose it'.

Arrigo Sacchi advised that his Italian side would be going all out for victory, but acknowledged that 'skill, passion, a will to win in the Irish team could be a deciding factor for them'. Sacchi's star man, Roberto Baggio, said that Italy would 'try to play very quickly, to break from midfield and to attack with speed'.

Despite the apparent indifference of the US media to the fact that their country was hosting the World Cup, the travelling Irish fans were more than happy to be experiencing the delights of New York, a city intertwined with the Irish emigrant story. However, New York could also be described as the most Italian city outside Europe and therein lay a potential problem from an Irish perspective. In the months leading up to the game, there were predictions that the significant Italian population would result in them out-numbering the Irish support in the Giants Stadium.

Such suggestions couldn't have been further from the truth. On a hot midsummer's afternoon, the borough of East Rutherford in New Jersey was invaded by a wonderful mixture of travelling Irish fans and the Irish-American diaspora. As kick-off approached, it was clear that the Irish supporters greatly outnumbered the Italians. In the days leading up to the game, Irish newspapers had suggested that somewhere in the region of 15,000 Irish fans had travelled for the opening fixture. Afterwards it was estimated that there were as many as 50,000 Irish supporters in the stadium.

Italy

1
Pagliuca

9
Tassotti

4
Costacurta

6
Baresi
(captain)

5
Maldini

16
Donadoni

11
Albertini

13
D. Baggio

17
Evani

10
R. Baggio

20
Signore

15
Coyne

11
Staunton

7
Townsend
(captain)

6
Keane

10
Sheridan

8
Houghton

3
Phelan

14
Babb

5
McGrath

2
Irwin

1
Bonner

Republic of Ireland

In a 2014 interview with *The 42*, Ray Houghton commented on the support as the squad made their way to the Giants Stadium:

> 'I remember going on the coach to the game and seeing the number of Irish fans en route. There was a real party atmosphere. There's nothing like it when you know people are shouting you on, that they've got your back and they're supporting you.'

A noteworthy incident occurred as the respective teams were about to depart their dressing-rooms. The Irish players were wearing their away kit – white jerseys, green shorts and white socks. To their surprise, they were informed that the Italians were also wearing white. It was, however, the Irish who had selected the wrong kit and they were ordered to change. The team frantically changed into their customary green jerseys, white shorts and green socks. Meanwhile, the Italian team was left standing in the tunnel waiting for their opposition to emerge. Some Irish players later ascribed importance to the kit-changing incident, observing that it helped to ease the team's nerves and that it may have upset the focus of some of the Italian players.

The teams finally emerged to a cacophony of sound, which coalesced into a rousing rendition of 'Amhrán na bhFiann' as the Irish fans made their voices heard. Ireland kicked off and started with intent. An immediate long ball forward was cleared to Staunton, whose left-footed volley flew well wide of the Italian goal. Italy soon settled and, after seven minutes, a through-ball sent Signori clear, but his run was tracked by McGrath. It took McGrath three or four strides to get going, but he soon caught up with Signori and made a vital tackle that directed the ball back to Bonner. The speed of McGrath's recovery helped to dispel some of the concerns over his fitness.

In the 11th minute, Ireland struck with a sucker-punch. John Sheridan took possession deep in the Irish half of the field and knocked a long ball forward, which was met by Costacurta, who headed it in the direction of Baresi, who in turn headed the ball back infield. The ball landed on the chest of the onrushing Houghton, who let it bounce before striking it with his weaker left foot. The shot lobbed over the head of the Italian goalkeeper Gianluca Pagliuca and into the Italian net. Six years and six days on from his goal against England in Stuttgart, Houghton had followed up with another early goal on the biggest stage of all.

Italy were suddenly in a position where they had to chase the game, but they had time on their side and plenty of attacking options. Despite the experience in their ranks, the Italians appeared to be rattled and their normally reliable defence was clearly unsettled. Ireland almost capitalised again when Andy Townsend beat the offside trap to meet a left-wing cross from Staunton, but Townsend's first touch was poor and Baresi recovered to clear. The *Azzurri* had their first attempt a minute later when a shot by Signori from outside the penalty area flew wide of Bonner's goal.

As the midway point of the first half approached, McGrath made three key interceptions within the space of ten seconds to deny both Dino and Roberto Baggio. Two clearing headers in quick succession were followed by a blocked shot as the centre-back got his face in the way. McGrath's interventions were inspirational and struck an important psychological blow for his team.

Italy began to build some momentum around the half-hour mark, with a slick one-two between Roberto Baggio and Signori resulting in a shot from the former, which fizzed over the Irish goal. As half-time approached, Roberto Baggio attempted another pass over the top of the Irish defence as Signori tried to steal in behind. However, Babb's headed clearance was indicative of a very disciplined first-half performance by the Irish back four.

One of the most notable aspects of the first half was that Ireland were intent on holding a high line in defence. There were occasions when the back four were pushed up close to the halfway line. The combination of a high defensive line and an extra player in midfield meant that Roberto Baggio was forced to drop deep in search of the ball. The Irish players were also working hard to support Tommy Coyne, with Houghton, Townsend and Staunton particularly prominent in getting forward to assist the front man.

At half-time, Sacchi made a substitution, with Daniele Massaro coming on for Alberigo Evani. Massaro's introduction took the AC Milan contingent to seven players and involved a switch to a 4-3-3 formation. For Sacchi to change from his trusted 4-4-2 was a tacit acknowledgement that Italy needed to do something different to counteract the Irish tactics. Massaro's introduction to a more central role required Signori to move towards the left wing but with a licence to drift inside.

The adjustments to the Italian team made an immediate impact as they assumed a greater command of possession in the early stages of the second half. Eight minutes into the half, a beautiful through-ball from Donadoni to Dino Baggio required Babb to make a sliding tackle in the penalty area. Babb's challenge was well-timed and cleared the ball for a corner. A minute later, Italy won a free kick, with a pre-rehearsed routine teeing up Dino Baggio, whose poorly struck shot was straight at Bonner.

The Irish team was struggling to contain Dino Baggio's runs from midfield. As the hour mark approached, the Juventus midfielder once again tried to get in behind the Irish defence and Denis Irwin was forced to make a crucial tackle. Signori was also seeing more of the ball on the left wing. A well-timed run and shot from the Lazio striker was too hot for Bonner to handle, with the Irish keeper batting the ball away.

Despite the increasing Italian pressure, Irish players were still looking to get forward. Sheridan's ability to hold possession was crucial. Houghton tested Pagliuca with a low shot before being substituted for Jason McAteer. The goal-scoring hero left the field to a rapturous reception and McAteer came on, marking his 23rd birthday with a first appearance in a competitive international. Although there was a perception that McAteer and Babb were the kids in the team, it is easy to forget that Roy Keane was the youngest Irish player on the pitch that afternoon. As both teams began to tire in the heat, McAteer's energy allied to Keane's drive and endurance, gave Ireland an added dimension in the last twenty minutes.

In what was probably the best passage of play in the second half, a triangle of intricate passes between Staunton, Townsend and Keane on the left wing released the latter, who powered his way to the end-line and pulled the ball back towards the middle of the penalty area. Coyne dummied the ball as it crossed his path, leaving Sheridan with a clear shot from just over 12 yards out. Sheridan's strike rebounded off the crossbar as Pagliuca looked on helplessly.

At this stage, Ireland were reasserting some control and McAteer's direct running and willingness to chase lost causes was making life difficult for Paolo Maldini, perhaps the most accomplished left-back of his generation. McAteer's energy also provided some much-needed support for Tommy Coyne and gave the Irish midfielders more time to get forward. In contrast, the Italians seemed to be running out of ideas. With eight minutes remaining, a long-range shot from Roberto Baggio went well over the top of the Irish goal, summing up an indifferent performance from the Juventus striker and the increasing desperation from his team.

As the clock passed the 90-minute mark and ticked agonisingly towards the final whistle, McGrath continued to exert his influence, making two key interventions in injury time. Firstly, he executed a well-timed tackle on Massaro before heading clear a subsequent cross from a short corner. In his compelling autobiography, *Back from the Brink*, McGrath recounted those closing minutes in the Giants Stadium with an eloquence that summed up the air of invincibility which accompanied his performance:

'Ninety-three Fahrenheit in the evening sun and time for just one last Italian corner. . . . Massaro played the ball short to his fullback. And that was when it happened. That was the moment somebody turned down the sound and everything slowed. The moment I felt unbreakable. As the full-back prepared to cross, I knew it no longer mattered where I stood. The ball would find me.'

The final whistle blew a minute later, and the Irish team had overcome the aristocrats of European football to register the country's first win against Italy.

In the post-match interviews, Ray Houghton described how Kevin Moran had encouraged him 'to go out and take more of a gamble,' which was rewarded with the all-important goal. In *Jack Charlton's American World Cup Diary*, the manager described the sense of achievement after the game: 'Of all the occasions we've celebrated success in our dressing room, this one is the best. We couldn't have asked for a better way to kick off our programme. Now, the sky's the limit.'

Arrigo Sacchi, clearly frustrated with the result, expressed a begrudging acknowledgement of the Irish performance and particularly the clarity of purpose from Charlton's team. 'Ireland proved a good, strong team,' said Sacchi. 'They were able to play a certain way. They had clearer ideas and were more incisive and they took their one chance.'

It was a career-defining performance from Paul McGrath, all the more remarkable as he was still feeling the effects of a shoulder virus. Given the stage on which he performed and the quality of the opposition, it remains perhaps the most iconic display from an individual player in an Irish shirt. Jack Charlton and the players heaped praise on their centre-back, with Andy Townsend describing McGrath's performance as 'awesome'. McGrath also had his admirers amongst the Italians, with Paolo Maldini stating that he 'already knew the man McGrath is world class and here was proof'.

Vincent Hogan of the *Irish Independent* reported that, after the game, the young Italian substitute, Lorenzo Minotti made his way to the Irish dressing-room door with a programme and pencil in his hand. Minotti was looking for McGrath and said: 'Today we faced a stone wall. This man McGrath was just unbreakable.'

Away from the football field, McGrath had endured a difficult childhood in Dublin orphanages and during his adult life, he fought an ongoing battle with alcohol addiction. As the rest of the Irish squad celebrated with the fans near the Giants Stadium that night, McGrath sat on the team bus, away from the public glare.

McGrath rightly received the plaudits, but the other three members of the Irish defence deserved huge credit for their assured performances, with Babb particularly prominent in shutting down the opposition attack. The five-man midfield was very efficient at closing down the Italian players when they were in possession. In the first half, Houghton and Staunton operated in advanced roles in their respective wing positions and were quick to get forward in support of Tommy Coyne. Italy's tactical shift at the start of the second half required Houghton and Staunton to play more defensively, but the attacking impetus was then provided by the central midfielders, with both Townsend and Sheridan pushing forward to good effect.

The Irish midfield was generally in control and aside from a fifteen-minute spell when Dino Baggio's forward runs proved difficult to contain, they adapted well to Italy's change in approach. Roy Keane's pace and energy were central to the team's performance as he cut out opposition attacks and powered forward when the opportunities presented.

As the lone striker, Tommy Coyne was selfless in running himself to the point of exhaustion until he was finally substituted for John Aldridge after 89 minutes. Although Coyne lacked the aerial prowess of Niall Quinn or Tony Cascarino, he competed effectively in the air.

149

Franco Baresi was not the tallest of centre-backs and Coyne made life difficult for the Italian captain, competing for every long ball sent in his direction. The Motherwell striker also worked continuously to close the angles for Baresi and Costacurta to pass out from the back.

In short, it was a deserved victory for Ireland, built on tactical discipline and hard work. The performance suggested that the Irish team had a maturity and growing sense of confidence on the international stage.

In the days that followed, the media was understandably glowing in its praise of Jack Charlton and his team. Frank Stapleton, one of the heroes of Euro '88, wrote in the *Irish Independent* that 'we have never had a better result in our soccer history'. Stapleton continued by stating that 'this victory over Italy and the way it was achieved has brought the Irish team to a new pinnacle of achievement'.

The Italian newspapers focused very little on the merits of the Irish performance, instead directing their attention to the perceived failings of the Italian manager and team. The headline in *Gazzetta dello Sport* read: 'What a disaster, Sacchi!' The Turin-based *La Stampa* adopted a similar tone and said that the Italian team's opening game was nothing less than a 'legendary fiasco'. The *Corriere dello Sport* went with the headline, 'Betrayal!' with the newspaper's main story strongly attacking Sacchi and his 'latest line-up which was invented on the eve of the game and failed piteously'.

The victory over Italy was comparable to the 1-0 win over England in Stuttgart six years earlier, not least because it was an early Ray Houghton goal that settled matters. Indeed, John Sheridan's second-half strike that hit the woodwork at the Giants Stadium was reminiscent of Ronnie Whelan's shot which rebounded off the crossbar in Stuttgart. However, while the win over England involved the team defending deep and hanging on for dear life, that was not the case in the Italy match. Ireland certainly had to contend with spells of Italian pressure, but it was notable that Italy only had one shot on target over the course of 90 minutes. The self-assurance of the Irish back four to push up and play a high defensive line throughout the game demonstrated their belief that they could squeeze the Italians and stifle their creativity.

The role of the Irish support in the Giants Stadium added to the occasion and the match report in the *New York Times* provided a colourful depiction of the setting:

'A crowd of 74,826 at Giants Stadium created a sense of pageantry in a place where American football is the normal fare and artificial turf is the normal surface. But today, the natural grass that was put on top of the turf looked as lush as any Irish hillside.'

The sheer elation which accompanied the victory was soon put into sharp perspective when news filtered through of a shocking massacre of innocent civilians as they watched the match in a pub in the small village of Loughinisland in County Down. The attack, which was carried out by members of the Ulster Volunteer Force, a loyalist paramilitary group, killed six people and wounded five others. It was a sombre reminder of the troubles that persisted back home.

As a one-off result, there was no doubting the magnitude of Ireland's win over Italy, but the subsequent performances at USA '94 meant that the result was tinged with some regret. Ireland travelled to Orlando for their next game against Mexico in the midday heat of the Citrus Bowl. Big Jack named the same starting eleven, but in temperatures that the Irish players were unaccustomed to, their normal pressing game was conspicuous by its absence. Mexico had too much pace and trickery, with two goals from Luis Garcia leaving Ireland in a perilous position. With tempers rising on the side-line, Charlton introduced McAteer and Aldridge in place of Staunton and Coyne. The decision paid off as McAteer crossed for Aldridge to power an emphatic header into the net. Despite a disappointing 2-1 defeat, the Aldridge goal was potentially crucial, as it meant that a draw against Norway in the final game might be enough to qualify for the last 16.

There was a general feeling of relief amongst the players and supporters that Ireland were returning to play their final group game at the Giants Stadium, where the temperatures would be somewhat more bearable. Charlton made three changes to the team, with Gary Kelly, Jason McAteer and John Aldridge drafted in. The changes were necessary, as Denis Irwin and Terry Phelan had each picked up two yellow cards in the previous fixtures and Tommy Coyne was suffering from the physical exertions of playing as the lone striker in difficult conditions.

Norway were managed by the pragmatic Egil Olsen. Of all the nations at the World Cup, the Norwegian style of play bore the most resemblance to that of Ireland. Olsen favoured a direct style, which revolved around their target man, Jostein Flo. The game was a tense encounter, with both teams effectively cancelling each other out. There was a lack of goal-scoring opportunities for either side, but John Sheridan went closest with a delicate chip over the Norwegian goalkeeper, which landed on the roof of the net. A dour game unsurprisingly ended in stalemate and with Italy and Mexico drawing 1-1 in the other fixture, all four teams ended up on four points. As the team with the poorest goal difference, Norway were eliminated, whilst Mexico, Italy and Ireland progressed to the last 16. The outcome of Group E remains the only time in World Cup history that all four teams in a group have finished level on points.

The last 16 presented Ireland with a return to Orlando where, for the third time at a major tournament, they would face the Netherlands. Phelan and Coyne were restored to the starting eleven, but Kelly retained his place ahead of Irwin. A misjudged header from Phelan early in the game let Marc Overmars in behind the Irish defence and he squared the ball to Dennis Bergkamp, who scored the opener. Wim Jonk made it 2-0 before half-time as a long-distance shot was fumbled by Bonner and rolled into the Irish net. There was plenty of Irish endeavour in the second half, but they never looked like overturning the two-goal deficit. And so, on 4 July, as the host nation celebrated Independence Day, Ireland's American adventure came to an end.

The squad returned home to another welcome party with tens of thousands of people waiting in Dublin's Phoenix Park. Although the reception was positive, the unbridled joy and sense of achievement was lacking in comparison to the homecoming of four years earlier. The public mood was tinged with a sense of anti-climax, indicative of the increasing level of expectation that now accompanied the Irish team.

Meanwhile, Arrigo Sacchi's Italian team advanced through the knock-out stages of the tournament, reaching the final against Brazil. A scoreless draw was followed by a penalty shoot-out which the Brazilians won, with Roberto Baggio missing the final penalty. Italy's only defeat in the tournament was the opening loss against Ireland.

The performance against Italy demonstrated the various elements of Jack Charlton's tactical approach that made Ireland so difficult to beat. There are perhaps a number of reasons why the team failed to build on that result as the tournament progressed. First and foremost, the high temperatures, particularly in Orlando, were prohibitive to an Irish team that relied heavily on a high-pressing game, which in turn placed demands on their energy levels. Secondly, the team was ageing, with several key players on the wrong side of thirty. Thirdly, the absence of Niall Quinn was compounded by the lack of fitness of Aldridge and Cascarino, weakening the team's attacking prowess, which lacked its normal physicality.

Another factor worth noting was the introduction of the back-pass rule in 1992, which prevented goalkeepers from picking up balls passed back by their own players. Ireland had used this tactic effectively at Italia '90, with both Kevin Sheedy and Niall Quinn scoring their goals following the mayhem caused by Bonner's booming kicks downfield. The combination of high-pressing and the use of the back-pass to take the sting out of games had allowed Ireland to control the pace, even against top level opposition. The Irish team adapted admirably to the rule change, but Bonner's kicking became less influential and some opposition teams, most notably the Netherlands, began to understand how best to counteract the Irish style.

Jack Charlton's team selection was also subject to some criticism after the 1994 World Cup. The decision to pick Gary Kelly and Terry Phelan in the full-back positions against the Dutch meant that there was no place in the team for Denis Irwin. The logic for picking Kelly and Phelan was that they were two of the quickest full-backs in the tournament and would provide the team with a strong attacking threat on either flank. However, it was a defensive mistake by Phelan that led to Dennis Bergkamp opening the scoring. Phelan's selection was widely criticised, as Irwin was generally regarded as one of the finest full-backs in English football, having just won consecutive league titles with Manchester United.

Most Irish fans and pundits would have selected Irwin as one of the first names on the team-sheet, but Charlton's decision to opt for Kelly and Phelan perhaps hinted at the manager's broader tactical philosophy. In the aftermath of the 1994 World Cup, Charlton claimed that the full-backs were the most important attacking players in a team. Such a view was certainly not commonplace in the mid-'90s, but the Irish manager realised that full-backs could avail of more space to run into than any other player in the team. Charlton's hypothesis would be borne out at the subsequent World Cup when France's Lilian Thuram and Bixente Lizarazu were two of the best attacking full-backs in the tournament and became integral to the French team's success.

Charlton's observations on football remained astute, but he was unwilling to adapt his style of play to reflect the changes taking place in the game. The 'route one' approach favoured by Charlton and other managers such as Egil Olsen, Graham Taylor and Joe Kinnear gradually proved to be less effective as the 1990s progressed, and opposition teams soon realised how to exploit the limitations of this approach.

Big Jack stayed on as manager after USA '94, with the stated ambition of taking Ireland to Euro '96, which was being hosted in England and would provide the ideal setting to bring down the curtain on his managerial career. Unfortunately, there was no fairy-tale ending. In June 1995, less than twelve months after beating Italy at the Giants Stadium, Ireland endured the ignominy of a scoreless draw away to the minnows of Liechtenstein. A week later, the team capitulated against Austria at Lansdowne Road, a result that would later gain notoriety due to the squad's visit to a Harry Ramsden restaurant for fish and chips on the day before the match. After that, the wheels came off and it became evident very quickly that an ageing Irish squad was in decline and in need of some fresh ideas.

The relative paucity of emerging young players meant that Charlton's squad lacked the energy and rejuvenation that every team requires. The continued reliance on a number of the old stagers from Euro '88 and Italia '90 also pointed to a general malaise in the underage structures. When Liam Tuohy, Noel O'Reilly and Brian Kerr vacated their positions with the underage teams in the 1980s, their role was largely fulfilled by Charlton's assistant, Maurice Setters. The underage teams under Tuohy and his assistants had qualified for various tournaments, but following their departure, there was a sense that the underage teams became an afterthought for Charlton and Setters. This neglect inevitably impacted on the pipeline of players being produced for the senior squad.

The Charlton era came to an end against the Netherlands in December 1995 when a young Patrick Kluivert and several prodigious graduates of the Ajax underage system clinically dispatched the Boys in Green in a Euro '96 play-off at Anfield. It was a meek ending to a wonderful decade of unprecedented success. According to Paul McGrath's autobiography, 'the magic of the Charlton era was on the wane by then,' with the hero of the Giants Stadium stating: 'I believe we came home from America a tired team, a little of the old ferocity had left us.'

Jack Charlton's tactical approach and style of play may not have been to everyone's liking, but he took Irish football to a level of success that may never be matched. At one point, his team was sixth in FIFA's world rankings. Charlton instilled discipline into the team and made them incredibly difficult for opposition teams to play against. Some commentators have argued that he might have achieved the same level of success by playing a more expansive brand of football. However, this line of argument overlooks the fact that Irish teams had played a more progressive passing style of football prior to his arrival but had fallen short of qualifying for tournaments. It is also worth noting that international football in the late '80s and early '90s was characterised by caution and a more defensive approach.

Charlton's game plan created a platform which allowed his players to control the pace of matches and, on occasions, their play in the opposition half of the field showed a degree of subtlety which is sometimes forgotten. Ultimately, the success of the Charlton era changed the parameters of what was considered possible for Irish football.

Chapter 10
Republic of Ireland v Netherlands
1 September 2001

'I've just said to them inside – be wound up for it, be passionate, but be calm as well. Calm heads will win the game today.'

– Mick McCarthy

Mick McCarthy succeeded Jack Charlton as Ireland manager in February 1996. At 37 years of age, McCarthy had almost four years of managerial experience at Millwall and had earned respect as captain of the national team, a role he handled with distinction during the halcyon days of Italia '90. Having served as captain under Charlton, there was a perception in certain quarters that McCarthy was a younger version of his former manager and some of the early commentary on his appointment referred to him as 'the son of Jack'.

McCarthy was, however, quick to dismiss suggestions that he would adopt a similar style of football to that of his mentor. 'Just because I played a certain way, it doesn't mean it is the way I most admire,' said McCarthy on the day that he was unveiled as the new manager. 'I have always loved to see good football played and it is what I always encourage.' McCarthy also advised that 'the Continental teams have caught up with our attributes of physical strength, fitness and spirit and we now have to try and match them in technical ability'.

It was evident from the outset that McCarthy would set out his stall to play a more possession-based style of football, with a clear preference for a 3-5-2 formation. The trend of playing three at the back with wing-backs was popular in the Premier League in the mid-'90s and was used by the likes of Liverpool and Aston Villa at a time when both clubs supplied some key members of the Irish squad. McCarthy also considered that the more traditional 4-4-2 formation left Irish teams susceptible to being over-run in midfield, whereas 3-5-2 provided an extra man in the engine room.

Although the Irish squad was in transition, their qualification group for the 1998 World Cup offered hope that the nation could return to another major tournament. Romania would pose the main obstacle, but Lithuania, Macedonia, Iceland and Liechtenstein were nations that Ireland were expected to overcome. After two impressive wins against Liechtenstein and Macedonia, the new formation encountered its first difficulties in October 1996, when Ireland endured a dour scoreless draw at home to Iceland, a game in which Roy Keane was deployed in a 'sweeper' role in the centre of the back three. Five months later, the team lost 3-2 away to Macedonia. The 3-5-2 formation was immediately consigned to the dustbin and McCarthy reverted to a more conventional four-man defence.

The team recovered to claim second place in the group and a play-off place for the World Cup in France. With Roy Keane recovering from a cruciate ligament injury, a side comprising a mixture of younger players and elder statesmen took on Belgium over two legs. A 1-1 home draw was followed by a courageous performance in Brussels, but Ireland went down 3-2 on aggregate. Belgium's winning goal followed on from a passage of play that should have yielded an Irish throw-in. It wasn't the first time that poor officiating had cost an Irish team in Brussels, but Belgium deserved to qualify.

At the end of his first campaign, McCarthy had taken a squad in transition to within striking distance of a World Cup and in doing so, he had placed his trust in a crop of promising young players. At the same time, the underage teams were experiencing a renaissance under the leadership of Brian Kerr and Noel O'Reilly. With Kerr at the helm, the Irish Under-20 team finished third at the 1997 World Youth Championship and the following year, the Under-16 and Under-18 teams completed an unprecedented double by winning the European Championship titles.

The underage successes were incredible achievements for a small football nation and the composition of those squads served to illustrate the quality of players emerging from the Dublin District Schoolboy League, as well as the increasing influence of rural parts of the country in producing young players. Indeed, it could be argued that the emergence of a crop of exciting young footballers owed much to the success of the Charlton era, as kids sought to emulate their heroes. Kerr was undoubtedly the right man in the right place at the right time, but it could also be argued that McCarthy was the right manager at senior level to give youth an opportunity.

The qualifying campaign for Euro 2000 saw a marked improvement in performances as McCarthy put his stamp on the team. The emergence of Mark Kinsella alongside the talented teenage duo of Damien Duff and Robbie Keane injected energy into the side. Duff was a precocious talent with a low centre of gravity, close control and dribbling ability. He had made his Premier League debut for Blackburn Rovers as a 17-year-old, winning the man of the match award in the process. Keane was a natural goal-scorer with the trickery of a street footballer. He had also burst on the scene as a 17-year-old, scoring two goals on his first team debut for Wolverhampton Wanderers.

The qualifying campaign started against Croatia, a team that had finished third at the World Cup two months earlier. In the first landmark result of McCarthy's tenure, Ireland brought Croatia tumbling back to earth, as the Manchester United pair of Denis Irwin and Roy Keane scored early goals to secure an impressive 2-0 win.

By the following autumn, the team was well positioned in the group and put themselves in the driving seat when they defeated a talented Yugoslavia 2-1 at Lansdowne Road. The Irish display was characterised by verve and attacking intent, with two wonderful second-half goals from Robbie Keane and Mark Kennedy proving decisive. The result put McCarthy's team at the top of the table, but a subsequent defeat to Croatia in Zagreb and a draw against Macedonia in Skopje undid the previous good work. On both occasions, the concession of injury-time goals cost Ireland the points, and Goran Stavrevski's headed goal for Macedonia with only twelve seconds remaining paved the way for Yugoslavia to top the group. It left Ireland with the prospect of a play-off for a third consecutive tournament.

Turkey provided the opponents on this occasion. The two-legged play-off ended in a 1-1 draw, with Turkey qualifying by virtue of the away goal they scored in Dublin. The final whistle in the Turkish city of Bursa was the cue for some unpleasant scenes between both sets of players and was an ignominious ending to a qualifying campaign that had included some notable highlights.

Despite the obvious progress being made by McCarthy and his young squad, the failure to qualify for Euro 2000 left the manager open to increasing levels of criticism. The disappointment of missing out on another tournament was particularly painful given the late goals conceded to Croatia, Macedonia and Turkey. The FAI opted to stick with their manager, despite much of the public criticism and pressure from some within the media.

The World Cup qualifying campaign for 2002 pitted Ireland in Group 2 with the Netherlands and Portugal. Both nations had reached the semi-finals of Euro 2000 and indeed, both were unfortunate not to have faced each other in the final. The prospects of Ireland qualifying for the World Cup appeared unlikely, given the calibre of players available to these top ranked sides. Prior to the start of the campaign, Mick McCarthy travelled to Manchester to meet with Roy Keane. The two men had endured an uneasy relationship from their time as teammates at the US Cup in 1992, but the meeting prior to the 2002 qualifying campaign was an opportunity for the manager and captain to discuss how the team's prospects of qualification could be optimised.

The campaign began with consecutive away fixtures against the group's heavyweights. The first match against the Netherlands in Amsterdam saw Ireland take the game to their more vaunted opponents. The Dutch seemed surprised by the quality of the Irish team's passing and movement. Two wonderfully crafted goals by Robbie Keane and Jason McAteer gave the team an unlikely but thoroughly deserved two-goal lead. However, two late goals salvaged a draw for the Dutch, much to the dismay of Roy Keane, who voiced his frustration in the post-match interviews.

The squad travelled to Lisbon to face Portugal the following month. Unlike the performance in Amsterdam, the Irish team faced wave after wave of attack from the home side, as they struggled to combat the midfield threat posed by Luis Figo and Rui Costa. Portugal took a deserved lead in the 57th minute, but second-half substitute Matt Holland equalised with a long range shot 15 minutes later. With a 1-1 draw secured in Lisbon, Ireland had managed to take points off both of their main opponents away from home.

By the time Portugal arrived at Lansdowne Road in June 2001, Ireland had beaten Estonia, Cyprus and Andorra to put themselves in serious contention within the group. In a tense game, the Portuguese dominated possession for long periods, but Ireland took a second-half lead through a goal from Roy Keane. Alas, Portuguese resilience was rewarded when the outstanding Luis Figo headed an equaliser with twelve minutes remaining. Keane's all-action display that afternoon is arguably one of the finest individual performances from an Irish player in any era.

A further win away to Estonia meant that Ireland had secured an impressive 18 points from their eight fixtures by the time the Netherlands travelled to Dublin in September 2001. The Portuguese had also amassed 18 points, but with a superior goal difference and an easier run-in, they appeared to be shoo-ins to top the group. The Dutch were four points adrift of Ireland with a game in hand, but knowing they needed a win in Dublin to secure a place in the play-offs.

In the week leading up to the game, FIFA took the unusual step of conducting the draw to determine the sequence of play-off fixtures. The draw confirmed that, rather than facing European opposition, the runners-up in Group 2 would play a team from the Asian qualification tournament. The prospective opponents were either Iran, Saudi Arabia or the United Arab Emirates, any one of which would have been considered a favourable proposition in comparison to facing a European opponent. The perception in the Irish media was that the outcome of the play-off draw would provide a psychological boost to the Netherlands, as a victory against Ireland would, in theory, pave the way for a straightforward qualification.

In devising a strategy for facing the Dutch, Mick McCarthy had a couple of key selection dilemmas. The first concerned who would play on the right side of midfield and, by extension, whether that would necessitate a change at right-back. Jason McAteer had featured on the right side of midfield throughout the campaign but was very much out of favour at Blackburn Rovers. His lack of club football led to calls for Gary Kelly and Steve Finnan to be selected on the right flank. In spite of the clamour, McCarthy remained loyal to McAteer and picked him in the starting eleven, with Kelly slotting in at right-back.

The second key decision was whether to start Niall Quinn or Damien Duff up front alongside Robbie Keane. Duff had performed impressively as a striker in the previous qualifier away to Estonia and McCarthy seemed to be toying with the idea of pairing the smaller duo of Duff and Keane. Given that Ireland had consistently relied on a strong and physically imposing centre-forward since the Charlton era, the prospect of Duff and Keane forming a strike partnership would represent a notable departure. McCarthy's thinking on the matter was at least partly informed by his attendance at a Premier League game between Manchester United and Fulham at Old Trafford two weeks earlier. United won the game 3-2, but McCarthy noted that their Dutch centre-back Jaap Stam struggled to contain the movement of Fulham's Louis Saha. McCarthy left Old Trafford believing that the movement of Duff and Keane could cause similar difficulties for Stam. He duly selected the young duo, with Niall Quinn on the substitutes' bench.

With those key selections made, the rest of the Irish team picked itself. Shay Given of Newcastle United had re-established himself in the team, having started the campaign as third choice behind Alan Kelly and Dean Kiely. The back four included the imposing presence of 21-year-old Manchester City centre-back Richard Dunne and three Louth men in the form of Steve Staunton, Gary Kelly and Ian Harte. Staunton was playing his club football with Aston Villa, whereas the uncle-nephew combination of Kelly and Harte were part of a strong Leeds United squad. McCarthy was missing three members of his first choice back four, as injuries had cost him the services of Stephen Carr, Gary Breen, and Kenny Cunningham.

In central midfield, Ireland could rely on two Premier League captains, with Manchester United's Roy Keane and Ipswich Town's Matt Holland forming an energetic and combative partnership. As the Irish captain, Keane had proved to be a driving force throughout the qualifying campaign, whilst Holland had impressed in a series of substitute appearances. With McAteer on the right flank, Sunderland's Kevin Kilbane was selected on the left wing. That left the front pairing of Damien Duff and Robbie Keane, two players whose careers had been inextricably linked since underage level.

When Ireland had faced the Netherlands twelve months earlier, the Dutch had been missing several key players. However, Louis van Gaal's squad was close to full strength when they arrived in Dublin, with the only notable absentees being Frank de Boer and Edgar Davids, who had both been suspended after testing positive for the banned substance nandrolone.

The Dutch were blessed with a wealth of attacking talent and had the luxury of leaving some world-class players on the bench. They had reached the semi-finals of the World Cup in 1998 and were only knocked out following a penalty shoot-out loss to Brazil. They had also reached the semi-finals of the European Championship in 2000, where they were once again eliminated on penalties. On that occasion, their failure to score against an Italian team which was reduced to ten men demonstrated that, despite all the attacking talent available to the Dutch, their wastefulness in front of goal could prove to be their undoing.

With Louis van Gaal at the helm, the expectation was that the Netherlands would play a possession-based game underpinned by the principles established during his time at Ajax. However, with Frank de Boer and Edgar Davids absent, only four of the starting eleven to face Ireland had come through the Ajax system – Edwin van der Sar, Mario Melchiot, Marc Overmars and Patrick Kluivert. Fewer Ajax players meant that van Gaal's Dutch team could sometimes appear less fluid and more rigid than the club side he managed in the mid-'90s. In his pre-match interview with RTÉ, van Gaal explained that his team formation was 'always three up front' and that Kluivert would occupy an advanced midfield role.

The Dutch team had struggled to click during the qualifying campaign and their disappointing draw against Ireland in Amsterdam was compounded by a subsequent 2-0 defeat and 2-2 draw against Portugal. Their form may have been unconvincing, but the Irish media and fans approached the game with a degree of trepidation, perhaps born out of a couple of chastening experiences against the Dutch towards the end of the Charlton era. Only three of the Dutch players remained from the side that had beaten Ireland in the one-sided play-off at Anfield six years earlier, whilst Gary Kelly and Jason McAteer were the only survivors from the Irish team that night.

Republic of Ireland

1
Given

2   4   5   3
Kelly   Dunne   Staunton Harte

7   6   8   11
McAteer   Roy Keane Holland   Kilbane
          (captain)

9   10
Duff   Robbie Keane

9
van Nistelrooy

11   10   7
Overmars   Kluivert   Zenden

8   6
Cocu   van Bommel
(captain)

5   4   3   2
Numan   Hofland   Stam   Melchiot

1
van der Sar

Netherlands

165

The Irish squad spent the week in the Citywest Hotel and on the morning of the game, the players went to the hotel golf course for their traditional pre-match walk before having lunch and travelling to Lansdowne Road. Mick McCarthy explained to his players the need for 'passionate hearts and calm heads'.

It was a pleasant Saturday afternoon in Dublin and there was a buzz of anticipation in the city. Both teams emerged to a rapturous welcome from the Lansdowne Road crowd, with those in attendance acutely aware that the prospect of World Cup qualification would likely hinge on the outcome of the following 90 minutes of football.

In the first minute, Roy Keane provided his own welcome to the visitors by unceremoniously clattering into the back of Marc Overmars. Keane's abrupt tackle deserved at least a yellow card. Remarkably, the experienced German referee Hellmut Krug decided not to book the Irish captain. The Dutch players appeared to be rattled by the audacity of Keane's transgression. A minute later, Marc van Bommel hacked down Kevin Kilbane, prompting a stand-off between several players from both sides. It was clear that both teams knew the stakes were high.

The Keane challenge was later acclaimed by many Irish fans and sections of the media as a case of the Irish captain setting the tone and sending a message to the opposition. Indeed, the tackle gained increasing prominence over the following years and is often cited as the seminal moment in the game. In truth, the tackle was rash and if the protagonist had been a different Irish player, it may have quickly faded from memory. Twelve months previously, Richard Dunne had swept the legs from under Patrick Kluivert in the opening minutes of the reverse fixture in Amsterdam, but that was quickly dismissed as an overzealous act from a young player making his first competitive start for his country.

Despite the tense opening exchanges, the Netherlands settled quickly into their stride and started to attack with some menace. The

Dutch urgency was apparent after only two minutes when Gary Kelly was caught in possession by Kluivert, but the Barcelona striker spurned the opportunity by shooting just wide from inside the Irish box. The sight of Kelly deliberating in possession should have been a salutary lesson to the Irish defence, but Richard Dunne would later be caught in similar circumstances during the second half.

Minutes after Kluivert's miss, van Bommel struck a low shot from outside the box, forcing Given into a save. With the Irish team struggling to gain a foothold in the game, it was the front pairing of Damien Duff and Robbie Keane who provided the initiative. Duff won a free kick when a trip from Kevin Hofland earned the Dutch player a yellow card. Robbie Keane then struck a low snapshot which forced a save from van der Sar.

The relative lack of pace in the Irish back four meant that the defence was sitting deep and inviting Dutch pressure. After 15 minutes, Boudewijn Zenden latched onto a backwards header from Staunton, but he too wasted another glorious chance as he shot straight at Given. The Netherlands were unfortunate not to be leading and Zenden's frustration was apparent when he became the second Dutch player to be yellow-carded for a foul on Kilbane.

As the first half wore on, Ireland slowly began to take the sting out of the Dutch attack and hold onto possession, without really threatening the opposition goal. Roy Keane's ability to retain possession was crucial, with both Duff and Robbie Keane providing useful outlets and bringing the Irish midfield into play. Prior to half-time, Kelly picked up a yellow card for a foul on Overmars. The resulting free kick from Zenden passed menacingly across the Irish six-yard line and should have been converted at the far post by Ruud van Nistelrooy, who saw the ball late and miskicked.

The half-time whistle provided a much-needed reprieve for the home side. There was little doubt that the Netherlands had enjoyed the better of the exchanges and could quite conceivably have scored two or three goals. Kluivert's failure to convert his chance in the opening minutes was particularly costly and may have added to the sense of pressure and collective anxiety within the Dutch team.

Ireland started the second half in a more composed manner, winning an early free kick in a position ideally suited to the left foot of Ian Harte. He struck it well, but it was caught by van der Sar at full stretch. A minute later, some sloppy defending presented the ball at the feet of Phillip Cocu, who threaded it through to van Nistelrooy, but the Manchester United striker produced a weak finish which was easily saved by Given.

Overmars' influence on the left wing was growing and Kelly was struggling to contend with his pace and movement. In the 54th minute, Richard Dunne lost possession and Overmars burst past Kelly before shooting to the foot of the near post where Given saved. Overmars then almost beat Given with a deceptive shot that bounced awkwardly and was turned around the post brilliantly by the Donegal man.

Van Gaal introduced his first substitution, withdrawing Zenden and replacing him with Jimmy Floyd Hasselbaink. Although Hasselbaink was naturally a striker, he took up an unfamiliar position on the right wing. Overmars continued to pose a threat on the opposite wing and Gary Kelly's unease at opposing the flying Dutchman manifested itself when he lunged in with a needless foul near the halfway line. Kelly left the referee with little alternative but to brandish a second yellow card to the Irish right-back. With the team reduced to ten men and over half an hour remaining, the task of holding out for a scoreless draw appeared increasingly difficult.

Mick McCarthy responded to the red card by sacrificing Robbie Keane for Steve Finnan. Finnan would slot in at right-back, so Ireland would effectively line up with a 4-4-1 formation for the remainder of the game. Duff was tasked with the responsibility of being the team's lone striker. While it was not a position that Duff was particularly familiar with, he had played as the lone front man during the latter part of the match against Portugal in Lisbon earlier in the campaign.

Following Finnan's introduction, he was immediately involved in what would be a key turning point in the game. Finnan lost the ball to Cocu, who played a pass in behind the Irish defence. Given and Staunton appeared to have the danger covered, but Staunton tried to head the ball back to his keeper, only to head it past him on the edge of the area. Van Nistelrooy was after it in a flash, but Given's subsequent collision with the Dutch striker allowed Richard Dunne to shepherd the ball past the far post. The stadium went silent as the referee considered his verdict before a roar of approval greeted his decision to award a corner. Whilst it looked as though Given's impeding of van Nistelrooy, unintentional or not, could have been penalised as a foul or obstruction, the referee's earlier decision to send off Kelly might have influenced his judgement. Given and his defenders looked relieved to have been given the benefit of the doubt, and it was another moment of good fortune for an Irish defence living on the edge.

The Dutch sensed their opportunity and van Gaal replaced his left-back Arthur Numan with a striker in the shape of Pierre van Hooijdonk. The Dutch team was now effectively playing with a 3-4-3 formation and their frontline comprised some of the most prolific strikers in European football.

Then, with 66 minutes on the clock, Roy Keane gained possession on the left wing and skipped past van Bommel, despite the Dutch midfielder's attempt to take him down. Rather than blowing his whistle, the referee played a sensible advantage and Keane powered forward before being met with a sliding challenge from Stam. Anticipating the tackle, Keane released the ball to Duff who quickly found Finnan in an advanced inside-right position. Finnan took the ball into the Dutch penalty area and with some useful footwork, he turned inside onto his weaker left foot before crossing. The ball eluded the Dutch defence and found its way towards the back post, where an unmarked Jason McAteer swept the ball majestically past van der Sar. Ireland had an unlikely lead and Lansdowne Road erupted in celebration.

The goal was certainly against the run of play and with 23 minutes remaining, the attention of the players immediately turned to the objective of holding onto their slender lead. It would require a backs-to-the-wall effort and the old stadium was rocking to its foundations as the home crowd sought to roar on what would be a famous Irish victory.

Van Gaal's response was to play his final card with the substitution of Overmars, who was replaced by Giovanni van Bronckhorst. Replacing Overmars was difficult to fathom, as he had tormented the Irish defence all afternoon.

Matt Holland later told Paul Kimmage, in an interview for the *Sunday Independent*, that he used a break in play during the second half to approach Patrick Kluivert – the hero of his son's Playstation game. Holland posed the question that he had been practising all week: 'Magik je shirt hebben alsjebliest, Patrick?' Kluivert might not have been accustomed to opposition players asking for his shirt in his native tongue, but he replied, 'Yeah, no problem'. Meanwhile, Gary Kelly was nervously watching the action unfold on a television monitor in the tunnel under the West Stand. He was joined momentarily by Larry Mullen, the U2 drummer, who was on his way to catch a helicopter ride to Slane Castle for the band's eagerly awaited concert.

The ten men of Ireland were defending deep, as the Dutch poured forward in an attempt to salvage their World Cup hopes. In the 78th minute, a goalmouth scramble led to Kluivert shooting into the side-netting from close range. The Dutch efforts were becoming increasingly frantic and they began to bypass the midfield, resorting instead to long, hopeful balls into the Irish penalty area, an approach that was at odds with the possession-based football associated with the Netherlands.

With five minutes remaining, Niall Quinn made his entrance in place of Duff, who had run tirelessly throughout and had eased the pressure on the Irish defence by winning important free kicks through his trickery and tenacity. As the clock approached the 90th minute, the Irish defending became increasingly resolute with the packed defence happy to simply clear the ball upfield. There was to be one final hearts-in-mouths moment, however, as the ball was crossed to van Nistelrooy, who headed wide.

When the final whistle blew, the sense of relief around the stadium quickly gave way to joyous scenes. An exhausted McAteer, his socks around his ankles, summoned the energy to make his way from the substitutes' bench to the far side of the field to take the acclaim of the Irish supporters. He might have had a lack of first team action at club level, but McAteer had repaid the faith shown in him by his international manager.

McCarthy's team had achieved one of the most significant victories in the history of Irish football against a star-studded team in a fixture of huge importance for both nations. The win guaranteed Ireland's passage to a World Cup play-off at the very least. The Dutch were facing into their first absence from a major tournament since 1986.

An Irish defence shorn of some of its first-choice players, had managed to keep some of the finest attacking talent in European football scoreless. The clean sheet might have required more than a slice of good fortune, but it is worth noting that, for the final 27 minutes of the game, the Dutch had a frontline of Kluivert, van Nistelrooy and van Hooijdonk, with Hasselbaink positioned on the right wing. As an indicator of their strength in depth, Roy Makaay of Deportivo La Coruña remained on the bench. Makaay might have been van Gaal's fifth-choice striker, but he would go on to win the European Golden Boot for his goal-scoring exploits the following season.

From a purist's perspective, it was certainly not the finest footballing performance of McCarthy's tenure. The back four sat deep and there were occasions when Gary Kelly and Richard Dunne were caught in possession when they might have been more assertive in clearing their lines. Kelly's sending off also displayed a lack of composure that belied his experience. The players appeared to be conscious that a defeat would cost them a play-off place and, as such, their attacking play lacked the crisp passing and conviction they had displayed in the away fixture in Amsterdam a year earlier.

Notwithstanding such criticisms, the win was McCarthy's finest hour as Irish manager and testament to his work in rebuilding the team over the course of five-and-a-half years. His willingness to put his faith in younger players and learn from his mistakes had provided the foundations for a consistent and impressive qualification campaign. With Roy Keane in inspirational form and providing the on-field leadership, the manager and captain had forged a mutually beneficial working relationship that appeared to be serving the team well.

As the Irish players and staff celebrated on the pitch that September afternoon, Roy Keane walked purposefully towards the sanctuary of the dressing-room. McCarthy jogged across to shake hands with and thank Ireland's talisman. One photographer managed to capture the moment, but his picture was somewhat deceptive as it caught the end of the handshake and showed Keane looking away from McCarthy. The picture would later become a symbol of the breakdown in the relationship between the pair and used as a reference point for the apparent lack of respect that Keane had for the manager. However, a viewing of the television footage illustrates that the handshake was more courteous and respectful, with Keane clearly turning to acknowledge McCarthy in a professional manner before continuing his walk to the tunnel.

In the post-match interviews, McCarthy described the result as 'the most satisfying win I've had as manager,' adding that the team was 'without five first team regulars and then had another sent off'. In contrast, Louis van Gaal cut a lonely figure as he sought to find an explanation for the result. 'We were lacking in organisation and structure,' said the Dutch manager. 'When Ireland scored, I thought it was their only chance in the match. But, at that time, we were worn out, we were broken.'

Writing in the following day's *Sunday Independent*, Dion Fanning described the result as 'a victory beyond the improbable'. Philip Quinn in Monday's *Irish Independent* referred to the team as 'green-clad heroes who showed courage in the line of fire, unrelenting honesty and enjoyed the odd ounce of old-fashioned luck, to record the finest international win for the Republic of Ireland in Dublin ever'.

The Dutch media was scathing in its criticism of their players and head coach. The Amsterdam-based *De Telegraaf* described the situation as 'a massive farce'. The Tilburg newspaper, *Brabants Dagblad*, stated that 'van Gaal should be ashamed of himself', whilst *De Volkskrant* pointed the finger at the players and said that 'too many of van Gaal's stars failed at decisive moments'.

It was the first time in sixteen years that the Netherlands had failed to qualify for the finals of a major tournament. The defeat in Dublin would force the Dutch Football Association to re-evaluate its approach to international football and the match would later be identified as a key turning point in the trajectory of Dutch football. In an article for *Sports Illustrated*, Simon Kuper later described how the defeat was referred to as 'het drama van Dublin' and that it led to a more pragmatic approach from Dutch teams, with an increased focus on results, rather than on the aesthetic quality of their play.

Ireland completed their qualifying group with a 4-0 home win against Cyprus on an evening when Niall Quinn celebrated his 35th birthday by scoring his 21st international goal, breaking Frank Stapleton's Irish goal-scoring record. Despite remaining unbeaten over the course of ten qualifying games, Ireland missed out on automatic qualification on goal difference to a very strong Portuguese team. The Boys in Green would enter the play-offs for a fourth consecutive tournament, hoping to achieve their first play-off success. Indeed, it was the eighth successive qualifying campaign in which Ireland had finished in the top two places in their group.

Although the squad had secured a hard-earned place in the play-offs, events further afield dominated the news headlines. Ten days after Ireland's victory over the Dutch, the world was rocked by the 9/11 terrorist attacks on the United States. Almost 3,000 people lost their lives and another 6,000 were injured. The events of that day put football into perspective, but the subsequent US invasion of Afghanistan added a layer of complexity to Ireland's imminent play-off assignment. Mick McCarthy's team would face Afghanistan's near-neighbours Iran over two legs, with Tehran as the last staging post in the pursuit of World Cup qualification.

The first leg was a tense occasion at Lansdowne Road, but Robbie Keane opened the scoring before an Ian Harte penalty sealed a 2-0 win. Shay Given made some outstanding saves in the second half to ensure that the team kept an all-important clean sheet. After the game, Roy Keane returned to Manchester to receive treatment for a recurring injury. It was a decision that would later resurface as a point of conflict between Keane and McCarthy.

A crowd of 95,000 in the Azadi Stadium in Tehran presented an intimidating backdrop for the Irish team in the second leg. Despite the absence of Roy Keane and Damien Duff, the team defended admirably and held onto possession in the early exchanges, which helped to quieten the crowd. Chances were at a premium throughout the game and Ireland looked comfortable for the most part. With the match scoreless after 90 minutes, the Iranian defender, Yahya Golmohammadi scored in injury time to inflict Ireland's first defeat of the qualifying campaign. Fortunately, the goal arrived too late for

Iran, and Ireland secured qualification for their third World Cup.

Ireland's qualification for the tournament was a significant achievement considering the quality of opposition they faced along the way. It also demonstrated that the manager and squad had become fortified by the previous setbacks and stiffened with an inner resolve. By integrating young players such as Given, Dunne, Duff and Robbie Keane with some of the older players from the Charlton era, Mick McCarthy had achieved a strong blend of youth and experience. The FAI also deserved credit for retaining McCarthy for a third qualification campaign, despite strong criticism from some quarters.

On 17 May 2002, as the country went to the polls for a General Election, the Irish squad began their World Cup adventure. The squad boarded a flight to Asia via Amsterdam, apparently using the same flight that the Netherlands had confidently pre-booked prior to their defeat in Dublin. However, within days of arriving at their pre-tournament base in Saipan, questions revolving around logistics, organisation and the quality of the training facilities came to the fore. The subsequent dispute between Roy Keane and Mick McCarthy would become one of the most infamous stories in Irish sporting history and set in motion a footballing 'civil war' between the two leaders. The context for the dispute, the opinions of both men and the views of several squad members have been publicised, debated and re-hashed in the years since. In a sense, the impact of Saipan has never fully dissipated.

The upshot of the dispute was that Keane returned home, with the rest of the squad travelling to Japan under a cloud of intense media coverage. There were fears that the team would struggle and had little chance of progressing from a group containing Cameroon, Germany and Saudi Arabia. Those fears appeared to be well founded in the first half of the opening group game against Cameroon, as Ireland struggled to contain the African champions. Trailing 1-0 at half-time, the Irish team emerged for the second half with renewed vigour and

Matt Holland equalised with a sweetly struck long-range shot.

The second match against Germany in Ibaraki was the pivotal fixture in the group and was likely to decide Ireland's fate. It was a particularly special occasion for Steve Staunton, who became the first Irishman to reach 100 caps. After a tentative start, the Germans struck first with a goal from Miroslav Klose. Ireland slowly worked their way into the game with some constructive passing and neat interplay. They created a number of opportunities but couldn't find a way past the German keeper, Oliver Kahn. Niall Quinn was introduced as a second-half substitute, as Ireland mixed up their game with some diagonal balls sent in his direction.

The German resistance was finally broken in the second minute of injury time when a knock-down from Quinn found its way into the path of Robbie Keane, who somehow contorted his body to direct the ball over Kahn and into the net. The goal was no more than the Irish team deserved and led to jubilant scenes from the players, management and supporters alike.

With two 1-1 draws secured, McCarthy and his squad knew that a win against Saudi Arabia by a margin of two goals or more would secure their passage to the last 16. The team duly obliged with goals from Robbie Keane, Gary Breen and Damien Duff earning them second place in the group behind the Germans.

The squad moved onto Suwon in South Korea for their last 16 match against a Spanish team that included Real Madrid's formidable strike partnership of Raúl and Fernando Morientes. The threat posed by the front pair materialised after only eight minutes when Morientes headed the opening goal. For the third time in the tournament, Ireland were in a position of having to chase an equaliser. It was a task that they set about with determination. Just after the hour mark, Duff won a penalty. The spot-kick was taken by Ian Harte and was saved, with the resulting rebound landing to Kilbane, who missed a glorious opportunity. It looked as though Ireland's World Cup dream was coming to an end, until they won a second penalty in injury time when Fernando Hierro pulled Niall Quinn's shirt. On this occasion, the penalty was taken by Robbie Keane, who duly scored despite the intense pressure.

The score-line remained at 1-1 after extra-time and for the first time since facing Romania at Italia '90, the Irish senior team faced into a penalty shoot-out. Robbie Keane once again converted, but three subsequent missed penalties from Holland, Kilbane and David Connolly proved costly. Spain advanced to the quarter-finals and Ireland exited the tournament, despite remaining unbeaten in normal time.

The quality of football played by the Irish team during the tournament had impressed many observers, with the front pair of Damien Duff and Robbie Keane receiving most of the plaudits. Indeed, Duff seemed to strike fear into the Spanish defence any time he received the ball. If Paul McGrath's performance against Italy at USA '94 is the best defensive display provided by an Irish player, it could be argued that Duff's performance against Spain is the finest attacking display.

A cursory glance at the statistics from the Germany game showed that Ireland had 58 per cent possession, whilst they enjoyed 55 per cent possession against Spain over the course of 120 minutes of football. McCarthy had overseen an impressive transition from a long-ball style of play to a more constructive passing game. Some elements of direct football remained, as illustrated by the role Niall Quinn played in Robbie Keane's injury-time equaliser against Germany. The use of Quinn in the tournament generally involved a second-half shift in formation from 4-4-2 to 3-4-3 with the Sunderland striker forming a three-man frontline with Duff and Keane. This demonstrated that the manager was not wedded to a particular philosophy but understood the need for a pragmatic approach, combining the traditional pressing and hard-running attributes with a more possession-based game.

There were, however, key moments during McCarthy's stewardship when more astute observations might have reaped dividends. One example was the failure to identify that Spain were playing with ten men during extra-time when David Albelda went off injured.

McCarthy's time in charge ended in the autumn of 2002, as two defeats against Russia and Switzerland at the start of the Euro 2004 qualifying campaign hastened his exit. By that stage, the Irish supporters and media were split over the Saipan controversy and the defeats led to calls for McCarthy's departure, with many hoping that it would facilitate Keane's return. It was a discordant endnote for McCarthy, whose commitment to the Irish team had been unfailing as both a player and manager. It is perhaps only with the benefit of time that the Irish public came to appreciate his achievements and the quality of football played during his first tenure.

Chapter 11
France v Republic of Ireland
18 November 2009

*'We feel cheated – we were the better team over the two legs,
every football fan in the stadium will say we were the
better team tonight.'*

– Sean St Ledger

Following Mick McCarthy's departure as Irish manager, Brian Kerr took over the role and was a popular choice amongst the fans and media. Kerr had achieved unprecedented success with the underage teams and seemed like the natural choice. During his time in the senior role, the team put in some solid performances, including an impressive display against France in Paris in October 2004. His team was unfortunate not to qualify for the 2006 World Cup, with a defeat to France in the reverse fixture at Lansdowne Road proving to be the difference in an incredibly tight group. Two earlier drawn games against Israel proved particularly damaging after Ireland surrendered the lead on both occasions.

Kerr's assiduous approach to the role ensured that the team was well organised and thoroughly briefed on the strengths and weaknesses of opposition teams. He continued to utilise the 4-4-2 formation favoured by his predecessors, but the tactical approach was more cautious than the latter half of the McCarthy era. In many respects, Kerr was unfortunate not to retain his job, with the FAI showing less patience than they had with McCarthy. The failure to qualify for the World Cup in 2006 served to highlight the thin line between what is perceived to be success and failure in international football. Kerr would later go on to manage the Faroe Islands, but the fact that the FAI never re-appointed him to a coaching or strategic role feels like a shameful waste of his experience and undoubted expertise.

Kerr was replaced as manager by Steve Staunton who was Ireland's most capped player at that time but a managerial novice. Staunton's tenure coincided with the historic opening of Croke Park to facilitate the FAI and the Irish Rugby Football Union (IRFU) during the redevelopment of Lansdowne Road. The GAA's Rule 42 had previously prevented the use of their grounds for association football and rugby, but the rule was modified in 2005. Given that Croke Park was steeped in sensitive political history, the opening of its gates to 'foreign games' was hugely significant in the context of a more progressive and modern Ireland.

Unfortunately, the stage provided by a world-class stadium was not matched by similar quality on the pitch. The Irish team struggled to capture the imagination of the capacity crowds which filled Croke Park. The team also struggled in the away fixtures during a qualifying campaign which was characterised by a series of abject and tactically inept performances. The results included a 5-2 loss away to Cyprus and a pyrrhic 2-1 win away to the part-timers of San Marino when an injury-time goal rescued the three points. Another poor performance and 1-1 draw at home to Cyprus in October 2007 brought an end to Staunton's managerial stint. It was a sad farewell for a man who had been an outstanding servant as a player, but there was a prevailing mood amongst many Irish fans that the national team required the appointment of an experienced manager with a track record.

In February 2008, the FAI announced with much fanfare the appointment of the legendary Italian manager Giovanni Trapattoni to the role. Trapattoni had managed some of Europe's biggest clubs, including AC Milan, Juventus, Inter Milan and Bayern Munich, as well as spending four years as manager of the Italian national team. This combination of top-level club football and international experience ticked all the relevant boxes as far as the FAI was concerned.

Trapattoni would be assisted by Marco Tardelli, who won the World Cup as a player with Italy in 1982 and was fondly remembered for his iconic goal celebration in the final of that tournament. The backroom team also included Liam Brady, who knew Trapattoni well from their time at Juventus. An important subtext to Trapattoni's appointment was the significant increase in the salary made available for the role, with a proportion funded by the Irish businessman, Denis O'Brien.

Trapattoni faced a stern test to qualify for the 2010 World Cup from a group containing Italy, Bulgaria, Cyprus, Georgia and Montenegro. His appointment generated excitement amongst the Irish public and his infectious personality engendered an early sense of affection from the supporters. Trap relied on a translator to communicate his message to the media and he used some interesting analogies to get his point across. His references to 'David and Goliath' in describing the challenge facing his Irish team against Italy and Bulgaria explained much about his outlook on the nation's overall standing within the world game.

The Italian's humour and courteous manner might have endeared him to the public and the media, but he demonstrated a ruthless streak in his dealings with certain players. Andy Reid was the first casualty of the new regime, with Trapattoni apparently taking umbrage with Reid's involvement in a late-night sing-song after the opening qualifier against Georgia. Reid was one of the best passers in the squad and one of the few Irish players with the vision and nous to unlock an opposition defence. Once Reid was cast aside, there was no way back for him. This created the sense that Trapattoni's issue was less about Reid's apparent misdemeanour and more to do with the Italian not fancying his attributes as a footballer. Indeed, Trap may well have identified Reid as a player that he could dispense with, while simultaneously demonstrating to the other players that he was a disciplinarian.

The general mood of optimism gathered momentum as the qualifying campaign for the World Cup progressed. After a solid start to the group, Trap's team secured an impressive 1-1 draw against his homeland on a memorable night in Bari when Robbie Keane provided a late equaliser. Both the home and away fixtures against Bulgaria also ended in 1-1 draws. By the time Ireland faced Italy in their penultimate game at Croke Park, they were well placed to secure a play-off as the second placed team in the group. A 2-2 draw against the Italians, while Bulgaria slumped to a defeat in Cyprus on the same night, earned the team a play-off.

Ireland were one of eight European teams that would enter the draw for the play-offs and their potential opponents included France and Cristiano Ronaldo's Portugal. Prior to the draw, FIFA made the controversial announcement that the play-offs would be seeded, with the four countries with the highest rankings kept apart. Shay Given publicly voiced his disapproval of FIFA's last-minute decision:

> 'Had they stated the rules from day one then that would have been fair on everyone. We deserved to finish second, Russia and Portugal deserved to finish second, so I do not see how it should be different for them and for us. You would just like to think it would be fair for everyone. Why should these teams get preferential treatment?'

Ireland were subsequently drawn against France, with the first leg to be held in Dublin and the second leg in Paris. The French team was managed by Raymond Domenech, who had the luxury of being able to select some of the leading players in Europe. Domenech had worked as France's U21 manager for eleven years before taking over the senior job in 2004. Under his management, France had reached the final of the 2006 World Cup, only losing out as a result of a penalty shout-out defeat to Italy. The French team qualified for the European Championship two years later but without their now retired talisman,

Zinedine Zidane, they were eliminated during the group stage. This apparent decline, allied to Domenech's general persona, meant that he was far from being universally popular in his homeland.

FIFA appointed a German referee, Felix Brych, to take charge of the first leg in Dublin, with Martin Hansson from Sweden appointed for the return leg in Paris. In the days prior to the first leg, Liam Brady recounted his memories of painful decisions that had gone against Irish teams during his own playing days. 'I have the experience of playing against the French before in tournaments gone by going back more than 20 years, and the one thing we didn't get was good referees,' said Brady. 'But now the focus is on the referees in these two games, particularly with the fact that FIFA changed the seeding arrangements, so they made it a bit easier for the more glamorous teams.' Brady noted that the referees would be 'thoroughly scrutinised because of what has gone on, and I fully expect to have better refereeing than when I was a player'.

The first leg of the play-off took place in front of an attendance of 74,103 at Croke Park. Ireland struggled to establish any foothold in the game and created very little. The team appeared to be inhibited by a fear of making mistakes or conceding a vital goal. Those fears were realised after 71 minutes when Nicolas Anelka struck a long-range shot, which deflected fortuitously off Sean St Ledger and beyond the reach of Shay Given. France had their all-important away goal and managed to keep a clean sheet. When the final whistle blew, there was an altercation on the pitch, as Keith Andrews took offence at comments allegedly made by the French midfielder, Lassana Diarra.

Losing the first leg at home was a huge disappointment, but the lacklustre performance left Irish supporters with little hope that the team could overturn the deficit in the second leg. The odds seemed stacked against them. No European team had ever won a World Cup play-off after losing the first leg at home and more worryingly, it was eight years since Ireland had last beaten a higher-ranked nation in a competitive fixture. One glimmer of hope lay in the fact that the more impressive performances under Trapattoni had come in the away fixtures.

Playing away from home seemed to suit Trapattoni's cautious approach, with less pressure on his team to take the game to the opposition. That was certainly the message that Robbie Keane conveyed when he spoke to the assembled media on the day before the second leg. 'The pressure is on them, they are playing at home and I'm sure the crowd will expect them to play well and score a couple of goals,' said Keane. 'We have nothing to lose. We have everything to gain so we will have to see how it goes.'

Trapattoni named the same side that had started the first leg, with the team lining up in his preferred 4-4-2 formation. Shay Given was very much the established No. 1 and was in outstanding form during the qualification group. Given had signed for Manchester City earlier in the year and was arguably at the peak of his powers. Both Trapattoni and Tardelli had spoken of their admiration for Given throughout the campaign, comparing him to Italy's Gianluigi Buffon.

John O'Shea was picked at right-back, having started the qualifying campaign in the centre of defence. O'Shea was the most decorated member of the squad with four Premier League titles and a Champions League winners' medal garnered as part of Alex Ferguson's Manchester United squad. Notwithstanding O'Shea's pre-eminence at club level, Richard Dunne was the heart and soul of the Irish defence. After a turbulent start to his career, Dunne had established himself as a consummate professional and had been voted as Manchester City's Player of the Year for four consecutive seasons. Dunne moved on to Aston Villa in the summer of 2009 at a time when Manchester City had started to invest heavily in the transfer market.

Dunne was partnered in central defence by Sean St Ledger, who was then on loan at Middlesbrough from Preston North End. St Ledger had made his international debut against Nigeria six months earlier and almost immediately established himself as part of Trapattoni's starting eleven. Kevin Kilbane was selected at left-back for what would be his 102nd international cap and his 60th consecutive competitive international in an Irish shirt. After spending most of his career on the left wing and in central midfield, Kilbane had transitioned into a solid left-back with a good understanding of his defensive duties.

Stoke City's Liam Lawrence was picked on the right side of midfield. Like St Ledger, Lawrence had also made his international debut against Nigeria earlier in the year. His Stoke City teammate Glenn Whelan formed the central midfield partnership with Keith Andrews of Blackburn Rovers. Whelan was a firm favourite of Trapattoni, whilst Andrews had broken into the international set-up a year earlier when the manager had rewarded his fine club form with a first cap. The midfield quartet was completed by Damien Duff, who had signed for Fulham earlier in the season. Aside from John O'Shea, Duff was the only player in the starting eleven to have won Premier League medals, as a member of José Mourinho's title-winning teams at Chelsea in 2005 and 2006.

The strike partnership of Kevin Doyle and Robbie Keane was undoubtedly Trapattoni's first-choice pairing and, although both were Premier League strikers, they had taken contrasting routes to get there. Doyle had played with St Patrick's Athletic and Cork City before earning a move to Reading in the summer of 2005. An instant success at Reading, he helped the club to gain promotion to the Premier League in his first season. The Wexford man signed for Wolverhampton Wanderers in June 2009 for a club record transfer fee. Robbie Keane, by contrast, had come through the youth system at Wolverhampton Wanderers and made his senior international debut at the age of 17. Keane had amassed almost twelve years of international experience and undergone a series of big-money moves at club level. The Tottenham Hotspur man was Ireland's leading goal-scorer and captain.

Raymond Domenech was able to name ten of the players who had started the first leg in Dublin. He was missing Barcelona's Eric Abidal, one of his first-choice centre-backs. Abidal's place in the team was taken by Julien Escude. The quality of the French team was evident in the fact that nine players in their starting eleven had featured in the group stages of that season's UEFA Champions League. The exceptions were the goalkeeper Hugo Lloris and centre-forward Andre-Pierre Gignac. Domenech had so much talent to choose from that Real Madrid's Karim Benzema had to console himself with a place on the bench.

Trapattoni might not have had the same riches to choose from, but his compact formation and defensive system could frustrate more illustrious opponents. Ordinarily, his system involved the central midfield partnership of Whelan and Andrews sitting deep and providing protection to the back four, with the creative spark provided by Lawrence and Duff in the wide positions. The full-backs also sat deep and rarely ventured beyond the half-way line, unless the team had a set-piece opportunity in the opposition half.

That approach was turned on its head for the second leg against France. It is now generally acknowledged that the senior players made a decision to deviate from the manager's safety-first approach and to play with the shackles off. Both Kevin Kilbane and Shay Given confirmed in their respective autobiographies that the senior players decided in advance of the game to adopt a more adventurous approach. This was reiterated by Damien Duff but in a less mutinous tone when speaking to the *Irish Independent* in November 2017. 'The talk amongst us in the dressing room and during the warm-up was that we'd nothing to lose,' explained Duff. 'You still work within the guidelines, but there was nothing coached. We just went for it and I think that showed in the performance.'

France

| 1 | Lloris |

| 2 Sagna | 4 Escude | 5 Gallas | 13 Evra |

18 A. Diarra

6 L. Diarra

9 Anelka

8 Gourcuff

12 Henry (captain)

11 Gignac

10 Keane (captain)

9 Doyle

| 11 Duff | 8 Andrews | 6 Whelan | 7 Lawrence |

| 3 Kilbane | 2 St Ledger | 5 Dunne | 4 O'Shea |

1 Given

Republic of Ireland

It had been 44 years since an Irish team had travelled to Paris for the nation's first ever World Cup play-off. On that occasion, Johnny Giles and his teammates were unfancied but provided a stern test for their Spanish opponents. In a similar vein, Trapattoni's team was not expected to upset the applecart, but an estimated 15,000 Irish fans travelled to the French capital, more in hope than expectation. The Stade de France was buzzing in the build-up to kick-off with an atmosphere of anticipation from an expectant home crowd.

Ireland started the game with purpose and launched their first attack in the third minute, with Lawrence providing a cross from the right wing, which was cut out by Julien Escude. Soon after, Doyle ran at the French back four before releasing Duff, and the winger's subsequent cross was almost met by the head of Keane. The Irish team had already shown more attacking conviction in the opening minutes than it had in the whole of the first leg.

The French team suffered a setback early on when Escude was forced to leave the field with a head injury. He was replaced by his Sevilla teammate Sébastien Squillaci. The substitution was followed by a brilliant piece of French counter-attacking as all four of their forward players combined. André-Pierre Gignac won the ball on the left wing before releasing Yoann Gourcuff, who found Nicolas Anelka, who in turn provided a through-ball for Thierry Henry. The resulting shot from Henry was blocked by Sean St Ledger, but the move was a sign of the attacking threat that the French team possessed.

As the midway point of the first half approached, Ireland began to exert control. The French defence was struggling to contain the movement of Keane and Doyle, whilst Duff was providing an important outlet for receiving the ball on the left wing. A 24th minute cross from Duff was headed down by Lawrence, but Hugo Lloris managed to punch the ball away just as Keane was about to pounce. A subsequent cross by Lawrence was met by a glancing header from Doyle, but the ball drifted past the far post.

188

The French players were looking increasingly ponderous, surrendering possession twice in quick succession. Firstly, Gignac failed to control an easy pass, which ran out for a throw-in. Then a simple misplaced pass from Lassana Diarra went out for another throw-in. Those errors were indicative of the hesitancy in the French performance and perhaps added to the sense of unease amongst the home team.

With France struggling to find their groove, Ireland capitalised. The breakthrough arrived in the 33rd minute, courtesy of some neat interplay from three of the most experienced Irish players. A clever one-two between Duff and Kilbane on the left wing allowed Duff to get to the end line, before cutting the ball back into the penalty area for Keane to side-foot his shot beyond the dive of Lloris. It was a priceless away goal and suddenly the French advantage from the first leg had been wiped out.

The build-up to the Irish goal demonstrated the rewards to be gained from a more positive and offensive approach. The initial move began with Lawrence winning possession on the right wing, then passing a square ball to Whelan, who moved it on to Andrews, who in turn found Duff. Each member of the Irish midfield was involved in the move, but that was only possible due to the more advanced positioning of Whelan and Andrews in central midfield.

With the home crowd silenced and an air of disbelief in the stadium, the Irish team was likely bracing itself for a French response. However, France continued to look disjointed, and aside from a deflected shot from Anelka, they struggled to create anything before the interval. When the half-time whistle blew, it was greeted by boos and whistles from the home crowd. In contrast, there was a sense of giddy excitement amongst the Irish fans, not only with the score-line, but with the quality of the team's display.

The Irish team started the second half at a similar tempo. With just over a minute played, they were awarded a free kick midway inside the

French half and on the left side of the pitch. Lawrence stood over the free kick and delivered a deep cross towards the back post where an unmarked John O'Shea had time to take the ball on his chest and shoot. O'Shea's shot went over the French goal when he could have taken more time to direct it on target.

Three minutes later, Keane provided a low cross from the left wing which required a last-ditch tackle from Patrice Evra, just as Lawrence was about to shoot. By this stage, there was a confidence coursing through the Irish team and their lack of inhibition was exhilarating. Their reluctance to sit back and defend was in marked contrast to their previous performances under Trapattoni.

France were struggling to carve out any decent goal-scoring opportunities apart from another long-range shot from Anelka. A subsequent shot from Gignac was blocked by St Ledger. That was to be Gignac's last involvement as he was replaced by Sidney Govou. The substitution involved some positional changes from the French, with Henry moving into the centre-forward position, Anelka switching to the left wing and Govou operating on the right wing.

With just over an hour played, Ireland were presented with a glorious opportunity to double the lead when Duff was put through by an incisive pass from Lawrence. Duff tried to place the ball past Lloris and shot with his weaker right foot, but the French keeper saved. The chance owed much to the persistence of Keane who had dispossessed Lassana Diarra in midfield. Duff's chance further highlighted the precarious position that France were in, as a second Irish goal would leave the hosts needing to score another two to avoid being eliminated on the away goals rule. The fact that the tie was so finely balanced also added to the air of nervous tension within the stadium.

Within the space of three minutes, Ireland were forced to replace two key players. Firstly, the injured Glenn Whelan was replaced by Darron Gibson and then John O'Shea hobbled off with Paul McShane coming on in his stead. The Irish substitutions coincided with a renewed sense of purpose from the French, which could be largely attributed to their positional changes following the Gignac substitution. Gourcuff started to see more of the ball and with Henry at centre-forward, the French frontline looked more dynamic. A shot by Gourcuff was blocked by McShane who threw his body in the way. Two minutes later, a right-wing cross from Sagna was met by a glancing header from Anelka which went wide of the far post.

The Irish team soon responded, carving out another great chance when a through-ball from Lawrence found Keane. The captain took a touch which brought him behind the French defence. Rather than shooting, he decided to go past Lloris, but eventually ran out of space.

The pace of the game slowed as it entered the final fifteen minutes of the second half. France sporadically sought to inject some urgency into their play, but the Irish players were quick to close down their approach avenues. Keith Andrews was particularly prominent, with the Blackburn Rovers man providing three key interventions in a ten-minute spell to dispossess French players. Andrews might have been facing more distinguished opponents, but he dominated the midfield exchanges with a display characterised by energy and athleticism.

As the game entered the 90th minute, Ireland won a throw-in deep in the French half of the field. Kilbane took a long throw into the French penalty area where four Irish players were waiting. Doyle managed to head the ball on to Robbie Keane, but Keane was adjudged to have handled the ball as he attempted to turn. That opportunity was quickly followed by a long range shot from Keane which flashed over the French goal. The Irish team were finishing the game with the same positive attitude that they had shown from the very start.

The referee blew his whistle to signal the end of normal time. With the aggregate score-line standing at 1-1, the two teams would face extra-time and potentially a penalty shoot-out to decide their fate.

The first talking-point of the extra-time period arrived after seven minutes when a defence-splitting pass from Lassana Diarra sent

Anelka clear. Anelka knocked the ball past Given and went to ground as he collided with the Irish keeper, which was quickly followed by French appeals for a penalty. The referee Martin Hansson ruled that there was no foul and awarded a goal-kick to Ireland. It was a fine example of strong refereeing from the Swedish official. Two minutes later, he waved the play on when Thierry Henry appealed for a free kick just outside the Irish penalty area. However, Hansson's inability to see Henry's transgression minutes later would prove to be the seminal moment in the play-off and would become one of the most infamous episodes in the history of Irish football.

The incident occurred with only two minutes remaining in the first period of extra-time when the home side were awarded a free kick. The set-piece was floated into the Irish box and the ball found its way towards the back post where Henry clearly controlled it with his left hand, before turning it across the six-yard box for William Gallas to score. As the French players wheeled away in celebration, a number of the Irish players immediately protested to the referee and his linesman, with Shay Given particularly irate.

It was a blatant handball and the television footage showed that Henry not only controlled the ball with his hand but took a second touch to steer it into his path. There was dismay amongst the Irish players, which was soon transmitted to the supporters. Most Irish fans were located at the opposite end of the stadium and for those who didn't see the handball in real time, they were soon made aware of it as text messages filtered through from those watching on their television screens back home.

When Hansson blew his whistle to signal the end of the first period of extra-time, some of the Irish players continued to remonstrate. Kevin Kilbane later recounted advising Hansson that he was 'massively wrong', but the referee maintained that he was '100 per cent right'. As the Irish players tried to make sense of what they had just witnessed, they perhaps lost sight of the fact that there was still the second period of extra-time to score another goal, which would have been sufficient to win the tie on the away goals rule.

Within the first minute of the second period, Trapattoni introduced Aiden McGeady in place of Liam Lawrence as his third and final substitute. The Celtic man went to the left wing with Duff switching to the right flank. McGeady was immediately involved, delivering a couple of corner-kicks into the danger area. His quick feet added a different dimension to the Irish attack.

It was apparent that the Irish players were beginning to feel the effects of their exertions and the fatigue was perhaps compounded by the sense of injustice following the Henry handball. The one obvious exception was Keith Andrews, whose stamina and work-rate ensured that the French midfielders had little opportunity to settle on the ball.

Richard Dunne pushed forward to add a physical presence to the attack, as they went in search of the all-important goal. As the game entered the final minute, he was joined by Shay Given, who raced forward for a free kick from McGeady. However, it wasn't to be, and a subsequent French counter-attack almost yielded a second goal for the home side, as Govou got on the end of a cross from Anelka.

At the final whistle, the French players and management started their celebrations, as the Black Eyed Peas' track 'I Gotta Feeling' was pumped out through the stadium's sound system. Some of the Irish players slumped to the ground in resignation, knowing that their dreams of performing at the World Cup were over. As Richard Dunne sat solemnly on the turf, he was joined by Henry, who sat alongside him and apparently explained that the handball had been an instinctive reaction and that it wasn't intentional. Dunne retained a respectful and dignified demeanour.

The Irish players then made their way to the southern end of the stadium to salute the banks of travelling away fans. Some of the players struggled to contain their emotions as the crowd showed their appreciation. The disappointment of the defeat seemed more pronounced for the older players, who likely realised that their last chance of playing at a World Cup had been snatched from their grasp.

After the game, Shay Given expressed his disgust at the referee's inability to see the handball incident and for the apparent failure to consult his assistants: 'I don't know if he spoke to the fourth official or the linesman or someone. It was so blatant, and we were so strongly protesting because we just felt somebody must have seen it, it was so blatant.' That sense of anger was echoed by Sean St Ledger:

> 'We got robbed, you can tell by the boys' reaction that it hit his hand blatantly. We feel cheated – we were the better team over the two legs, every football fan in the stadium will say we were the better team tonight. It's cost a lot of us our dreams – as a boy I used to dream of playing in the World Cup, and now I'm not.'

For Liam Brady, it must have felt like the latest in a series of refereeing injustices affecting Irish teams he was involved with over the course of his career. In the post-match interviews, Brady was forthright in his views: 'With the draw FIFA wanted France and Portugal to go through and that's what happened. You saw the goal and that's enough said. It's a bad day for football. When it comes to the crunch, the big teams always seem to go through.'

The frustration at Henry's offence and the failure of the officials felt particularly dispiriting, given the quality of Ireland's display. Previous Irish hard-luck stories might have centred on the idea of a moral victory, but the performance in the Stade de France combined controlled aggression with attacking intent.

In his match report, Liam Mackey of the *Irish Examiner* described it as 'a display of super-human endeavour, raw courage and no little skill'. David Kelly in the *Irish Independent* wrote that the team's performance 'should remain the template as Irish manager Giovanni Trapattoni and his team of warriors plot for a brighter future despite the indignities heaped upon the perennial underdogs'.

The handball incident generated newspaper headlines across the world. It was of particular interest to the Italian media, given the esteem with which Giovanni Trapattoni was held in his native land. The *Gazzetta dello Sport* reserved its front page for events at the Stade de France, under the headline: 'Trap – what a robbery!'

Martin Hansson and his assistants were also subject to scathing criticism in their homeland, with the Swedish newspaper *Aftonbladet* stating:

> 'There are approximately 80 million Irishmen around the world. We guarantee they all feel pretty bad today. But I sincerely hope there are three Swedes that feel even worse. They are Martin Hansson and (referee's assistants) Stefan Wittberg and Fredrik Nilsson.'

The article in *Aftonbladet* concluded that 'there will be no World Cup for Ireland and I assume that Team Hansson has also forfeited its right to continue to take charge of major international matches'.

It was an egregious error on Hansson's part, but there was a sense that it was a genuine mistake. After all, Hansson had waved away Anelka's claims for a penalty five minutes earlier. In 2010, Swedish filmmakers made a documentary entitled *Rättskiparen* ('The Referee') in which they followed Hansson's career for a year. The documentary demonstrated an awareness on Hansson's part that the failure to see Henry's handball would be likely to endure as the defining moment of his career.

In the days following the play-off, the handball incident was on the verge of becoming a diplomatic issue, as politicians from both nations weighed in to express their views. French President Nicolas Sarkozy apologised to Taoiseach Brian Cowen, while the French economy minister, Christine Lagarde expressed her sadness that France had qualified through what she described as 'cheating'. Lagarde told France's *RTL* Radio: 'I think that FIFA would do well to look at the rules because I think it would be good, in such circumstances, to decide maybe to replay the match.' The Irish Minister for Justice, Dermot Ahern also demanded a replay, which he felt was owed to 'the thousands of devastated young fans around the country'.

Two days after the game, Henry broke his silence with a statement in which he claimed that a replay would be the 'fairest solution'. Henry explained that he felt 'embarrassed at the way that we won and feel extremely sorry for the Irish who definitely deserve to be in South Africa'. Robbie Keane responded by thanking Henry for his 'courage and honour' in making the statement and said:

> 'As captain of the Republic of Ireland team, I would also be happy for a replay to happen in the interest of fair play so that whichever team qualifies, can do so with their heads held high. We can only hope that the French Football Federation might accept the wishes of both captains in the best interests of the game.'

The statements by Henry and Keane coincided with letters which the FAI sent to FIFA and the French Football Federation requesting a replay, but their calls were rejected. On 27 November 2009, nine days after the play-off defeat, the FAI met with FIFA, apparently to convey the damage done to Irish football and to discuss a football solution. Three days later, FIFA President Sepp Blatter spoke at a press conference and referred to an apparent request by the FAI to be the 33rd team at the World Cup. Blatter's mocking tone showed a distinct lack of respect or empathy, and indeed a certain air of contempt, given that the issue arose from the failure of FIFA's match officials.

Irrespective of the context or the manner in which the FAI may have framed such a request, the suggestion of being the 33rd team at the World Cup displayed a misguided sense of entitlement. The FAI's request, allied to some of the pronouncements from political figures and members of the public, were unbecoming and lacked perspective. If nothing else, the Irish players and supporters had left the Stade de France holding the moral high ground, but the subsequent involvement of the football administrators deflected attention away from what had been a performance of real substance.

In June 2015, almost six years after the play-off, it emerged that the FAI had subsequently convened a meeting with FIFA during which Blatter personally apologised to the FAI delegation for his remarks about Ireland seeking to be the 33rd team. It was reported that FIFA offered the FAI a €5 million interest-free loan by way of compensation in exchange for ending protests about the loss of qualification. The document, signed on 15 January 2010 by senior FAI and FIFA officials in Switzerland, guaranteed the FAI immediate delivery of €5 million on the strict condition that Irish officials never revealed existence of the deal. In June 2014, a letter from FIFA's deputy secretary general, Markus Kattner, informed the FAI that it no longer needed to repay any of the purported loan.

The news of the FIFA payment added another dimension to a fixture that had already generated its fair share of newspaper headlines. It certainly raised questions for both FIFA and the FAI, not least from an ethical standpoint. The counter argument was that securing €5 million in funds represented a pragmatic outcome for an association that was undergoing financial struggles.

With all the political involvement and hearsay that followed the play-off, the more precise details of the match itself became somewhat obscured. Some commentators presented Ireland's qualification for the World Cup as a *fait accompli* that had been dashed by the treacherous intervention of Henry. It was forgotten by some that even if France had not scored following Henry's handball, there were no guarantees that Ireland would have progressed to the World Cup. After all, they would have faced the prospect of a penalty shoot-out against a French team playing in front of their home crowd.

Perhaps the sense of sporting injustice was accentuated by the perception that qualification for the World Cup meant less to the French. There was a feeling that, despite all their talent, the French squad was dysfunctional and combustible, with a manager who lacked the confidence of his players. That precarious balance within the French set-up would be borne out the following summer in South Africa when the relationship between the players and management collapsed in the midst of a succession of poor performances.

Nicolas Anelka was sent home by the French Football Federation after the second game following a half-time argument with Raymond Domenech. That decision was followed by further rows and recriminations within the French camp, which led to the players refusing to train. This extraordinary episode was played out in front of the international media at their training base in Knysna. The French would go on to lose their final game of the group against South Africa, although they did manage to score their only goal of the tournament. Henry was introduced as a second-half substitute in what was to be his final appearance for his country. Despite finishing his international career as France's all-time leading goal scorer, the handball controversy and his apparent lack of leadership in Knysna still obscures the public perception of Henry in his own country. Thierry Marchand and Philippe Auclair wrote in the December 2014 publication of *The Blizzard* that 'Henry could and should have nipped that pathetic rebellion in the bud, but he chose to keep his own counsel'.

The ignominious behaviour of the French squad during the 2010 World Cup might have felt like comeuppance for the manner in which they qualified. However, the sad reality of Henry's handball was the significant opportunity cost it had for the Irish players and management. Several of the players were at the peak of their careers around the time the 2010 World Cup was taking place. The team would later qualify for Euro 2012, but by then, Kevin Kilbane was no longer a part of the squad and the senior players were past their peak.

In the subsequent years under Trapattoni, the performance in Paris would become a point of reference that fans and media regularly used to question why the Italian continued to adopt such a cautious tactical approach. Was he simply ignoring the attacking verve demonstrated with such conviction in the Stade de France? There was considerable frustration that the team continued to play a defensive style of football and had failed to build on that performance.

In the Euro 2012 qualifying campaign, Trapattoni's team continued to beat the weaker nations but were exposed when they met stronger and more technically proficient sides. The sight of Ireland being overrun in midfield became increasingly common. The frailty of their system was cruelly exposed by Russia in both Dublin and Moscow, although a heroic defensive effort from Richard Dunne secured an unlikely scoreless draw in the latter fixture. Qualification for the European Championship in Poland was a notable achievement, but the fact that Ireland went to the tournament as the only participating nation without a Champions League player in their squad was indicative of the challenge they faced.

Euro 2012 would prove to be a chastening experience for the Irish squad, as they succumbed to the superior technical qualities of Croatia, Spain and Italy. The team was outclassed in each of their three matches. The UEFA Technical Report for the tournament referred to the Irish team's 'frequent use of back-to-front passing and long diagonals'. Aside from Sean St Ledger's goal against Croatia, the only memorable aspect of the tournament was the contribution of the large travelling contingent of Irish fans who continued to support their team and behaved well wherever they went.

Speaking in February 2018, Kevin Doyle expressed his views on the tournament. 'That Euros was two years too late,' said Doyle. 'That squad of players was at their peak in the France play-off game. Had we gone to that World Cup . . . I think we'd have put up a better show.'

The performances at Euro 2012 should have probably signalled the end of the Trapattoni era, but his tenure limped on into the subsequent campaign for the 2014 World Cup. A deepening sense of malaise crept into the set-up and the team stuttered its way through the group with a series of poor performances, including a record 6-1 defeat at home to Germany. The slim hopes of qualification came to an end with a defeat to Austria in September 2013, after which Trapattoni departed.

The legendary Italian had certainly effected a change in Irish football and achieved success in taking the nation back to its first major tournament in a decade. In terms of performance, the play-off in Paris marked the apex of his tenure. The uninhibited approach displayed in the Stade de France would ultimately be viewed as a one-off performance, with much of the Trapattoni era characterised by a lack of fluency in the style of play. The stop-start approach of Trap's team felt sterile at times and was seemingly devoid of the urgency and high-tempo approach displayed by previous Irish teams.

Chapter 12
Italy v Republic of Ireland
22 June 2016

'I grew up dreaming about this stage and to go and do it in front of my family is the best feeling in the world.'

– Robbie Brady

Martin O'Neill succeeded Trapattoni as manager in November 2013, by which time the Republic of Ireland were ranked 67th in the world and confidence was low. As a player, O'Neill had won two European Cups under the management of Brian Clough at Nottingham Forest and had captained Northern Ireland at the 1982 World Cup in Spain. O'Neill's management career had included spells at Leicester City, Celtic and Aston Villa. During his time at Leicester, he won the League Cup twice, whilst his five seasons at Celtic included three league titles and an appearance in the UEFA Cup Final. O'Neill's stock was high after his success at Celtic and he had been strongly linked with the England manager's job in 2006 before Steve McClaren was eventually appointed.

The Derry man was renowned for his man-management skills and his ability to motivate players. Much like Brian Clough, he was not known for his day-to-day coaching on the training ground. John Robertson had assisted with the coaching duties for most of O'Neill's management career, but Robertson had stepped away from football after their time together at Celtic.

In accepting the Ireland job, O'Neill surprised many by announcing Roy Keane as his assistant manager. Keane's own management career had started promisingly at Sunderland where he had secured promotion to the Premier League, but he later departed the club in acrimonious circumstances. In his subsequent managerial role at Ipswich, the club's performances and results were inconsistent and eventually led to his sacking in January 2011.

The new management team had almost a year to prepare for the start of the qualifying campaign for Euro 2016. Their prospects of qualification were helped by the expansion of the European Championship to 24 teams, which meant that the top two teams in each group would qualify automatically, with the third-placed teams entering the play-offs. Ireland were faced with a difficult group that included Germany's newly crowned World Cup winning team, as well as Poland and a resurgent Scotland.

The campaign started well and included an unexpected 1-1 draw against Germany in Gelsenkirchen. O'Neill's men benefitted from an injury-time goal, with John O'Shea marking his 100th international cap by scoring the equaliser. However, Ireland's campaign was subject to a major setback the following month when an anaemic performance accompanied a 1-0 defeat to Scotland in Glasgow.

The team then had the benefit of two home fixtures against Poland and Scotland, their main opponents for the second and third place positions in the group. Both matches ended in 1-1 draws, with Shane Long's injury-time equaliser against Poland continuing the theme of late goals. The team was clearly demonstrating its never-say-die attitude by salvaging results, but the failure to beat Poland or Scotland in Dublin left many Irish supporters feeling a sense of frustration at the inability to capitalise on home advantage.

With four games remaining, the prospect of securing qualification seemed like a long shot, but two surprise results changed the shape of the group. Firstly, Scotland lost away to Georgia in September 2015 and, the following month, Ireland shocked Germany with a 1-0 win on a famous night at the Aviva Stadium. A goal from Shane Long in the 70th minute and some heroic defending were sufficient to defeat the world champions – some 59 years after Ireland had beaten Sepp Herberger's world champions at Dalymount Park. The win against Germany provided the stimulus that Martin O'Neill's stewardship was crying out for. Remarkably, it was the first time Ireland had beaten a higher-ranked nation in a competitive fixture since Jason McAteer's goal defeated the Netherlands in September 2001, a gap of over fourteen years.

Despite a subsequent loss to Poland in Warsaw, Ireland progressed to the play-offs with confidence and a steely belief that qualification could be secured. Drawn against Bosnia and Herzegovina, another higher-ranked team, the Boys in Green were the underdogs. A positive 1-1 draw on a foggy night in Zenica left the team well placed for what would effectively be a cup final in Dublin. In the second leg, Ireland played with a conviction that had become increasingly rare during the previous decade. A 2-0 win was secured, with both goals scored by Jonathan Walters.

Northern Ireland had already qualified, thereby meaning that the IFA and FAI would be sharing the stage at the finals of a major tournament for the first time. The Republic of Ireland were drawn in Group E and would face Sweden, Belgium and Italy. It was another ominous draw, but unlike four years earlier, the new tournament format offered a glimmer of hope. The 24-team tournament would be based on the same format that FIFA used for the 1990 and 1994 World Cups. This meant that the top two teams from each of the six groups would qualify automatically for the second round, with the four best third-placed teams also securing their passage.

With the tournament being held in France, the team would be roared on by the travelling hordes of Irish fans. However, fears of a repeat of Euro 2012 meant that many Irish supporters approached the tournament with a combination of trepidation and cautious optimism.

The first match against Sweden in the Stade de France was identified as the key fixture and the one that O'Neill's men had the best chance of winning. On a beautiful afternoon in the Parisian sun, Ireland took the game to Sweden, with Jeff Hendrick particularly prominent in the first half. The Irish endeavour was rewarded early in the second half when a Seamus Coleman cross was met by Wes Hoolahan, who smashed a half-volley into the Swedish net. The intensity of the Irish performance dropped off after the goal and the Swedes started to build a series of menacing attacks. With just under twenty minutes remaining, Zlatan Ibrahimovic dribbled the ball into the Irish penalty area before crossing into the danger zone in front of Darren Randolph. The cross was met by Ciaran Clark, who inadvertently turned the ball into his own goal. After the equaliser, Ireland tried to rally to score a winner, but the team looked fatigued in the closing stages and ultimately settled for a draw.

The next match pitched O'Neill's team against Belgium in Bordeaux. Belgian football had gone through a revolution during the previous decade, with high quality coaching structures providing the national team with a change in playing style and culture. The Belgian squad boasted some of the most valuable players in Europe.

From the opening whistle, Ireland never looked like they believed they could upset their more vaunted opponents and their performance was underpinned by caution and negativity. The game was scoreless at half-time and Ireland should have been awarded a penalty early in the second half when two Belgian defenders challenged Shane Long with recklessly high feet. A quick counter-attack followed, which resulted in Romelu Lukaku opening the scoring. Axel Witsel doubled the lead just after the hour mark and Lukaku added a third after 70 minutes. The result and performance were painfully redolent of Euro 2012 and suddenly the team and supporters seemed deflated, with any optimism about qualifying for the last 16 slowly fading.

In the days after the defeat to Belgium, there was a re-appraisal of the tactical approach and mindset within the Irish camp. Roy Keane was particularly vocal in expressing his views on the type of single-minded approach that he felt was needed. As the assistant manager observed, 'we're not here to make friends'; he expected a player to 'do whatever you can to get the right result'. 'You might get a yellow card, you might even get a red, but your team might win,' said Keane. 'Sacrifices. You have to make sacrifices for your team.'

Keane didn't mention any specific incident from the Belgium game, but his thought process might well have been informed by the third Belgian goal. The goal was scored following a counter-attacking move in which Eden Hazard had run half the length of the field before setting up Lukaku. The only Irish player who attempted a challenge was Ciaran Clark, whose lunging tackle took neither the ball nor Hazard.

Keane's comments also hinted at the lack of dominant personalities within the Irish team. It was certainly difficult to identify players with the ruthless streak sometimes required during the heat of battle. One exception was Jonathan Walters, who had earned a reputation as a hard-working professional and a tough opponent for Premier League defenders. Walters had become Ireland's talisman during the qualification campaign, scoring crucial goals and holding the ball up when the team needed some respite. Unfortunately, he had picked up a calf injury in training before the tournament began and, although he started the opening game against Sweden, he was patently unfit. The team missed the hard-nosed edge that Walters could have provided.

The loss to Belgium meant that the squad and management approached their final group game against Italy knowing that they needed a win to qualify from the group and even then, qualification would depend on how the third-placed teams fared in other groups. Italy had won their two previous group games against Belgium and Sweden and looked like a well-drilled and cohesive unit. The team was managed by Antonio Conte, who was renowned for his competitive instinct and ferocious intensity. Conte had taken over the national team in August 2014 after managing Juventus to three successive

Serie A titles. Of his twelve competitive games in charge of Italy, the team had won nine and drawn three.

There was little doubt that Conte would be keen to retain the team's unbeaten record and he said: 'If you think this is a dead rubber for us then that's not the case; winning breeds additional victories and I am going to pick my side based on that feeling.' The Italian manager also recognised the significance of the fixture for the Irish players when he observed that 'this will be life and death for them, the biggest game of their careers'.

Italy's success in winning their first two group games allowed Conte the luxury of shuffling the deck, making a total of eight changes to the starting team which played against Sweden. On one hand, this meant that the Italian side was weakened, but it also meant that Ireland would face fresh players who would be eager to impress. The Italian team also remained stacked full of talented individuals from leading clubs in Serie A, including four players from Juventus.

Throughout his managerial career, Conte had demonstrated tactical adaptability and an inclination to utilise different formations. His success at Juventus was built on a system with three at the back with two attack-minded wing backs. The 3-5-2 formation that Conte employed involved high pressing and the control of possession. Italian football has historically been characterised by defensive solidity, which has its roots in the *Catenaccio* system and the role of a defensive sweeper. In many respects, Conte's 3-5-2 formation helped to satisfy the Italian desire for security. When playing against a conventional 4-4-2 formation, it offers a spare man in both defence and midfield. When faced with a team playing a lone striker, it leaves two spare men at the back, allowing one of the centre-backs to step forward into midfield when in possession.

At Juventus, playing three at the back allowed Conte to make effective use of the experienced trio of Giorgio Chiellini, Leonardo Bonucci and Andrea Barzagli, who played in front of Gianluigi Buffon in goals. It made sense for Conte to build his Italian team around the Juventus defence and retain the same formation. The team he picked to face Ireland included both Bonucci and Barzagli, with Buffon and Chiellini rested. In midfield, Alessandro Florenzi of Roma retained his place from the win over Sweden and he was joined by Thiago Motta of Paris St Germain. The strike partnership of Ciro Immobile and Simone Zaza had scored a combined total of 17 goals for their clubs during the domestic season and were certainly not Conte's first-choice pairing.

In the days before the game, an interview with Marco Tardelli appeared in *Gazzetta dello Sport* in which he spoke about his experience of working with the Irish players during his time as Giovanni Trapattoni's assistant. Tardelli was complimentary of the Irish players' attitude and character, but when discussing the defeat to Belgium, he claimed that the Irish players 'have trouble handling the game tactically' and that 'they don't get that football is also an intellectual matter'.

Tardelli's comments were picked up by the Irish newspapers, but much of the media speculation centred on Martin O'Neill's key selection decisions, most notably whether he would retain James McCarthy in midfield. McCarthy had been replaced after just over an hour of the Belgium game, looking visibly shaken as he left the field to take his seat on the bench. The other player at risk of losing his place was Ciaran Clark who had scored an own goal against Sweden and was exposed for the third Belgian goal.

O'Neill's starting eleven was announced less than an hour before kick-off and was not what the fans and pundits were predicting. The team included four changes from the side that lost to Belgium, with Shane Duffy, Richard Keogh, James McClean and Daryl Murphy replacing John O'Shea, Ciaran Clark, Glenn Whelan and Wes Hoolahan. The fact that McCarthy was retained ahead of Whelan surprised many, whilst few anticipated that O'Neill would drop the two central defenders who had started the tournament.

Darren Randolph retained his position as the team's goalkeeper. The West Ham netminder had established himself as O'Neill's first-choice keeper after he replaced Shay Given as a substitute in the famous win over Germany, on a night when he provided the assist for Shane Long's goal.

Everton's Seamus Coleman was selected at right-back and was given the honour of captaining his country for the first time. Coleman had been surplus to requirements four years earlier when Trapattoni named his squad for Euro 2012, but the reputation of the former Sligo Rovers man had continued to grow, a testament to his professionalism and application. The central defensive pairing of Shane Duffy and Richard Keogh would be playing together for the first time. Duffy played his club football for Blackburn Rovers and this would be his first competitive international. Keogh was at Derby County, but, unlike Duffy, he had featured in some pivotal fixtures for his country, including both legs of the play-off against Bosnia and Herzegovina. The back four was completed by Burnley's Stephen Ward who had established himself as Ireland's left-back during Trapattoni's tenure.

In midfield, James McCarthy was picked in the holding role. The Glasgow-born midfielder had shown fleeting glimpses of his ability with Everton in the Premier League, and occasionally in the green of Ireland, but he was often criticised for not imposing himself enough on games. McCarthy was joined in midfield by Jeff Hendrick and Robbie Brady – both products of the St Kevin's Boys club in Dublin. Hendrick was a teammate of Richard Keogh at Derby County, whilst Robbie Brady played alongside Wes Hoolahan at Norwich City.

Southampton's Shane Long was selected on the right of the front three. The former Tipperary minor hurling star provided an abundance of pace but sometimes lacked the requisite finesse and instinct in front of goal. James McClean on the left wing had featured regularly for West Bromwich Albion during the Premier League season and he offered a direct approach and strong running which Martin O'Neill valued. Daryl Murphy of Ipswich Town was picked in the centre-forward role. At 33 years of age, the Waterford man was the oldest player in the starting eleven and, remarkably, he had never scored for Ireland.

The team was set-up in what appeared to be a flexible 4-3-3 formation when going forward, with a more defensive 4-1-4-1 formation when defending. McClean and Long were tasked with providing width and support to Murphy, as well as being expected to track back and offer defensive support to the full-backs.

Only three of the starting eleven – Ward, Long and McClean – had been part of Trapattoni's squad at Euro 2012. The team had since undergone a period of transition, with a gradual changing of the guard which culminated in O'Neill's selection to face the Italians. During his time in the job, O'Neill had vacillated between different formations and personnel. This was undoubtedly a bold selection from the manager and a judgement that appeared to be based on instinct and the need to win the game.

The manager had decided to put his faith in a more physical and athletic team, which probably explained the decision not to start Wes Hoolahan. At 34 years of age, Hoolahan was one of the elder statesmen in the squad, but he had regularly struggled to find a place in O'Neill's starting eleven. As a result, the Norwich City midfielder had become a *cause célèbre* for Irish supporters, much as Andy Reid had been during the Trapattoni era. Hoolahan was a player of undoubted talent and one of the few Irish players with the ability to unlock an opposition defence.

Italy

1
Sirigu

15
Barzagli

19
Bonucci
(captain)

5
Ogbonna

21
Bernardeschi

14
Sturaro

10
Motta

6
Florenzi

2
De Sciglio

7
Zaza

11
Immobile

7
Murphy

11
McClean

9
Long

19
Brady

8
McCarthy

13
Hendrick

17
Ward

5
Keogh

12
Duffy

2
Coleman
(captain)

1
Randolph

Republic of Ireland

The game was staged in Lille in the northwest of France, but there was some concern about the state of the pitch at the Stade Pierre-Mauroy. A combination of rain, humidity and lack of sunshine over the previous weeks had left the pitch in poor condition. UEFA considered that the weather conditions had caused 'irreversible damage' to the playing surface and they made the decision that the pitch would be replaced following the game between Italy and Ireland.

The stadium roof was closed, and the teams walked out to a cauldron of noise, with the Irish crowd in the majority. When the national anthems were complete, the Irish players gathered for their customary huddle and Seamus Coleman assumed the speaking duties. Coleman later described it as 'an emotional speech' in which he talked about what the Irish team and fans meant to him.

Italy kicked off and, within nine seconds, Coleman was leading by example as he raced into a tackle to dispossess Mattia De Sciglio. Coleman's challenge was late, and the referee awarded an Italian free kick, but the Donegal man had made it clear that his team was willing to scrap for everything. James McClean followed up with a couple of biting tackles and Jeff Hendrick went in with a hard challenge on Alessandro Florenzi. Those early exchanges suggested that Roy Keane's words were ringing in the players' ears.

From the opening minutes, it was clear that Ireland intended to play on the front foot. The caution and negativity that had characterised their previous performance against Belgium were replaced by intensity and physicality. The team fashioned its first chance in the ninth minute, as Stephen Ward hit a long ball forward towards Daryl Murphy, who in turn knocked the ball down for Hendrick to rifle a 25-yard shot just wide of the goal. With 20 minutes on the clock, Murphy was once again involved, meeting a Brady corner with a powerful header that was tipped over by the Italian keeper.

By the midway point in the first half, the Irish team was in the ascendency. James McCarthy was quietly but effectively helping to dictate the pace. McCarthy's athleticism and ability to read the game was demonstrated in one passage of play in which he beat Simone Zaza to secure possession in the opposition half, and within fifteen seconds he was once again retrieving the ball from a headed clearance. The Everton midfielder's ability to cover large tracts of ground facilitated Brady and Hendrick in pushing forward to support Murphy, whose physicality kept Bonucci occupied. Murphy's presence allowed Long and McClean to find pockets of space between the Italian back three and wing-backs. For all the benefits that a 3-5-2 formation offers, it is often that space between the back three and wing-backs where the system is most vulnerable, and Ireland were cleverly finding ways to exploit it.

The Irish approach yielded a series of free kicks and corners in the first half, which allowed Robbie Brady to provide some dangerous deliveries into the Italian penalty area. With just over half an hour played, Brady took a short corner to Hendrick before delivering a deep ball to the back post, where Duffy and Long were queuing up. Duffy got his head to the ball but couldn't direct his header downwards. McClean later collected the ball in a left-wing position and ran direct at Sturaro and Barzagli before the latter clipped his wings with an unceremonious foul.

Italy had their first attempt on goal in the 43rd minute when Immobile took a shot from just outside the Irish box, but his low right-footed strike flew wide. With the half-time whistle approaching, the Irish team launched one final attack. Hendrick threaded a neat pass through to Murphy, who released McClean on the edge of the Italian box. McClean took a touch, but the Derry man appeared to be nudged in the back by Bernardeschi and fell to the ground. The referee waved play on, but the television replays showed that McClean should have been awarded a spot-kick. For the second time in consecutive games, Ireland had been denied what appeared to be a clear-cut penalty.

The Italians started the second half looking stronger, but it took them just over seven minutes to conjure up their first decent chance. A cross from De Sciglio was met by a left-footed volley from Zaza which flew over Randolph's goal. That was followed by a pacey Irish attack which led to a shot from Coleman, but it was blocked by Bonucci. On the hour mark, Hendrick had another shot from the edge of the area which flew narrowly wide.

Ireland continued to work hard, but an experienced Italian defence was proving difficult to break down. O'Neill introduced his first substitution with twenty minutes remaining, with Aiden McGeady replacing Daryl Murphy. Murphy had repaid O'Neill's faith in him by putting in an industrious performance and being a handful for a physical Italian defence. Murphy's departure meant that Shane Long moved into the centre-forward position to allow McGeady take up the role Long vacated on the right wing. The hope was that McGeady would provide some trickery and offer the team something different as they went in search of the all-important goal. On the opposite flank, McClean continued to provide an attacking threat and he delivered a dangerous cross which Sirigu attempted to punch, but the keeper struggled to connect with the ball and was fortunate that an Irish player didn't capitalise.

A three-minute spell followed which shifted the dynamic of the match. Firstly, Antonio Conte substituted Ciro Immobile for the diminutive figure of Lorenzo Insigne. A short time later, James McCarthy was withdrawn for Wes Hoolahan. As Hoolahan ran onto the field, Insigne gathered possession in a midfield position and ghosted past McGeady before continuing his run towards the Irish box and then curling a right-footed shot beyond the reach of Randolph. Fortunately, from an Irish perspective, the ball bounced back off the post.

Insigne's introduction had added pace to the Italian frontline, but it was no coincidence that he found space to run into just as McCarthy left the field. McCarthy had patrolled the area in front of the Irish defence up to that point and Hendrick was now being asked to take up the defensive duties. McGeady and Hoolahan added a creative spark to the Irish midfield, but their introduction meant that the game would inevitably open-up and Ireland needed to be mindful of the Italian team's ability to counter-attack.

Although the team had struggled to create any clear-cut chances in the second half, the Irish crowd remained optimistic that they could conjure up one final opportunity. With seven minutes remaining, it felt as though that opportunity arrived. Bonucci attempted to dribble the ball out of defence and lost possession as he came under pressure from McGeady. The ball arrived at the feet of Hoolahan who advanced into the Italian penalty area. Hoolahan had time and space – more than he could have conceivably imagined – and he tried to place a left-footed shot past Sirigu, but the shot was tame and comfortably saved.

At that moment, it felt like Ireland's chance had passed and that the team's participation in the tournament was coming to an end. The television commentary from RTÉ's George Hamilton and Ronnie Whelan summed up how most Irish fans must have felt at that moment. 'Well, was that the chance?' asked Hamilton. 'Ah, that was the chance. You couldn't have got a better chance,' responded an exasperated Whelan.

Fortunately, there was to be one final roll of the dice, with Hoolahan once again playing a pivotal role. The move started with Randolph rolling the ball out to Brady, who passed to McGeady on the half-way line. After a short burst of pace through the middle, McGeady found Hoolahan in space near the right wing. Hoolahan turned inside onto his favoured left foot and whipped in a beautifully flighted ball that was met by the on-rushing Brady who headed to the Italian net. The Norwich City duo had found a way of breaking the Italian resistance and the goal provided the cue for wild celebrations.

The goal was crafted by Martin O'Neill's two substitutes, but Brady's energy and willingness to make the run from deep inside his own half of the field was impressive, particularly after 84 minutes of football on a heavy pitch in humid conditions. Brady never broke his stride and attacked the ball, despite the risk of a collision with Sirigu, as the Italian keeper advanced from his goal.

Ireland now needed to hold out and prevent the Italians from equalising. The stadium reverberated to the sound of an Irish crowd buoyed by an appreciation that their team was on the brink of a famous result. As the clock ticked towards the 90th minute, Stephen Quinn was introduced to provide a fresh pair of legs in the midfield.

After an agonising five minutes of injury time, the final whistle was met by an outpouring of emotions, as the Irish squad and management celebrated their achievement. The players made their way to the end of the stadium where most of the Irish fans were located. In some of the most memorable television footage from the tournament, the goal hero Robbie Brady was embraced by his girlfriend and brothers.

The winning goal owed much to the guile and technique of McGeady, Hoolahan and Brady, but the foundations for the result were put in place by a performance underpinned by hard work, honest endeavour and physicality. There was an aggression about the Irish approach, and they were helped when a series of robust early tackles went unpunished by the Romanian referee, Ovidiu Haţegan. The pace offered by Long and McClean troubled the Italian wing-backs, but it was noteworthy that over 40 per cent of Irish attacks were down the left flank where Ward and McClean dovetailed effectively with Brady.

After the game, Martin O'Neill heaped praise on his team. 'The whole team was terrific,' said O'Neill. 'It would be hard to find a weakness. There wasn't a player that didn't perform heroically.' An emotional Robbie Brady, cognisant of the significance of his goal, said: 'I grew up dreaming about this stage and to go and do it in front of my family is the best feeling in the world.' The squad of players had, for the most part, achieved modest success at club level and James

McClean summed up the prevailing mood when he described it as the 'best night of my football career, hands down'.

Antonio Conte was less than complimentary of the Irish approach, describing the match as 'a very physical contest against a side that played a lot of long balls, made heavy, powerful challenges, [and contested] second balls'. The Italian manager was also critical of the playing surface. 'The pitch helped them a lot more in this situation than it did us,' said Conte. 'I don't think they deserved to win. A draw would have been a fair result.'

The following day, Daniel McDonnell wrote in the *Irish Independent* that Robbie Brady's 'composure was in keeping with the contribution of the youngsters that inspired the victory – with a little bit of help from the brilliance of late substitute Wes Hoolahan'. The result was defined by the energy that the younger players injected into the performance. In particular, the midfield duo of Brady and Hendrick linked up well and demonstrated an on-field understanding which could be traced back to their time as schoolboy players with St Kevin's Boys.

The Italian press praised the Irish team spirit and determination, with *Gazzetta dello Sport* opening their match report with the words, 'What heart, Ireland'. The *Corriere della Sera* referred to the 'head, heart and legs' shown by the Irish team. With the large contingent of Irish fans continuing to make a good impression on their French hosts, it was perhaps unsurprising that the front and back pages of *L'Équipe* included one large picture of the Irish supporters in Lille, accompanied by the headline: 'Let the party begin.'

The French interest in the Republic of Ireland's passage through to the last 16 of the tournament was heightened by the fact that O'Neill's team would provide the opposition for the host nation in Lyon. With only three days to prepare for the fixture, the Irish team would need to overcome the physical and mental fatigue following the victory in Lille. They were also at a distinct disadvantage, as France had a full week to prepare.

In the build-up to the game, the media in both Ireland and France focused on the previous meeting between the sides, including Thierry Henry's infamous handball. The last 16 match was seen by many as an opportunity for an Irish team to exact revenge.

The fixture was played at the impressive home of Olympique Lyonnais, with a comparatively small crowd of Irish fans able to access tickets. The match got off to a dramatic start as Ireland were awarded a penalty inside the first minute when Shane Long was pushed over. After being denied penalties in the two previous outings against Belgium and Italy, it seemed as though justice had finally prevailed. Robbie Brady stepped up to take the spot-kick and duly converted to give Ireland an unlikely lead and 88 minutes to hold onto it.

The Irish team was playing with confidence and there was a sense that they were continuing where they had left off against Italy. They could quite conceivably have scored another before half-time, but the game changed in the second half. France substituted one of their defensive midfielders at the interval for the more attack-minded Kingsley Coman. As the Irish team visibly tired, Antoine Griezmann pounced to score two goals in the space of three minutes. Shane Duffy received a subsequent red card when he took down Griezmann on the edge of the box and Ireland's hopes of making the quarter-finals soon faded.

It was a disappointing outcome, but the team had shown enough quality against France to suggest that they had grown over the course of the tournament and could evolve further under the leadership of Martin O'Neill. The performances also helped to exorcise some of the grim memories from Euro 2012.

In terms of playing style, Ireland's appearances at Euro 2016 marked a notable improvement from the performances in Poland four years earlier. UEFA's Euro 2016 Technical Report indicated that the Irish team enjoyed an average of 45 per cent possession over the course of their four games at the tournament, with an average passing accuracy of just over 77 per cent. In contrast, Trapattoni's team had averaged less than 40 per cent possession and a passing accuracy of 58 per cent over the course of the three games in Poland. Although the respective strengths of the opposition teams were a factor, the evidence on the pitch indicated that O'Neill's team showed more of a willingness to retain possession than that of his predecessor.

Possession and passing accuracy are not necessarily indicators of success, but they do serve to illustrate a team's offensive approach and use of the ball. At Euro 2016, five teams registered lower possession statistics than the Republic of Ireland, including Iceland (36 per cent) and Northern Ireland (37 per cent), both of whom also qualified through their respective groups.

What was perhaps more surprising about the Republic's performances at the European Championship was that the team covered an average distance of 103 kilometres in each game. This was the lowest total of any competing nation at the tournament. The lack of distance covered might seem at odds with the characterisation of the Irish team as a hardworking unit, but this statistic could be attributed to the team's approach with and without possession of the ball. An observation of their four matches would suggest that the Irish team was comfortable covering distance without the ball, but in possession, their play was often distinguished by a lack of movement. In contrast, the stronger technical teams at the tournament demonstrated an ability to create angles for passing and to find space between the lines through the fluid movement of their players.

Euro 2016 was the first time Ireland had qualified through the group stages at a European Championship. The victory against Italy was only the second time the country had won a game at a European Championship, the previous win coming against England in Stuttgart 28 years earlier. Indeed, it was only the country's fourth win at the finals of a major tournament.

In the grander scale of Irish football achievements, there may be some debate about its true standing. The victory over Italy came with the caveat that it was achieved against a team that had already qualified from the group and rested some of their key players. Some critics would point to the fact that reaching the last 16 of Euro 2016 meant that O'Neill's team progressed no further than Trapattoni's team did by qualifying for the previous 16-team iteration of the tournament. The success of 2016 certainly fell short of Jack Charlton's team qualifying for the eight-team tournament at Euro '88. It could even be argued that the Irish team which defeated Austria on its way to qualifying for the last eight of the 1964 European Nations' Cup was closer to the European elite when they missed out on what was then a four-team tournament.

Notwithstanding the relevance or otherwise of such comparisons, the success of O'Neill's team in qualifying through their group at Euro 2016 was that it provided a landmark result and an important reference point for a new generation of Irish players and fans.

O'Neill remained in charge for the qualification campaign for the 2018 World Cup. The team put themselves in a strong position in the group, with some valuable early victories, including an impressive win against Austria in Vienna. The all-important goal arrived courtesy of James McClean who finished an excellent counter-attacking move, orchestrated by Wes Hoolahan. Remarkably, it was the first time in 29 years that Ireland had defeated a higher-seeded nation in a competitive qualifier away from home, with the previous occasion generally acknowledged as the defeat of Scotland in Glasgow on the road to qualifying for Euro '88. O'Neill's team repeated the trick in their final group game away to Wales in Cardiff. In what was described as a classic away performance, McClean once again provided the goal and secured Ireland a place in the World Cup play-offs.

Despite some impressive results achieved in the qualifying campaign, the Irish team had failed to grasp the initiative in the group, with a series of listless performances in Dublin proving costly in their pursuit of automatic qualification. There was an increasing sense that the team was relying on defensive solidity, physicality, and a long-ball approach to secure results. The apparent willingness to cede possession proved particularly frustrating, with the game plan seemingly based on containment rather than possession retention.

Such failings were in evidence at the start of the campaign when the Irish team managed to salvage a 2-2 draw against Serbia in Belgrade, despite only completing 94 passes over the course of 90 minutes of football. A similar trend was again in evidence twelve months later when they completed 152 passes and managed 31 per cent possession in a 1-1 draw against Georgia in Tbilisi.

These frailties ultimately proved costly in the World Cup play-offs when a scoreless draw against Denmark in Copenhagen was followed by a humiliation in Dublin. Trailing 2-1 at half-time, O'Neill decided to replace his two defensive midfielders, David Meyler and Harry Arter, with the more attack-minded Wes Hoolahan and Aiden McGeady. Some pundits subsequently saw the double substitution as evidence that O'Neill panicked. Whether that was the case is open to conjecture, but it is also quite plausible that the manager was casting his mind back to the game against Italy in Lille when he introduced Hoolahan and McGeady during the second half. On that occasion, the duo had provided a creative impetus as the team threw caution to the wind, but against Denmark their introduction removed the side's defensive discipline. The lack of midfield cover in front of the Irish back four provided an invitation which Christian Eriksen and his Danish teammates ruthlessly exploited, ultimately winning 5-1.

The nature of the defeat to Denmark illustrated the lack of a consistent and coherent tactical approach from O'Neill. The technical limitations of his squad also came into sharp focus, particularly when faced with more expansive opposition. Over the course of the twelve games played during the 2018 World Cup qualifying campaign, the

Irish team only scored thirteen goals. This poor return could be partly attributed to the retirement of Robbie Keane, as it was the first campaign in almost twenty years that the country's record goal-scorer had been absent from the squad. However, as Ken Early pointed out in the *Irish Times* in October 2018, O'Neill's repeated references to Ireland's lack of a natural goal-scorer belied the fact that 'even the "natural" scorers need to be surrounded by a team structure that is designed to play to their strengths'.

The absence of a discernible pattern of play was apparent in an Irish team which looked increasingly uncomfortable in possession, even against modest football nations such as Georgia and Moldova. The play-off defeat increased the spotlight on O'Neill and questions were raised about his management style and preparation for games. Some of the criticism focused on the manager's insistence on announcing his starting team an hour before kick-off, which created the impression that the starting players were not being drilled as a unit in the days prior to games.

It seems reasonable to suggest that a country with a deficit in playing resources needs to compensate through coaching and attention to detail. One of the criticisms of Giovanni Trapattoni was the rigidity of his coaching style and the tactical responsibilities he demanded of his players, whereas O'Neill adopted a more flexible approach by placing his trust in the players and offering them greater autonomy on the pitch.

O'Neill demonstrated a willingness to use different formations, but without ever establishing what could be described as a clear identity for the team. Variations of 4-5-1 and 4-3-3 were used with differing degrees of success, depending on the personnel available. A midfield diamond was also used on occasions, which facilitated the use of Wes Hoolahan in an advanced midfield role. In the latter part of O'Neill's tenure, he experimented with a 3-5-2 formation, which on paper appeared to be suited to some of the individual players at his disposal.

UEFA introduced their Nations League as a new competition for European nations, which was intended to replace friendly matches previously played during the international calendar. By the time the new competition began in the autumn of 2018, the Irish team looked rudderless and bereft of confidence. O'Neill's credibility had not been helped by speculation earlier in the year linking him to the managerial job at Stoke City and his apparent willingness to engage in discussions with the club. His difficulties were compounded by tensions within the camp, with Roy Keane allegedly directing an expletive-laden rant towards Harry Arter and Jonathan Walters. A dour scoreless draw against Denmark in November 2018 finally signalled the end for O'Neill and Keane.

In truth, O'Neill's managerial reign had run its course a year earlier following the play-off defeat. It is important to acknowledge that O'Neill was working with a more limited pool of talent than his predecessors and he was not directly responsible for the relative lack of young players emerging through the system. The failure of the FAI to provide sufficient investment in grassroots and underage football during the previous decade had taken its toll on the national team. The gradual decline in the quality of playing resources and indigenous talent also served as a painful reminder of the long-standing structural flaws in Irish football and how its development had been left behind by other European nations.

Martin O'Neill's legacy as an Irish manager may only be judged in the fullness of time, but some of the results achieved during his tenure were highly credible. For a period of over fourteen years, Ireland had failed to beat any higher ranked nation in a competitive fixture, but the Derry man led the team to victories over Germany, Bosnia and Herzegovina, Italy, Austria and Wales. The style of football might not have satisfied the purists, but O'Neill's reign brought about some big results and created excitement for a period of time.

Epilogue

When the Republic of Ireland travelled to Gelsenkirchen in October 2014, German manager Joachim Löw spoke about what he considered to be the strengths of Irish football. Having faced Ireland on four previous occasions in his managerial career, Löw advised that 'there's nothing new for us', before explaining that 'the Irish are good fighters, they have commitment and fantastic fighting spirit, and they know how to defend'. Löw's words might have seemed prescient, as Martin O'Neill's team subsequently salvaged a draw against the world champions with an injury-time goal and would go on to beat their more illustrious opponents in Dublin later in the campaign. Nevertheless, Löw's comments were instructive, as they echoed the sentiments expressed by his compatriot Sepp Herberger over half a century earlier when he spoke about 'a hard fight' for his World Cup-winning team when they lost at Dalymount Park.

Such platitudes are not simply reserved for use by successful German managers. The opinion that heart and fighting spirit are the great strengths of Irish teams is regularly trotted out by opposition managers, players and media outlets. It has remained a constant throughout the history of Irish football, irrespective of how tangible or measurable those characteristics might be. Indeed, UEFA's Technical Report published in the aftermath of Euro 2016 listed the key tactical and stylistic features of the competing nations and, in the case of the Republic of Ireland, the report referred to the team's 'outstanding work ethic, team spirit, [and] never-say-die attitude'.

The repeated references to fighting spirit and work ethic can sometimes feel like back-handed compliments, representative of an international perspective of Irish football as lacking in technical quality. The emphasis on such characteristics in a footballing context also serves to create a narrative around the team's style of play and an apparent lack of finesse.

Ireland's greatest period of success was certainly based on a robust style of football which relied on a 'route one' approach and pressurising the opposition. The Charlton era left a legacy, part of which is a playing style that regularly relies on a long-ball approach as its default setting. During the height of Charlton's success at Italia '90, Eamon Dunphy wrote in the *Sunday Independent* that 'international football teams are not really teams at all, rather coalitions of players, ideas and styles'. Dunphy's words may be thirty years old, but they remain relevant to Irish football in a contemporary context, as the nation has perhaps failed to progress new ideas and styles, or indeed keep pace with the innovations taking place in the global game.

Since the end of Charlton's tenure, the country has qualified for three major tournaments under three different managers, with the two latter qualifications for Euro 2012 and Euro 2016 relying on what some commentators would consider to be relatively crude playing styles. A simplistic style of attacking play lends itself to the notion that Irish football is largely underpinned by that famed fighting spirit.

If Irish football has indeed become synonymous with a direct or long-ball approach, this overlooks the more subtle style of play that existed prior to the Charlton era, as illustrated by the short passing and possession retention espoused by both Johnny Giles and Eoin Hand during their respective managerial reigns. Going back further, an examination of the results achieved, and the key protagonists involved in Irish teams from the late-1940s through to the mid-1960s, suggest that there was a discernible style of football in evidence during that period. That style existed within a framework which typically involved using strong and physically imposing defenders, with smaller, more skilful players in the midfield and forward roles. The victory over West Germany in 1956 was distinguished by the speed and skill of the Irish players, which proved too much for the physical prowess of the Germans. Diminutive midfielders and forwards capable of manipulating the ball are not readily associated traits of modern-day Irish players; and yet, it could be argued that there is a line of correlation linking Arthur Fitzsimons to Johnny Giles to Liam Brady to Damien Duff.

There is certainly a long history of smaller, skilful players that have emerged from schoolboy clubs but, increasingly, there appears to be a distrust of such players in the international set-up. During the managerial reigns of Trapattoni and O'Neill, the creative talents of Andy Reid and Wes Hoolahan were regularly cast aside in favour of options that offered greater athleticism and physical strength. Such preferences may simply be a by-product of modern football, which places an emphasis on players covering longer distances, but it is also perhaps indicative of an Irish football culture that fails to attach sufficient weight to the technical proficiency of players.

Trapattoni and O'Neill could, with some justification, contend that they fulfilled the brief laid down by the FAI; both qualified for the European Championships and both took their teams to the World Cup play-offs. And yet, as their respective tenures progressed, there was a sense amongst many fans and media pundits that their tactical approaches had a stultifying effect on the players and any inclination those players might have had to play expansive football. The inevitable debate has tended to revolve around whether the players were following the instructions of their managers, or whether the national team simply cannot call upon the calibre of players capable of executing a more progressive brand of football. Mick McCarthy's ephemeral second stint as manager, underpinned by the short-term objective of qualifying for the European Championship, did little to resolve this debate.

The public discourse surrounding Irish football has increasingly been characterised by a false dichotomy: one that places 'pragmaticism' in opposition to 'flair', 'caution' in opposition to 'expression', and 'physicality' in opposition to 'technique'. The best teams generally strike a balance and for a nation of Ireland's size and playing resources, there will always be a need for some level of pragmatism. However, for more than a decade, Irish supporters have become accustomed to the sight of mid-ranking nations arriving in Dublin, retaining possession, and showing a level of ambition which is often lacking in the home side.

A myriad of reasons can be used to explain why Irish football has failed to keep pace with other European nations in producing high-quality technical players, not least the lack of investment in coaching and the complex structural issues that exist between domestic schoolboy football and the League of Ireland. For decades, Irish football could rely on exporting its better players to the English leagues, which provided the platform for their further development. However, the globalisation of the English Premier League has shifted the paradigm and means that there is a sharp decline in the number of Irish players breaking through. Moreover, there are fewer English players making the grade in the top-flight, meaning that English-born players of Irish descent are under greater pressure to represent the country of their birth, as evidenced by the high-profile defections of Jack Grealish and Declan Rice.

This confluence of factors has clearly squeezed the available talent pool and led to an increasing number of players who have spent their formative years in the League of Ireland before moving cross-channel and breaking into the international set-up at a later age. The likes of Kevin Doyle, Seamus Coleman and James McClean have demonstrated that young players can use the domestic league as a launchpad for a successful international career. In the short-term, this might make it more difficult for Ireland to challenge the stronger nations and may result in an older age profile for the senior team.

However, in the longer-term, it provides an opportunity to create a more sustainable production model for Irish football. This includes fostering stronger links between schoolboy clubs and the League of Ireland, thereby affording young Irish players a more viable alternative that allows them time to mature and to secure an education. The creation of the League of Ireland underage leagues is a step in the right direction and should, in theory, provide more young players with the platform to transition from schoolboy football to senior level.

Increased investment in underage coaching and structures is paramount to delivering greater autonomy for Irish football in this changing landscape. However, such investment is likely to prove extremely challenging given the well-publicised failings of the planning and organisation structures within the FAI and the severe financial difficulties that have resulted. The failure of the association to provide meaningful leadership and capitalise on the popularity of the sport has become a recurring theme and reached its nadir over the past decade. Following the recent overhaul in some of the key administrative positions within the FAI, there is hope that the new leadership will provide a brighter and more transparent future for Irish football.

With the FAI approaching its 100th anniversary, the appointment of Stephen Kenny as manager presents an opportunity for a recalibration of Irish football and its future priorities. Kenny's appointment marks a step-change in the FAI's approach to the senior managerial role. Rather than being solely focused on the short-term goal of qualifying for major tournaments, there is hope that Kenny's emergence will result in a more progressive and fluid playing style, which places a renewed emphasis and trust in the technical capabilities of the players. It also provides an opportunity to harness the impressive style of football exhibited by the Irish underage teams in recent years and ensure continuity for younger players graduating to the senior squad.

When his appointment was officially confirmed in April 2020, Kenny asserted that his ambition will be to control matches and that 'no matter who we are playing, home or away, it will be about trying to establish control'. The new manager also stated: 'Ideally I would want every schoolboy team looking at the senior international team and thinking "that's how we want to play".' If he can achieve that aspiration, then the Irish senior team will certainly be in a healthy position.

Irish football stands at a crossroads where it needs to negotiate a period of transition, while remaining relevant to a public that has grown tired of negative news stories and become increasingly discerning in its choice of sport and entertainment. In other countries, the attraction of international football has faded somewhat, largely due to the suffocating spread of the club game and the unrelenting efforts of sponsors, television companies and social media.

Despite this, the large travelling support that made its way to the European Championships in Poland and France demonstrated that the Irish team remains an intrinsic part of the country's sporting psyche and still has the capacity to captivate the nation. The emergence of new leadership within the FAI, together with the appointment of Stephen Kenny and what appears to be an emerging generation of promising young players, offers hope that there may be many more memorable occasions to come in the history of the Republic of Ireland football team.

BIBLIOGRAPHY

1)   Archives

Archives of the Football Association of Ireland (University College Dublin, 2010).

Leinster Football Association Archives (University College Dublin, 2010).

2)   Official Reports

FAI (2016), *Strategic Plan 2016–2020.*

FIFA (1990), *World Cup Italia 90 Official Report.*

FIFA (1994), *World Cup USA 94 Official Report.*

FIFA (2002), *2002 FIFA World Cup Korea/Japan Report and Statistics.*

Genesis Strategic Management Consultants (2002), *Football Association of Ireland: Preparation and Planning for the 2002 FIFA World Cup – Evaluation Review.*

UEFA (2012), *Euro 2012 Poland-Ukraine Technical Report.*

UEFA (2016), *UEFA Euro 2016 France Technical Report.*

3) Newspapers, Magazines and Periodicals

ABC (Spain)

Aftonbladet (Sweden)

Bihari Napló (Romania)

Brabants Dagblad (Netherlands)

Cork Examiner

Corriere della Sera (Italy)

Corriere dello Sport (Italy)

Daily Express (UK)

The Daily Telegraph (UK)

L'Équipe (France)

Evening Herald

Football Sports Weekly

France-Soir (France)

Gazzetta dello Sport (Italy)

The Guardian (UK)

Het Laatste Nieuws (Belgium)

Irish Examiner

Irish Independent

Irish Press

Irish Soccer Magazine

Irish Times

Kickin'

La Libre Belgique (Belgium)

The Liverpool Echo (UK)

The Manchester Guardian (UK)

New York Times (USA)

Le Soir (Belgium)

Sovetskii Sport (USSR)

Der Spiegel (Germany)

Sports Illustrated (USA)

La Stampa (Italy)

Sunday Independent

Sunday Tribune

Sunday Times

De Telegraaf (Netherlands)

The Times (UK)

De Volkskrant (Netherlands)

Die Welt (Germany)

Westmeath Independent

The Wicklow News-Letter

World Soccer (UK)

4)   Theses and Dictionary Entries

Agnew, Paddy, 'Irish Football's Two Contrasting States', in *Fortnight*, No. 200 (1984).

Carey, Tadhg, 'Ireland's Footballers at the Paris Olympics, 1924', in *History Ireland*, Vol. 20 No. 4 (July-August 2012).

Finnegan, Laura et al, 'Somewhat united: primary stakeholder perspectives of the governance of schoolboy football in Ireland', in *Managing Sport and Leisure*, Vol. 23, Nos. 1-2 (July 2018) pp. 48-69.

Garnham, Neal, 'Accounting for the Early Success of the Gaelic Athletic Association', in *Irish Historical Studies*, Vol. 34, No. 133 (May 2004), pp. 65-78.

Rouse, Paul, 'The politics of culture and sport in Ireland: a history of the GAA ban on foreign games 1884-1971. Part one: 1884-1921', in *The International Journal of the History of Sport*, Vol. 10, No. 3 (December 1993), pp 333-60.

Slattery, Lynda, 'Two Bishops and a Football: Ireland and the Balkans in the 1940s and 1950s', in *History Ireland*, Vol. 15. No. 5 (September-October 2007), pp. 41-43.

Tynan, Mark Patrick, *Association Football and Irish Society during the Inter-War Period* (PHD Thesis, NUI Maynooth, September 2013).

5) Books

Agnew, Paddy, *Forza Italia: The Fall and Rise of Italian Football* (Ebury Digital, 2012).

Aldridge, John, *My Story* (Hodder & Stoughton Ltd, 1999).

Alexander, Duncan, *Outside the Box: A Statistical Journey through the History of Football* (Century, 2017).

Auclair, Philippe, *Thierry Henry* (Macmillan, 2013).

Bairner, Alan (ed.), *Sport and the Irish: Histories, Identities, Issues* (UCD Press, 2005).

Ball, Phil, *Morbo: The Story of Spanish Football* (WSC Books Limited, 2003).

Bate, Richard, *The Sweeper* (Reedswain, 1999).

Bolger, Dermot, *In High Germany* (Gemma Open Door, 2008).

Bonner, Packie, *The Last Line: My Autobiography* (Ebury Press, 2016).

Borst, Hugo, *O, Louis: In Search of Louis van Gaal* (Yellow Jersey Press, 2014).

Brady, Liam, *So Far, So Good: A Decade in Football* (Readers Union, 1980).

Brodie, Malcolm, *The History of Irish Soccer* (Arrell Publications, 1963).

Brodie, Malcolm, *100 Years of Irish Football* (Blackstaff Press Ltd, 1980).

Burns, Jimmy, *La Roja: How Soccer Conquered Spain and How Spanish Soccer Conquered the World* (Nation Books, 2012).

Byrne, Peter, *Football Association of Ireland: 75 Years* (Sportsworld, 1996).

Byrne, Peter, *Green is the Colour: The Story of Irish Football* (Carlton Books Ltd, 2012).

Byrne, Peter, *From the Press Box: 70 Years of Great Moments in Irish Sport* (Liberties Press, 2014).

Charlton, Jack with Byrne, Peter, *World Cup Diary* (Gill & Macmillan Ltd, 1990).

Charlton, Jack with Byrne, Peter, *Jack Charlton's American World Cup Diary* (Gill & Macmillan Ltd, 1994).

Charlton, Jack with Byrne, Peter, *Jack Charlton: The Autobiography* (Partridge Press, 1996).

Clerkin, Malachy with Siggins, Gerard, *Lansdowne Road* (O'Brien Press, 2010).

Cox, Michael, *The Mixer: The Story of Premier League Tactics, from Route One to False Nines* (HarperCollins, 2018).

Cox, Michael, *Zonal Marking: The Making of Modern European Football* (HarperCollins, 2019).

Cullen, Donal, *Ireland on the Ball: A complete record of the international matches of the Republic of Ireland soccer team, March 1926 to June 1993* (ELO Publications, 1993).

Cullen, Donal, *Freestaters: The Republic of Ireland Soccer Team 1921–1939* (Desert Island Books Ltd, 2007).

Curran, Conor and Toms, David (eds), *New Perspectives on Association Football in Irish History* (Routledge, 2018)

Doyle, Roddy, *The Van* (Secker & Warburg, 1991).

Dunphy, Eamon, *Only a Game? The Diary of a Professional Footballer* (Penguin, 1987).

Dunphy, Eamon, *The Rocky Road* (Penguin, 2014).

Foley, Theo with Foley, Paul, *Theo Give Us A Ball: A Life in Football* (Apex Publishing Ltd, 2018).

Foot, John, *Calcio: A History of Italian Football* (Harper Perennial, 2007).

Garnham, Neal, *Association Football and Society in Pre-Partition Ireland* (Ulster Historical Foundation, 2004).

Gibney, Eugene with Gibney, Siobhan, *Handball* (Brandon/Mount Eagle Publications, 2010).

Giles, John with Lynch, Declan, *A Football Man: The Autobiography* (Hodder & Stoughton, 2010).

Giles, John with Lynch, Declan, *The Great and the Good – The Legendary Players, Managers and Teams of Fifty Years of Football* (Hachette Ireland, 2012).

Given, Shay, *Any Given Saturday: The Autobiography* (Trinity Mirror Sport Media, 2017).

Glanville, Brian, *Soccer Nemesis* (Secker & Warburg, 1955).

Goldblatt, David, *The Ball is Round: A Global History of Football* (Penguin, 2007).

Goldblatt, David, *The Age of Football: The Global Game in the Twenty-First Century* (Macmillan, 2019).

Hart, Simon, *World in Motion* (De Coubertin Books, 2018).

Hand, Eoin with Browne, Jared, *First Hand: My Life and Irish Football* (The Collins Press, 2017).

Hand, Eoin with O'Neill, Peter, *The Eoin Hand Story* (Brophy Books, 1986).

Hannigan, Dave, *The Garrison Game: The State of Irish Football* (Mainstream Publishing, 1998).

Hayes, Dean, *Ireland's Greatest: 60 Years of Football Heroes* (Appletree Press Ltd, 2006).

Hayes, Dean, *The Republic of Ireland International Football Facts* (The Collins Press, 2008).

Healy, John, *No One Stopped Shout* (House of Healy, 1988).

Heighway, Steve, *Liverpool: My Team* (Souvenir Press Ltd, 1977).

Hesse, Uli, *Tor! The Story of German Football* (WSC Books Limited, 2013).

Holmes, Jimmy, *The Day My Dream Ended* (Apex Publishing Ltd, 2017).

Horgan, Neal, *The Cross Roads – Rise of the Rebel Army and Crisis at the FAI* (Sportsproview, 2019).

Howard, Paul, *The Gaffers: Mick McCarthy, Roy Keane and the Team They Built* (O'Brien Press, 2002).

Hughes, Charles, *The Winning Formula* (Collins, 1990).

Keane, Roy with Doyle, Roddy, *The Second Half* (Weidenfeld & Nicolson, 2015).

Keane, Roy with Dunphy, Eamon, *Keane: The Autobiography* (Penguin, 2002).

Keane, Trevor, *Gaffers: 50 Years of Irish Soccer Managers* (Mercier Press, 2010).

Kilbane, Kevin with Merriman, Andy, *Killa: The Autobiography of Kevin Kilbane* (Aurum Press Ltd, 2014).

Kimmage, Paul, *Full Time: The Secret Life of Tony Cascarino* (Simon & Schuster Ltd, 2000).

Kormelink, Henny with Seeverens, Tjeu, *The Coaching Philosophies of Louis Van Gaal and the Ajax Coaches* (Reedswain Incorporated, 1997).

Kuper, Simon, *Football Against the Enemy* (The Orion Publishing Group, 2003).

Langan, Dave with Keane, Trevor and Conway, Alan, *Running Through Walls: Dave Langan* (DB Publishing, 2012).

Leatherdale, Clive, *Ireland: Quest for the World Cup – A Complete Record* (Desert Island Books Ltd, 1994).

Lynch, Declan, *Days of Heaven – Italia 90 and the Charlton Years* (Gill Books, 2010).

McAteer, Jason, *Blood, Sweat and McAteer: A Footballer's Story* (Hachette Books Ireland, 2016).

McCarthy, Kevin, *Gold, Silver and Green: The Irish Olympic Journey 1896-1924* (Cork University Press, 2011).

McCarthy, Mick with Dervan, Cathal, *Mick McCarthy's World Cup Diary 2002* (Pocket Books / TownHouse, 2002).

McGrath, Paul with Hogan, Vincent, *Back from the Brink* (Arrow Books, 2007).

McLoughlin, Alan with Evans, Bryce, *A Different Shade of Green: The Alan McLoughlin Story* (Ballpoint Press, 2014).

Menton, Brendan, *Beyond the Green Door: Six Years Inside the FAI* (Blackwater Press, 2003).

Metcalf, Mark, *Charlie Hurley: The Greatest Centre Half the World Has Ever Seen* (Sportsbooks, 2008).

Moore, Cormac, *The Irish Soccer Split* (Atrium, 2015).

Needham, David, *Ireland's First Real World Cup: The Story of the 1924 Ireland Olympic Football Team* (Manuscript Publisher, 2012).

O'Kelly, Shay and Blair, Derek, *What's the Story?: True Confessions of the Republic of Ireland Soccer Supporters* (Elo Publications, 1992).

O'Mahony, Eddie, *40 Shades of Green* (Lettertec, 2018).

Quinn, Niall, *Niall Quinn: The Autobiography* (Headline, 2002).

Robson, Bobby with Hayward, Paul, *Bobby Robson: Farewell but not Goodbye – My Autobiography* (Hodder Paperbacks, 2006).

Rouse, Paul, *Sport and Ireland: A History* (OUP Oxford, 2015).

Rowan, Paul, *The Team That Jack Built* (Mainstream Publishing, 1994).

Ryan, Sean, *The Boys in Green: The FAI International Story* (Mainstream Publishing, 1997).

Ryan, Sean with Burke, Stephen, *The Book of Irish Goalscorers* (Irish Soccer Co-op, 1987).

Sheedy, Kevin with Keith, John, *So Good I Did it Twice: Kevin Sheedy, My Life from Left Field* (Trinity Mirror Sport Media, 2014).

Stapleton, Frank, *Frankly Speaking* (Blackwater Press, 1991).

Taylor, Matthew, *The Association Game: A History of British Football* (Routledge, 2008).

The Irish Times, *Olé Days: Italia '90 25 Years On* (The Irish Times, 2015).

Tomlinson, Alan and Young, Christopher (eds), *German Football: History, Culture, Society* (Routledge, 2006).

Townsend, Andy with Kimmage, Paul, *Andy's Game: The Inside Story of the World Cup* (Tiger Books, 1994).

Trapattoni, Giovanni, *Coaching High Performance Soccer* (Reedswain, 2000).

Walsh, Thomas P., *Twenty Years of Irish Soccer 1921–1941* (Sports Publicity Services, 1941).

Ward, Adam, *The Republic of Ireland – Gifted in Green* (Hamlyn, 1999).

West, Patrick, *Beating Them at Their Own Game: How the Irish Conquered English Soccer* (Liberties Press, 2014).

Whelan, Daire, *Who Stole Our Game? The Fall and Fall of Irish Soccer* (Gill & Macmillan Limited, 2006).

White, Colin, *Dalymount Park: The Home of Irish Football* (Curragh Press, 2015).

Wilson, Jonathan, *Behind the Curtain: Travels in Eastern European Football* (The Orion Publishing Group, 2006).

Wilson, Jonathan, *Inverting the Pyramid: The History of Football Tactics* (The Orion Publishing Group, 2008).

Wilson, Jonathan, *The Anatomy of England: A History in Ten Matches* (The Orion Publishing Group, 2010).

Wilson, Jonathan, *The Outsider: A History of the Goalkeeper* (The Orion Publishing Group, 2012).

Winner, David, *Brilliant Orange: The Neurotic Genius of Dutch Football* (Bloomsbury Publishing PLC, 2001).

Yallop, David, *How They Stole the Game* (Constable, 2011).

Young, Colin, *Jack Charlton: The Authorised Biography* (Hero Books, 2016).

6)   Films and Documentaries

Ceasefire Massacre (ESPN 30 for 30 Series, 2014).

Division: The Irish Soccer Split (RTÉ, 2019).

Euro 2016: Two Shades of Green (RTÉ, 2016).

Going to America with Jack Charlton (Carlton Visual Entertainment, 1994).

Green is the Colour – History of Irish Football (RTÉ, 2012).

Have Boots, Will Travel (RTÉ, 1997).

Ireland in Euro 88 (RTÉ, 1988).

Ireland's World Cup 2002 Qualification Campaign (RTÉ, 2001).

Italia '90 – Highlights of the 1990 World Cup (Stylus Video, 1990).

Italia 90 Revisited with Jack Charlton (Decent Suit Productions, 2008).

Jack Charlton – The Irish Years (Decent Suit Productions, 2005).

Jack's Heroes – The Republic of Ireland: Italia '90 (Stylus Video, 1990).

June 17th 1994 (ESPN 30 for 30 Series, 2010).

Kerr's Kids (Eir Sport, 2018).

McCarthy's Park (Setanta Sport, 1998).

Mick McCarthy's Irish Dream (Sky Sports, 2001).

Paul McGrath – My Life and Football (A Bruno Dog Production, 2010).

Rättskiparen (Sveriges Television, 2010).

Reeling in the Years – 1988 (RTÉ, 1999).

Reeling in the Years – 1990 (RTÉ, 2000).

Reeling in the Years – 1994 (RTÉ, 2000).

Reeling in the Years – 2002 (RTÉ, 2010).

Republic of Ireland – Campaign America (Universal, 1994).

Rising Sons – Ireland's Eastern Odyssey (RTÉ, 2002).

Seven Games from Glory: The Official Film of 2002 FIFA World Cup Korea/Japan (TWI, 2002).

Soccer Shoot-Out: The Official Film of the 1990 FIFA World Cup Italy (Drummond Challis, 1990).

Tales of the Fans (RTÉ, 2000).

The Boys in Green (A Loosehorse Production for RTÉ, 2020).

The Miracle of Bern (Soda Pictures, 2005).

The Road to America (Treasure Films for RTÉ, 1993).

The Road to Asia (RTÉ, 2002).

The Road to Germany – Euro 88 Preview (RTÉ, 1988).

The Road to Italy (RTÉ, 1989).

The Score: The UEFA EURO 2012 Official Film (Go Entertain, 2012).

They Call Him God (RTÉ, 1998).

TOR! TOTAL FOOTBALL European Football Championship 1988 (Worldmark Productions Ltd, 1988).

Two Billion Hearts: The Official Film of 1994 FIFA World Cup USA (Sport Target Media Productions, 1994).

UEFA Euro 2016 Official Film (Noah Media Group).

7)   Websites

www.balls.ie

www.eire.guide

www.fai.ie

www.fifa.com

www.opeljersey.com

www.pogmogoal.com

www.rte.ie

www.secondcaptains.com

www.si.com

www.soccer-ireland.com

www.theathletic.co.uk

www.theblizzard.co.uk

www.the42.ie

www.uefa.com

www.ybig.ie

INDEX

246

249

Printed in Poland
by Amazon Fulfillment
Poland Sp. z o.o., Wrocław